Re-Vision

A New Look at the Relationship between Science and Religion

Edited by Clifford Chalmers Cain

University Press of America,® Inc.
Lanham • Boulder • New York • Toronto • Plymouth, UK

Dedicated to our past, present, and future faculty colleagues,
staff, and students at Westminster College
in Fulton, Missouri

"The real voyage of discovery consists not in seeking new landscapes, but in having new eyes."

—Marcel Proust

Contents

Foreword

Clifford Chalmers Cain, Harrod-C.S. Lewis Professor of Religious Studies at Westminster College, and his scientific and philosophical conversation partners have offered access for the undergraduate reader, and for other educated, non-specialist, general readers, to several topics at the interface of science and religion, and their treatment makes this a very attractive volume. It is a skill to convey complex material compellingly and accurately, and these writers have accomplished this.

By use of models for understanding the science and religion relationship in our culture—adapted from the late physicist and theologian, Ian Barbour, and refined by others as well—this cooperative book project shows readers very clearly how we arrive at differing interpretations that occur on the religious landscape. The use of these models is fair-minded, but clear and unequivocal in perspective.

In the process of unfolding the "conversation" possible between astrophysics and theology, for example, this volume shows an appreciation for the common interests in the two domains in cosmic origins. In his response chapter, Professor Cain states how contemporary cosmology supports the theological value of continuous creativity. The nature of mathematical language in science is explored, on the one hand, and the symbolic language of theology, which often *depicts* but never *defines* transcendent reality, is examined, on the other hand. This is a sample of the kind of teaching this book can do as it views the goals and outcomes of each domain in the conversation.

In moving toward a theological engagement with biological evolution, the book points to the resources of process theology. It is a picture of the continuous processes of a physical universe influenced but not determined by the presence of God. Professor Cain risks the classic theological tradition's understanding of divine power and transcendence at this juncture in order to present a God whose power is expressed as one cause among other finite causes, but he does this with eyes open to the conceptual problem in relating finite causality to divine cause. The second risk at this juncture is that of entering into the language system of process theology—a considerable challenge indeed, but worth the effort for those who will enter into, and proceed through, this thicket.

The reader is, at various crossroads, drawn into the classic question of the meaning of God's action. On the one hand, the book asserts that God is always beyond the God of our language; on the other hand, God is pictured as finite cause among finite causes, as "struggling" with finite forces. This work, in other words, throws us into classical dilemmas, even paradoxes, and does not pretend to solve them for the reader, but rather to make the reader conscious of them.

Ultimately, the moral and spiritual capacities of the human species, the capacity to guide and influence natural ecologies in a way that reflects a divine intention, is part of the fruit of the evolutionary process. This volume raises, but does not presume to resolve, the problem of suffering and evil issuing from evolutionary processes, and their fit with affirmations of God as loving creator of the universe.

In another one of the conversations between science and religion, the book addresses the question that haunts many at the interface of contemporary science and religion: Does the evidence from genetics contradict the historical claim about the human agent in the ethical monotheisms of religions such as Judaism, Christianity and Islam? Are we moral agents or products of genetic determinants? But there are moral dilemmas in applied genetics, as well, and in the power we now possess to use and misuse bio-technology at this level. This book provides intriguing resources on these issues for the reader.

The last issue taken up is about the status of 'intelligent design' with respect to both science and religion. The authors educate the reader on these issues, but also state their own views clearly and reasonably.

The book concludes by returning to the issue of theodicy which casts its shadow widely, especially in our understanding of contemporary evolutionary sciences. One can make the case that theodicy has always been with us and without definitive solution; evolution only makes the issues more graphic. In his conclusions in the final chapter, Professor Cain tips his hand on this large problem, and I leave it to the reader to discover his point-of-view, only to add that he states it again with clarity and conviction.

The reader will find a great deal to chew on in this volume, and will learn about some of the most important issues at the interface of science and religion in our day.

W. Mark Richardson, Ph.D.
President and Dean, Church Divinity School of the Pacific
Berkeley, California

Preface

This book is the outgrowth of a conversation between religion and science made possible by the generous and gracious collaboration of three scientists, a philosopher, and a theologian. Experts in their given fields, physicist Laura Stumpe, biologist Gabe McNett, geneticist Jane Kenney-Hunt, and philosopher Rich Geenen have written introductory chapters on cosmic origins, evolutionary biology, genetic endowment, and intelligent design, respectively, to which I have attempted religious/theological responses. Each has constructed her or his contribution to stand on its own; in no way were the chapters assembled to set-up a/any particular theological or religious response.

This book is intentionally directed toward a general, non-specialist audience, because the contributors believe that the attempt to relate science and religion should not be reserved for, or monopolized by, experts talking only to each other. Rather, persons on the street, persons in the pew, and persons in the classroom are invited to reflect with us on the important issues of the Big Bang and creation by God, evolution and divine activity in the world, genetic inheritance and human freedom, and whether Intelligent Design is good science and good theology. The writers hope that our addressing the interface of these issues will stimulate the reader to take our insights as intentionally and merely a catalyst for his or her own further thoughts.

Indeed, the collaborators represent a wide array of worldviews and do not, and would not, fully agree with one another's positions and conclusions, especially mine! That has made the assembly of this book a "difficult delight," and has made my religious/theological responses "contentiously creative."

Thus, this book represents a starting point and not an arrival at any finish line. Each of us would wish that more chapters and greater depth and fuller breadth were possible within the confines of a book that is modest in length. Further, in my response chapters, our book reflects a Western religious framework, more specifically Christian theology, since any attempt to include an adequate representation of the perspectives and responses of all the world religions, both Eastern and Western, would have resulted in a work that is multiple times its present length and unfathomably complex.

Although I have expressed on the Acknowledgments page my gratitude to my four colleagues and friends for their excellent work and challenging exchanges, I would do so again here: It is a tremendous joy to know them, to work with them, and to share thoughts and feelings with them.

Clifford Chalmers Cain
Westminster College
Fulton, Missouri
2015

Acknowledgments

Cliff Cain would like to thank the following persons:

Ms. Nicolette Amstutz, Assistant Acquisitions Editor, for her guidance, encouragement, and quick responses to numerous questions throughout the "concrescence" of *Re-vision.*

Dr. Laura Stumpe, Dr. Gabe McNett, Dr. Jane Kenney-Hunt, and Dr. Rich Geenen, whose critical comments and willingness to take-on this project leave him deeply in their debt.

The Very Rev. Dr. Mark Richardson, President and Dean, Church Divinity School of the Pacific, who graciously wrote the Foreword in the midst of much busyness.

The Most Rev. Dr. Katharine Jefferts Schori, Presiding Bishop of the Episcopal Church in the United States, who somehow found time in her saturated schedule to read the manuscript.

Dr. James R. Curry, Professor *Emeritus* of Biology, Franklin College of Indiana, long-time friend, former co-teacher, and author of *Children of God, Children of Earth*, who read the manuscript once and a couple sections twice in order to make them better.

Dr. Nick Steph, Professor *Emeritus* of Physics, Franklin College of Indiana, long-time friend and former co-teacher, who read the manuscript and helped him think about things in some different and helpful ways.

Dr. Ted Jaeger, Professor of Psychology, Westminster College of Missouri, whose expertise in neuroscience helped him sort through the complexity of neurons and genes in relation to the issue of determinism vs. freewill.

Dr. Kimberly K. Leon, Activities Director, Lenoir Woods Healthcare Center, Columbia, Missouri, who read a section at his request and pointed-out, and then helped straighten-out, his writing peculiarities; and whose computer expertise made this work and his life easier.

Ms. Enni Kallio, Westminster College ('13), whose wonderfully-creative photography graces the cover of this book.

The late Ian Barbour (October 5, 1923–December 24, 2013), physicist and theologian, who pioneered the initial conversation between science and religion.

Laura Stumpe would like to thank her husband and children and extended family for their encouragement and support. Also, she would like to thank her Westminster College colleagues for their work and willingness to engage in this dialogue. Lastly, she indicates that she owes her inspiration to study science to the Roman Catholic Church, without which she would not have entered this pursuit of truth.

Gabe McNett would like to thank, in alphabetical order, Dr. Paul De Luca, Dr. Jane Kenney-Hunt, students Kyle Klahs and Travis Niemeier, Dr. Karthik Ramaswamy, Dr. Laura Sullivan-Beckers, and student Chris Stiegler for reading his chapter and sharing their insightful responses.

Jane Kenney-Hunt would like to like to thank Cliff Cain, Gabe McNett, and Neil Hunt for their helpful comments.

Rich Geenen would like to thank Siri Geenen for her support and student Chris Givan for his helpful comments.

Chapter One

Introduction

Clifford Chalmers Cain

Why have a conversation between science and religion? Why would such a dialogue be profitable? Why might it be worth the trouble? Why could it possibly be fruitful?

What is the benefit of a conversation, from religion's side?

One of the things science may teach religion is that the conception of God must be re-imagined, or re-imaged, throughout time. As a matter of fact, theologian Paul Tillich argued that each generation must re-interpret religion/theology (in his case, Christianity/Christian theology) for its specific, historical time and for that time's particular, pressing issues. In fact, Tillich at one point, even suggested that, since the notion of "God" carried so much baggage, it ought to be shelved for fifty years until that time when appropriate, relevant content could be given once again to such a concept! He went on to suggest that "God" was "our symbol for 'God,'" meaning that the reality of God exhausted and exceeded the thought categories of any given period in time.[1] The mystery that is God is greater than the rational understanding we have of God in any given moment in history.

As a result, the concept of God—the image of divine Reality—is ever influx and must necessarily be so.

The awareness of the need today for re-imaging God is therefore not unprecedented: In hunter-gatherer times, the forces of nature were divinized as the greatest powers imaginable. So, lightning, thunder, rain, and sun were perceived as gods. The various dynamics of nature were explained in supernatural terms. The gods—plural in number—needed to be appeased, or survival was contested by forces beyond human control. "Every hunter-gatherer culture [had a] belief in supernatural beings—and always more than one of them; there is no such thing as an indigenously monotheistic hunter-gatherer society."[2]

1

When hunter-gatherers settled down and started taking care of the farm, fertility goddesses rose in prominence. These female gods were responsible for the soil's productivity, the abundance of crops, the rotation of the seasons, and the bounty of nature. Indeed, the copulation between goddesses and their god-consorts caused the fertility of the soil and the fecundity of nature. This Agricultural Revolution occurred 10,000 years ago in approximately 8000 BCE.

With the emergence of city-states, power became centered in rulers. Echoing one's king or one's lord, a local god was now portrayed as the divine King or the transcendent Lord. Just as each earthly king ruled over a particular political kingdom, so each heavenly king/god ruled over an earthly kingdom, a people. When peoples battled, so did their respective gods—king vs. king, divine king vs. divine king, god vs. god.

After a long period of theological struggle, innovation, and recidivism, the Hebrews came to affirm that their divine king was the *only* divine king, what has been termed "Yahweh-alonism."[3] The perception now was that there was a single deity; there was believed to be only one God. Through this relatively-new imagining of divinity, monotheism began to replace polytheism as the dominant world theology.

This ethical monotheism (goodness was rewarded and evil was punished by this one God) interpreted failure as due to the people's own shortcomings, not the workings of another deity. And when this interpretive schematic didn't always work (e.g., the Book of Job, in which apparent evil happens to an innocent man—bad things in that instance befall a *good* person), there developed a tag team wrestling match among various theological options:

One option is the traditional "evil as a *punishment*" option. This view regards the suffering that one experiences as a just recompense for immoral actions that that person has performed, or moral actions that that person has failed to perform.

Another option emanates from the figure of "Job" in the Hebrew Bible. The suffering that befalls Job is a "test." Is Job's faith sufficient to endure the pain? Will he continue as a faithful person, even though what happens to him is not deserved? This is the *faith-perseverance* view.

Another option suggests that there is another transcendent or supernatural power at work here. In the Book of Job, that power is named *ha Satan*, literally the "accuser" or the "adversary" or the "celestial prosecutor." The full-blown notion of the Devil, or the Demonic, has not yet been fully developed, since *ha Satan* has no power of independent action, but rather, requires God's permission. So, *ha Satan* is the precursor of "Satan." This is the beginning of the Satan/Devil/Demonic option, the start of conceiving another cosmic power that is opposed to God and is the source of evil, pain, and suffering in the world.

Yet another option is that pain and suffering strengthen one's character. Just as fire galvanizes metal, thus making it stronger, so pain is "ultimately good for you" and "makes you stronger." This is the *character development* view of suffering.

The final option to be briefly described is the "we just don't know why God would do this" view. This alternative accents the distinction between God's reality and human reality: We humans are not capable of understanding why God would cause or allow pain and suffering. As the book of the prophet Isaiah reminds humans, "'For my thoughts are not your thoughts, neither are your ways my ways,' declares the Lord" (Isaiah 55:8). Thus, how it can be that a good and all-powerful God exists, and so do evil and suffering, is unsolvable. The answer is unknown, incapable of being known by humans. It remains a mystery, and this is the *mysterious* view of pain and suffering.

These various options, though quite different in outlook and resolution of the issue, nevertheless underscored the conceptualization of God in terms of "ethical monotheism."

Later, in the historical figure of Jesus, God became re-imagined as "Daddy," "Father" (*Abba* in Aramaic, the language Jesus spoke), a more-connected authority figure and deity whose intimacy was chiefly characterized by love: "God is love" (John 3:16; I John 4:8). The early Church Father, Clement of Alexandria, represents this "now familiar profile of Western religion as belief in only one God, a fundamentally good God who focuses on the moral improvement of human beings, not the gratification of his own desires, and who cares about all people everywhere. That is, a *monotheism* that has an *ethical* core and is *universalist*."[4] As writer James Carroll puts is, "Hebrew religion was revivified as a religion of compassion and empathy, its god a God to be honored in acts of loving-kindness toward the neighbor."[5]

By the late medieval period, the image of God was one characterized by power, absolute power—God's *potential absoluta*. God's omnipotence was stressed over against other divine characteristics such as love and goodness. This time period's over-emphasis of divine power hearkened back to the fifth century and St. Augustine, who wrote in the *Confessions*, "[God is] the omnipotent, all-creating and all-sustaining maker of heaven and earth."[6] As German theologian Jurgen Moltmann captures the point, "This was the new picture of God offered by the Renaissance [and following]: God is almighty, and *potential absoluta* is the pre-eminent attribute of his divinity."[7] In the midst of the uncertainties of life and death, especially occasioned by frequent and widespread outbreaks of the bubonic plague beginning in the fourteenth century, the security afforded by the "faith-certainty" that God was ultimately and absolutely in-charge was comforting in the here-and-now and therefore essential. God controlled what was happening, and what was happening was either punishment for sin or the work of the Devil (as a collaborator in justice whom God lets so punish, or as an accomplice in the testing of faith, or as the source entirely of the evil) or the evil scheming of the Jews (who were charged with poisoning wells) as scapegoats.

In the post-Copernican era, the intimate, immanent, and loving God forwarded and promoted by Jesus was pushed to the periphery by the theological response to the seventeenth century emergence of science and the results of the scientific method. Nature was no longer understood to be the arena of the Devil who sent the plague for his own purposes—or by God's permission administered the plague in God's behalf—but an arena in which scientific observation and experimentation were undertaken. Still dangerous to one's body but no longer harmful to one's soul, nature was perceived by science as working in clockwork efficiency according to natural laws which God had made. Isaac Newton (1642–1727) is a prime example of this perspective, for Newton saw God as the masterful Creator whose existence could not be denied in the beauty and intricacy of nature as divine creation. [8]

So, the creation ran like clockwork. Indeed, in the following century, Englishman William Paley would propose that nature ran like a clock, like a watch. Therefore, there must have been a clock-maker, a watch-maker, who created what is, started it in motion, and then retreated to another area or dimension. William Paley's 1802 book, *Natural Theology: Evidences of the Existence and Attributes of the Deity, Collected from the Appearances of Nature*, was regular and required reading in university classrooms. In this conception of divine reality, God was still transcendent, but no longer immanent—God functioned as a sort of "absentee landlord," who got things going, but now is nowhere to be found.

Today, and in light of the findings of astrophysics (the Big Bang theory), evolution (descent from common ancestry through modification), and genetics (the relationship of genotype to phenotype), and the controversy concerning intelligent design (Is it good science? Is it good religion? Is it both? Is it neither?), it would appear that God is to no longer be conceived as completely-transcendent or immutable, but as ever-changing, ever-present, ever-suffering, and ever-growing—just as we humans change and are present to one another, suffer, and grow.

However, as Robert Wright chimes-in,

> You might think this [the evolutionary development of the concept and character of God] is impossible, If, like me, you grew up with a Sunday School understanding of the scriptures, then you think of God as not having "taken shape" at all. He was there in the beginning, fully formed, and he then gave form to everything else. That's the story in the Bible, at least. What's more, [some serious biblical scholars] have analyzed the Bible and come away with a similarly dramatic account of Yahweh's birth. [9]

This early and abrupt emergence of monotheism, however, does not jibe with a holistic reading of the Bible. For Wright continues, "If you read the Hebrew Bible carefully, it tells the story of a God in evolution, a God whose character changes radically from beginning to end." [10]

A dialogue between religion and science could facilitate such a re-imagining and re-imaging of "the highest power we know"—a re-visioning of God—for our time. This re-visioning would be quite relevant, for it would inform religion and theology at the very least and help transform religion and theology at the very most. In the process, religion and theology would be adjusted and made more plausible and relevant to the worldview, life, and issues of the twenty-first century. As Roman Catholic scholar, David Tracy, has put it, "The systematic theologian's major task is the reinterpretation of the tradition for the present situation." [11] Or as Protestant scholar, Ted Peters, captures the point,

> How can the Christian faith, first experienced and symbolically articulated in an ancient culture now long out of date, speak meaningfully to human existence today as we experience it amid a worldview dominated by natural science, secular self-understanding, and the worldwide cry for freedom? [12]

Of course, the relationship between science and religion has been tenuous at best. At times, the Church has suppressed science, for instance in the trial of Galileo: When the telescopic findings of Galileo Galilei confirmed the theory of Copernicus that the earth orbited the sun—a heliocentric conception of the universe (rather than *vice-versa*, a geocentric conception of the universe)—Galileo was summoned to Rome in 1632, forced to recant his views publicly in 1633, and then decreed to live in seclusion for the rest of his life until his death in 1642.

And at times, science has been dismissive of religion, when it has claimed that the *only* way of knowing anything about the world and about life is through the scientific method. This ontological reductionism asserts that any other method/source is unhelpful and misleading at the least and totally bankrupt and false at the most. This "scientism" has often been accompanied by an accomplice—the philosophical school of logical positivism—which proclaimed that any statement which could not be logically or empirically verified was a totally meaningless assertion. Thus, by their very nature, statements of faith and belief were rendered devoid of meaning.

Yet, ironically, when science emerged in the seventeenth century, most of the early scientists were persons of faith, who saw nature in their investigation as a "Second [revealed] Book," to be held alongside the "First [revealed] Book," the Bible. [13]

So, despite past moments of historical contention, it could be a propitious moment now for the conversation between science and religion. If religion were open to considering the theological implications of science's discoveries and assertions, it could benefit in the ways outlined above, especially and chiefly the revising, reimaging, of the concept of "God."

And what is the benefit of a conversation, from science's side? In a good and genuine conversation, both parties are served, and each party benefits. So, what might science gain?

One thing that religion could underscore for science is Western culture's assertion or assumption that the world—the physical world—is "real" and "good" (i.e., therefore can be engaged) and also "reasonable" or "knowable."

Both science and religion in the West affirm that the reality of the physical world, what we humans sense—see, hear, taste, touch, and smell—is truly real. It is not an illusion; it is not a mirage. It truly exists, and our perception and investigation of it are neither deceptive nor unproductive.

Religion also affirms the goodness of nature. In the Judeo-Christian-Islamic tradition, religion affirms that nature is good (Hebrew, *tov*), which is an intrinsic goodness, since God in Genesis 1 pronounces the creation good a *number* of times before the advent of humankind. Though nature could *appear* evil and was, in its *fallen* state, evil—the Plague could kill you (in fact, it *did* kill one-third to one-half of Europe's human population)—it was originally and basically *good*. This assertion shifted the late Middle Ages' perspective on nature as the Devil's playground (the Devil now became responsible for the Plague, and not God as using disease and death to mete out divine punishment) to a regard for nature as capable of investigation and redemption.[14] Nature was no longer and *necessarily* dangerous territory in which to place one's soul as well as one's body.[15] This shift invited examination and association rather than deterring involvement.

Religion also underscores the reasonableness or know-ability of the universe, the comprehensibility of nature. Einstein maintained that the universe is rational and that this faith that the universe is rational is a *religious* faith:

> There also belongs the faith in the possibility that the regulations valid for the world of existence are rational, that is, comprehensible to reason. I cannot conceive of a genuine scientist without that profound faith. The situation may be expressed by an image: Science without religion is lame, religion without science is blind. . . . The most incomprehensible thing about the universe is that it is comprehensible.[16]

Einstein again affirms, "I assert that the cosmic religious experience is the strongest and the noblest driving force behind scientific research. . . . What a deep faith in the rationality of the structures of the world and what a longing to understand even a small glimpse of the reason revealed in the world there must have been in Kepler and Newton to enable them to unravel the mechanism of the heavens in long years of lonely work!"[17]

In short, Einstein acknowledges "a profound reverence for the rationality made manifest in existence."[18]

In terms of real-ness, good-ness, and rational-ness, religion affirms science's basic assumptions or presuppositions. Here religion does not break new ground for science, but ploughs the same field as science: Religion's assertions match science's presuppositions.[19]

Thus, in these suggestive ways (at the very least), science and religion could benefit from a relationship with one another.

In light of this contention about such a connection, what, then, have been, and might be, the various models of relationship between science and religion in contemporary times?

Georgetown University Roman Catholic layman, John Haught, suggests four models—Conflict, Contrast, Contact, and Confirmation.[20] Carleton College Physics Professor *Emeritus* and Professor *Emeritus* of Religion and Science, the late Ian Barbour, points to a "fourfold typology"—Conflict, Independence, Dialogue, and Integration.[21] Dutch theologian, Willem Drees, argues for no fewer than nine categories.[22] Princeton Theological Seminary Professor, Wentzel van Huyssteen, argues that models of interaction must be contextually examined and that no broad categories at all may be established (he regards Barbour's "fourfold typology" above as too generic, too universal).[23]

For the purposes of this study, and drawing from the options above, the following models will be considered in an introduction to the relationship between religion and science for a general audience—*conflict, contrast,* and *conversation*. These three alternatives will present a fertile, suggestive beginning, and the reader is encouraged to conceive, to be stimulated to consider, additional models or "takes" on the relationship between science and religion.

The "conflict model" regards the two fields as fierce opponents. In this view, science and religion make polar-opposite assertions about reality, and one must choose between the two mutually-contradictory, mutually-exclusive worldviews. If a person has a religious commitment, he/she cannot be scientific. If a person is committed to the scientific method, she/he cannot be religious. This is a very common, even popular, perspective on the relationship between religion and science in the United States and often is fed by the debate over evolution *versus* creation. "Victory" is the goal, and "aggression" is the *modus operandi*.

Here, religion and science are mortal enemies.

However, this "warfare thesis" or "battleground thesis" for the relationship of religion and science skews the historical evidence. "The idea that scientific and religious camps have historically been separate and antagonistic is rejected by all modern historians of science."[24] Though there have been instances of antagonism and outright onslaughts, there have also been examples through the centuries of attempts to dialogue and to effect reconciliation.

"When religion first met modern science in the seventeenth century, the encounter was a friendly one. Most of the founders of the scientific revolution were devout Christians who held that in their scientific work they were studying the handiwork of the Creator."[25] For example, the aforementioned Isaac Newton was a deeply religious man, who believed that his scientific investigation brought one inevitably into contact with the grandeur of the creation. This grandeur suggested and gave evidence to him that there was a Creator. Newton brought together his scientific view on motion and nature with his religious sensitivities:

> When I wrote my treatise about our Systeme, I had an eye upon such Principles as might work with considering men for the beliefe of a Deity, and nothing can rejoice me more than to find it usefull for that purpose.[26]

And in the twenty-first century, Francis Collins—the doctor and Ph.D. who is director of the National Human Genome Research Institute and who headed the Human Genome Project (the successful attempt to map the human genetic inheritance)—is a deeply religious man. After reading C.S. Lewis and witnessing the role religion played in granting buoyancy to his gravely-ill patients, he came to religious faith. In his book, *The Language of God*, he asserts that religion and science can "co-exist in one person's mind." In fact, he acknowledges that our own DNA instruction-book has made it possible to compare our DNA with the DNA of many other species. He affirms that "the evidence supporting the idea that all living things are descended from a common ancestor is truly overwhelming."[27]

Another option is the "contrast model," which regards the two fields as fully and necessarily unfamiliar with each other. In this view, religion and science have different domains of inquiry, and these separate investigations allow for peaceful co-existence but no relationship between them. The late Harvard paleontologist, Stephen Jay Gould, in agreement with a number of fellow scientists, once labeled this as NOMA—"Non-overlapping magisteria"[28]—in other words, the two disciplines are like two, individual, distant, parallel circles which each has its own space or domain or field. "Conflict" only occurs when one field mistakenly or presumptuously makes claims that are properly the prerogative of the other. So long as religion keeps to "things religious" and science to "things scientific," there is no need for a battle.

Thus, according to the contrast model, science is rightly concerned with the value of facts; religion is rightly concerned with the fact of values. Science deals with causal relations among events in the world, while religion deals with moral meaning and purpose in life. In short, science is dedicated to the natural and empirical, and religion is dedicated to the supernatural and the ethical. In the words of biologist James R. Curry, "The power in the Bible [and hence, religion] lies not in its historical accuracy, but in its [ethical] guidance and [psychological or spiritual] reassurance."[29] So long as this dichotomy is preserved, and each one keeps its nose out of the other's business, there is no issue. In fact, they have nothing to say to each other. "Independence" is the goal, and "avoidance" is the *modus operandi.*

Here, religion and science are strangers.

However desirable, it is not so easy for the two fields to be kept neatly and tidily separate and compartmentalized. Religion's articles of faith regularly bump up against the real world in which people live their lives and hold their faith, and this goes far beyond just the field of ethics, values, and morals. In fact, a number of theological doctrines make claims about the world—for example, that the natural world was created (and had a beginning), that it is good (and knowable), that God is involved in the world through a "doctrine of providence" ("miracles" being but one expression and "symbol" of this activity), that history is going somewhere (fulfilling some sort of *telos* or purpose), and that hope is credible (and not merely wishful thinking).

As the Very Rev. Dr. Mark Richardson, President and Dean of the Church Divinity School of the Pacific, has remarked,

> If God is one, then the universe the scientist explores must be the same universe about which we [theologians] make assumptions from the standpoint of faith under different descriptions.[30]

In addition, and in terms of the previously-mentioned realm of ethics, the work of science often bumps up against morals and values questions which its methodology is not prepared to address. "Can we?" questions of capability and applied technology push scientists into the realm of "Should we?" questions of ethics and moral values. These "meta-questions" or "boundary questions"[31] could benefit from contact between the two fields. In this way, sometimes science can be the primary beneficiary of the interaction. Debates over what direction to go and what steps to take can be informed by the work and reflections of religion. For the "wise use of knowledge" is an ethical, social, cultural concern, not just a scientific one.

Lastly, the "conversation model" envisions the two fields as capable of dialogue and pledged to engage in it. In this model, the two disciplines talk to each other. The discussion is for the purpose of exchange to advance potential mutual knowledge. Each field can learn from the other through such intentional contact. For example, and to religion's benefit, religion can learn from science about the ways in which genetic inheritance can shape persons' behavior, orientation, and appearance. And for example, and to science's benefit, science can learn from religion about concerns that certain scientific discoveries or capabilities could be misused and thereby render harm rather than health, evil rather than good.

"Friendship" is the goal, and "discussion" is the *modus operandi.*

As indicated, sometimes religion can be the primary beneficiary of the conversation: Conceptions of divine realities and understandings of doctrine may be re-thought and re-vamped. Reformulation of ideas about God and about human nature, informed by the findings of contemporary science while still holding to (or attempting to hold to) the messages of one's religious tradition, may be attempted.

As has been noted,

> There have been many unsettling [scientific] discoveries . . . , but always some notion of the divine has survived the encounter with science. The notion [of God] has had to change, but that's no indictment of religion. After all, science has changed relentlessly, revising if not discarding old theories, and none of us thinks of that as an indictment of science. On the contrary, we think this ongoing adaptation is carrying science closer to the truth. Maybe the same thing is [or could be] happening to religion.[32]

Biology Professor *Emeritus* James Curry observes in his book, *Children of God, Children of Earth*, that as a discipline, science is ever and necessarily immersed in the process of change(ing).[33] Scientific hypotheses are put forth, tested, assailed, tried to be disproved, revised if inaccurate in details or insufficient in explanation, and then set forth again to undergo rigorous tests of "verification" or "falsification." Science is dynamic. Sometimes change comes quickly, other times more slowly.

For example, the Steady-State Universe theory proposed by Fred Hoyle enjoyed prominence in the court of scientific opinion and held sway for a number of years before being replaced by the Big Bang theory. But the point is clear: When the evidence was forthcoming that the universe was expanding (based on red-light shift)[34] and that the universe had a beginning, science dramatically adjusted its conclusions and its world-view.

However, Professor Curry goes on to acknowledge critically that religion, by contrast, "seems" not to change. The late philosopher Bertrand Russell makes it a duet: "A religious creed differs from a scientific theory in claiming to embody eternal and absolutely certain truth, whereas science is always tentative, expecting that modifications in its present theories will sooner or later be found necessary, and aware that its method is one which is logically incapable of arriving at a complete and final demonstration."[35]

But, in fact, it can be successfully argued that religion *does* change, but not "typically" at the rate of speed of science. Sometimes, indeed, religion is stubbornly resistant to adjustment, even when the evidence or necessity for modification is substantial if not overwhelming.

For example, as previously noted, Galileo was summoned before the Inquisition of the Roman Catholic Church in the seventeenth century, found guilty, and forced to live in strict seclusion for the rest of his life. It was not until the twentieth century that Pope John Paul II issued an apology for the Church's action and an exoneration of Galileo. This took but 300 years!

Be that as it may, and moving slowly over a (much) longer period of time, religion/theology *does* change. And perhaps the conversation between science and religion can assist religion to refine its understanding of God, thereby moving or changing the religious worldview closer to "truth."

This is what Robert Wright argues in his ambitious and wide-ranging book, *The Evolution of God*. He delineates the various theological revisions/adaptations/dramatic changes that religion/theology has undergone throughout history: From animism (nature—both animate and inanimate—is filled with spirits) to polytheism (many, many gods exist) to henotheism/monolatry/tribal deity (rejecting the worship of all gods but Yahweh; i.e., many gods exist, but we have loyalty to just one, and devotion to the others is forbidden) to theological monotheism (there is one God, but is this one deity nasty or nice?) to ethical monotheism (originally considered a god of vengeance, now this one God is conceived as loving and expects humans to be and do likewise in obedience to God's commandments) to ? Clearly, "monotheism turns out to be . . . a very malleable thing."[36]

These alterations or adjustments were not made in a vacuum, but in the context of political, historical, economic, social, religious, and scientific forces. "Facts on the ground—facts about power and money and other crass things—have often been the leading edge of change, with religious belief following along."[37] For example, God's "divine upward mobility" from and through the polytheism of ancient Israel to universal monotheism was occasioned or stimulated or caused in (great) part by the northern kingdom of Ephraim's fall to the Assyrians and the southern kingdom of Judah's exile to Babylon.[38] "Israelite thinkers adjusted theology to their exilic predicament."[39] In other words, "circumstances change, and God changes with them."[40]

In the conversation model, then—just as it is in human friendship—a conversational friendship between science and religion can sometimes be contentious, sometimes affirming. For friends disagree as well as agree, disappoint as well as inspire, criticize as well as support.

But here, in this model, religion and science are partners.[41]

For example, in his day, Galileo re-thought biblical hermeneutics in an attempt to harmonize his scientific findings and his understanding of biblical texts. He was not unprecedented in this approach. Thirteen hundred years before him, Augustine of Hippo had advocated a similar resolution of apparent conflict: When or where there is a disagreement between the demonstrated knowledge of nature and the world that scientific investigation produces with the literal reading of the biblical texts, then the text in question is to be interpreted metaphorically, not literally. The text in question in Galileo's case (indicated in his "Letter to the Grand Duchess Christina")[42] was the passage in Joshua 10 in the Hebrew Bible (Old Testament) in which God commands the sun to stand still in the sky so that the Israelites can exact a more devastating victory on the battlefield against their opponents.

Galileo and Augustine both agreed that we can learn about the world and about life through two sources—the Book of Scripture and the Book of Nature: Religion and Science.

Mathematician and philosopher, Alfred North Whitehead, realized nearly 100 years ago the importance of a conversation between science and religion and also the difficulty of that dialogue:

> When we consider what religion is for mankind, and what science is, it is no exaggeration to say that the future course of history depends upon the decision of this generation as to the relations between them. We have here the two strongest general forces which influence men, and they seem to be set one against the other—the force of our religious institutions, and the force of our impulse to accurate observation and logical deduction.[43]

Harald Fritzsch was optimistic that this opposition would shortly come to an end:

> It is only a question of time before everyone, not only those involved in [scientific] research, will become concerned about the relationship of science and religion. The time of reciprocal exclusion [conflict model] or division into discrete competencies [contrast model] is past. The world of belief and the world of science are complementary, interdependent worlds. To draw a sharp dividing line between them, as many theologians [and scientists] have done in the past and still do today, is absurd.[44]

This time has come. Consequently, while acknowledging historically and philosophically the three models of Conflict, Contrast, and Conversation, this book will especially and specifically advocate and play-out the third model of interaction—"conversation" (friendship, partnership)—and will explore the relationship between religion and science on four important, contemporary topics/issues:

Cosmic Origins
Evolutionary Theory
Genetics
And
Intelligent Design

Scientific experts have written chapters describing the best and latest that science has to offer in understanding our world based on these four topics or issues. The work of each writer—physicist Laura Stumpe, biologist Gabe McNett, geneticist Jane Kenney-Hunt, and philosopher Rich Geenen—stands on its own. Though a specific author may have included her/his opinion or point-of-view on the subject matter of that chapter, the professors' work was not written *for* a religious or theological response. That is, their work in no way *sets things up* for a specific religious reply. Indeed, the writers represent a spectrum of belief and unbelief, religiosity and non-religiosity, faith and doubt, affirmation and agnosticism. In that regard, it will be no surprise that the writers may, or may not, stand in agreement with the religious and theological responses that have been made to their respective chapters.

Though their writing and friendship have influenced me—and I am deeply grateful for both—they are not responsible for any perspectives or points-of-view—or errors or misstatements or misinterpretations, for that matter—contained in the response chapters.

NOTES

1. Paul Tillich, *Systematic Theology*, Vol. I (Chicago: University of Chicago Press, 1951), 19f; *Dynamics of Faith* (New York: Harper and Row, 1957); "On the Idea of a Theology of Culture," in Paul Tillich, *What is Religion?*, ed. by James Luther Adams (New York: 1969). The film character, Catherine Holly (portrayed by the late actress, Elizabeth Taylor), makes the same point in the 1959 movie, *Suddenly Last Summer*, when she exclaims, "People try to spell 'God' with punctuation marks."

2. Robert Wright, *The Evolution of God* (New York: Little, Brown, and Co., 2009), 17; cf.; Forrest Church, *Love and Death* (Boston: Beacon Press, 2009), 124f.

3. *Ibid.*, 150.

4. *Ibid.*, 71.

5. James Carroll, *Jerusalem, Jerusalem* (Boston, New York: Houghton, Mifflin, Harcourt, 2011), 110.

6. Gijsbert van den Brink, "God's Absolute Power and Late Medieval Extremism," in *Almighty God: A Study of the Doctrine of Divine Omnipotence* (Kampen, the Netherlands: KOK Pharos Publishing House, 1993), 83–86, 92.

7. Jurgen Moltmann, *God in Creation* (San Francisco: HarperCollins, 1991), 26.

8. Isaac Newton, *Principia*, Book III, *Newton's Philosophy of Nature*, ed. by H.S. Thayer (New York: Hafner Library of Classics, 1953), 42; R.K. Winn, "The Emergence of Rational Dissent," in *Enlightenment and Religion* (Cambridge, England: University of Cambridge Press, 1996), 19.

9. Wright, *op. cit.*, 101; cf. Robert K. Gnuse, *No Other Gods: Emergent Monotheism in Israel* (Sheffield, England: Sheffield Academic Press, 1997), 66.

10. Wright, *loc. cit.*

11. David Tracy, *The Analogical Imagination: Christian Theology and the Culture of Pluralism* (New York: Crossroad, 1981), 64.

12. Ted Peters, *Playing God* (New York and London: Routledge, 1997), 157–158.

13. Examples of such early scientists are Francis Bacon, Copernicus, Galileo, and Isaac Newton.

14. Francis Bacon believed that nature, though "fallen," was able to be examined without putting the examiner's soul in jeopardy. He thought that nature could be interrogated in order to have "her" secrets revealed.

15. The work of Carolyn Merchant is notable, and recommended, on this theme. See her book, *The Death of Nature* (San Francisco: Harper and Row, 1980).

16. Albert Einstein, *Out of My Later Years* (The Estate of Albert Einstein, 1956).

17. Albert Einstein, *The New York Times Magazine* (November 9, 1930); cf. Walter Isaacson, *Einstein: His Life and Universe* (New York: Simon and Schuster, 2007), 2–3.

18. Albert Einstein, *Out of My Later Years* (The Estate of Albert Einstein, 1956).

19. The goodness of reality, an assertion of religion in the West, could and would attract investigation. While scientific engagement today with the natural world does not necessarily depend on nature's goodness (indeed, most contemporary scientists would just assume that the world simply "is" and is "indifferent"), the assumption that it is not *evil*—as construed in the Middle Ages—would be a motivation for learning as much as possible about it, rather than avoiding it in fear for one's soul as well as for one's body.

20. John Haught, *Science and Religion* (New York: Paulist Press, 1995).

21. Ian Barbour, *When Science Meets Religion* (New York: HarperCollins, 2000), 7–38; cf. Ian Barbour, *Religion in an Age of Science* (San Francisco: HarperCollins, 1990).

22. Willem Drees, *Science and Naturalism* (Cambridge, England: Cambridge University Press, 1996), 43–49.

23. Wentzel van Huyssteen, *Duel or Duet?: Theology and Science in a Postmodern World* (Harrisburg, PA: Trinity Press International, 1998).

24. Lawrence M. Principe, *Science and Religion* (Chantilly, VA: The Teaching Company, 2006), 22f., 96–111; cf., Lawrence M. Principe, *The Scientific Revolution* (New York: Oxford University Press, 2011). See also, Gary Ferngren, *Science and Religion: A Historical Introduction* (Baltimore, MD: Johns Hopkins Press, 2002), which explodes the myth of the warfare thesis between science and religion.

25. Ian Barbour, *When Science Meets Religion* (New York: HarperCollins, 2000), xi.

26. Isaac Newton, *Philosophiae Naturalis Principia*, quoted in Stephen D. Snobelen, "To Discourse of God: Isaac Newton's Heterodox Theology and His Natural Philosophy," in *Science and Dissent in England, 1688–1945*, ed. by Paul B. Wood (Aldershot, Hampshire, England: Ashgate Publications, 2004), 39.

27. Francis S. Collins, Interview: "God Is Not Threatened by Our Scientific Adventures," www.beliefnet.com/News/Science-Religion/2006/08/God-Is-Not-Threatened-By-Our-Scientific-Adventures; cf. *The Language of God* (New York: Free Press, 2006).

28. Non-overlapping magisteria (NOMA) is the view that science and religion each has "a legitimate magisterium, or domain of teaching authority," and that these two domains do not overlap. Gould suggests that "NOMA enjoys strong and fully explicit support, even from the primary cultural stereotypes of hard-line traditionalism" and that it is "a sound position of general consensus, established by long struggle among people of goodwill in both magisteria." Stephen Jay Gould, *Rocks of Ages: Science and Religion in the Fullness of Life* (New York: Ballantine Books, 2002); cf. Ian Barbour, *ibid.*, 99–101.

29. James R. Curry, *Children of God, Children of Earth* (Bloomington, IN: AuthorHouse, 2008), 165.

30. W. Mark Richardson, "Presentation at All Saints Episcopal Church" (Pasadena, CA, May 6, 2012), 1. This was also a common theme in the writing of Arthur Peacocke, Anglican priest, theologian, and biochemist, in *Theology for a Scientific Age* (Minneapolis: Fortress Press, 1993).

31. Karl Rahner, *Foundations of Christian Faith* (New York; Seabury Press, 1978), 11f.

32. Wright, *op. cit.,* 5.

33. Curry, *op. cit.*

34. Edwin Hubble, in the late 1920's, formulated the Law that bears his name when he examined the "red shift" of light from nebulae far, far away—"The velocity of recession of a nebula is proportional to its distance from us." This is quoted in Ian Barbour, *When Science Meets Religion*, 39; see also the next chapter on cosmic origins by physicist Laura Stumpe.

35. Bertrand Russell, *Religion and Science* (Oxford: Oxford University Press, 1935).

36. Wright, *op. cit.*, 186. Wright's book is heartily recommended to the reader. Though controversial, it is thoroughly researched and compellingly written. Anglican Bishop John A.T. Robinson makes a similar point to Wright's in his classic, ground-breaking book from over 50 years ago, *Honest to God* (Philadelphia: Westminster Press, 1963). In that forthright and transparent set of reflections, he argues that our God-concept changes over time in response to

historical, political, cultural, ethical, and theological developments. For example, he proposes that a supranatural depiction of God ("God [only] 'out there'") was no longer persuasive in the last two-fifths of the twentieth century and that an emphasis on God's immanence (presence) was needed to balance God's transcendence (otherness).

37. Wright, *op. cit.,* 133.

38. *Ibid.,* 117f.

39. *Ibid.,* 183.

40. *Ibid.,* 187.

41. It has been pointed out that this partnership seems "asymmetrical," in that religion may be giving-up more, or conceding more, as a result of the conversation: 'Science determines the truth about the world, and religion adjusts to it.' However, a partnership does not assume 50-50 at all times in order for there to be a conversation. And there appears to be a need, since the two fields have avoided having a conversation for so long, for religion to "catch up"—that is, to allow its assertions about God and the world to be informed by the very best of what science has to offer. This does not mean, however, that religion has acquiesced to any one-sided claim that only science, and its scientific method, can determine, or arrive at, "truth."

42. Galileo Galilei, "Letter to the Grand Duchess Christina (1615)," in *The Essential Galileo,* trans. and ed. by Maurice Finocchiaro (Indianapolis: Hackett Publishing Co., 2008), 109–145.

43. Alfred North Whitehead quote is from John Haught, *op. cit.,* 2.

44. Harald Fritzsch, "Science and Religion Are Complementary," in *Science and Religion: Opposing Viewpoints* (San Diego: Greenhaven Press, 1988), 58; cf. Harald Fritzsch, *The Creation of Matter: The Universe from Beginning to End* (New York: Basic Books, 1984).

Chapter Two

The Big Bang Theory

Laura Stumpe

Close your eyes and try to picture where you are right now in the universe. How do you picture yourself? To be in keeping with our current state of knowledge, picture yourself on a blue-green ball immersed in the blackness of space, a ball that spins around as it circles a giant ball of fire at the rate of about 19 miles per second. If you could tell that you were traveling at this speed, your day-to-day existence on the earth would rival all roller coaster rides. In addition, picture yourself and the Earth swirling around the center of our spiral-shaped galaxy containing billions of stars like the sun in the gigantic black sea of space full of millions of other galaxies. Is this not absolutely amazing to think about! You don't even feel like you are moving at all!

You have just pictured your place in the universe for a short snippet of time, but what do you picture if you "rewind the tape"? What took place before you were born? Before any humans existed? In addition, what will happen to the universe in the future? Has the universe always existed? Will it come to an end? Many disciplines seek to provide answers to these questions, and science is certainly one of them. The current theory of the origin of the universe that is accepted by most scientists today is called the Big Bang Theory. In this chapter, I would like to provide you with an introduction to this theory—what it is, where it came from, the evidence for it, and how it has been modified recently. Before we get started, I would like to review with you how science works today.

THE METHOD OF SCIENCE

If you had lived in the 1400's, your picture of yourself in the universe would have been quite different. Without the equipment or knowledge that we have today, it made perfect sense to think that the earth was stationary. Even today we speak as if the earth were stationary when we say that the sun is rising or that the sun is going down. It is easy to look back and laugh at what people believed years ago, but it is important to keep in mind that people in the future may look back at us and laugh at what we believe today. This idea brings us to the first of four points I want to make about the field of science as we practice it today—theories in science are not absolutes. In the field of science, we have to be open to being wrong.

The second point is related to the first: Theories are constructed using the scientific method. We bring forth a hypothesis that can be tested, that can be proven wrong by an experiment. A theory is an explanation of a large number of phenomena that has been tested over and over again. We cannot say that a theory is absolutely correct, because more evidence may come-in to show that it is not. For example, even though scientists accept the theory of relativity, you will find that experiments are being conducted at this very moment to test relativity theory. However, if we don't like a theory, we should not brush it off as "just a theory." A theory after all requires a lot of hard work and has to pass the inspections of many distinguished scientists. Indeed, the scientific spirit compels one to get in the game and offer a hypothesis that could prove the theory wrong or to come up with a different theory that could be tested.

Many people in the history of science have disliked or liked a certain theory, and here we arrive at the third point: In science we appeal to reason. Scientists have many different backgrounds, but what we appeal to is reason. A scientist who wants to offer a new theory must convince other scientists that the theory is correct through reason (based on observations and mathematical calculations).

Finally, the fourth point is that some of the principles under which we operate in science are not "proven"; we just take them to be true. One is that the universe is reasonable. Otherwise, what is the point of science?! Another principle is that the simplest explanation that fits the data is the best explanation. A third principle is that the laws that are true here on earth are also true "out there" in the remote areas of the universe. This third principle is called the cosmological principle and is testable (it can be proven wrong). In fact, the cosmological principle helped scientists to form the Big Bang Theory. If the laws are different in space, then we are at a loss when it comes to constructing a theory of how the present state of the universe came to be. However, by assuming that physical laws are universal and with our knowledge of how those laws work on earth, we are able to piece together an understanding of why things are as we observe them and make predictions about future observations.

Therefore, when we approach the Big Bang Theory, we need to keep in mind that the theory is not to be taken as an absolute truth in science, but that it deserves great respect as it has been built by the hard work of many people. Based on reason, it has had to gain the approval of many scientists. And finally, the Big Bang Theory was developed using the cosmological principle. With these four points in mind, we will proceed to a description of the Big Bang Theory.

WHAT IS THE BIG BANG THEORY?

The Big Bang Theory is the theory that the known universe was once an extremely dense fireball only a few millimeters across in size, and that it expanded to its current size and continues to expand. Some people mistakenly think that the Big Bang indicates an explosion like a bomb that goes off with pieces flying out in all directions. However, this view is not correct. In the theory, there is no center of the universe. Also, the theory doesn't require the universe to be finite or infinite. Instead, you can loosely think of the process like a chocolate chip cake. When the cake is cooked in the oven, it expands. The chocolate chips don't expand but the distance between any two chips increases. In this analogy, the chocolate chips are the galaxies. The cake batter is empty space. Space itself *expands* or stretches. Figure 2.1 illustrates this effect.

If space is expanding as described, then if we rewind the tape, we will find the galaxies all merging together. Therefore, the Big Bang Theory indicates that the universe had a beginning. With this theory, we can discuss the state of the universe from the very first few seconds of time. However, the theory is not able to offer answers as to what happened before those first few seconds. The Big Bang Theory is able to give an age for the universe (12–14 billion years old) and is able to give an answer as to what may happen to the universe in the future based on experimentally-determined variables (continuous expansion or Big Crunch). We will delve more into how the theory can

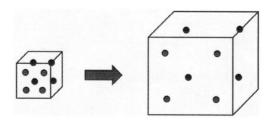

Figure 2.1.   The box on the left illustrates a densely packed universe where the dots represent galaxies. Upon expanding, the universe looks like the box on the right. The galaxies are the same sizes as before but the distances between galaxies have increased.

help us determine the age and fate of the universe later, but first, you may be wondering how this theory began and why scientists accept it. [1]

THE ORIGIN OF THE BIG BANG THEORY

Where did the theory come from? In the early 1900's, the prevailing theory of the universe's origins was known as the Steady State Theory. This theory championed the view that the universe is static and has always been in the state that it is in now. Two key discoveries overturned this prevailing view and ushered in the era of the Big Bang Theory—new *solutions* of Einstein's General Relativity equations and new detailed *observations* of the radial velocities and distances of galaxies. The former is a theoretical result, and the latter an experimental one. Let's take a look at these two main discoveries and some of the people who discovered them. [2]

First, let's look at the new solutions of Einstein's General Relativity equations. Before doing so, we have to go back to Isaac Newton. Newton recognized that any two pieces of matter are attracted to each other with a force proportional to the mass of each and inversely-proportional to the distance between them squared. The force is called the force due to gravity, and using this force, he was able to explain the motion of different objects not only on earth, but also in space. (This is the cosmological principle in action. The objects in space are subject to the same laws as objects on earth.) However, Newton's force law breaks down for objects that move near the speed of light. Einstein came up with a new description of the motion of objects and gravity that expanded on Newton's work and gives a more accurate description of the motion of objects, including those moving near light speed. His theory is known as General Relativity. In this theory, space and time are not independent of each other and so a concept was born called space-time. In this theory, instead of thinking of masses moving differently due to forces, you look at masses moving differently based on the curvature of space-time. Matter, by its presence, tells space-time how to curve. Think of a ball rolling in a funnel. If you give the ball a sideways push, it will roll in a circle in the funnel, like a planet orbiting a star. This analogy gives you a rough idea of how space-time affects the motion of bodies. See Figure 2.2. [3]

The key idea here is that in Einstein's conception, empty space has physical properties. What I mean by physical properties is that space can bend, curve, and stretch even though it is not made of material. Many people are puzzled to learn that the Big Bang Theory says that space is stretching, but this fits right-in with Einstein's theory.

The theory of General Relativity has been very successful in explaining observations in space and has not been disproven. In formulating the theory, Einstein put a number (called the cosmological constant) into his equations

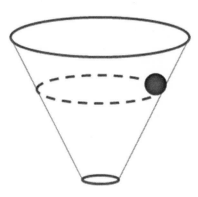

Figure 2.2. In Einstein's General Relativity Theory space-time tells matter how to move in a way similar to a funnel telling a ball how to roll in the picture above.

that gave solutions supporting a static universe, the prevailing view of the time (he later called this his greatest blunder, even though scientists today are seeing that the cosmological constant may have some significance). However, Alexander Friedmann, a Russian cosmologist, discovered in 1922 that solutions could also support a dynamical universe if the number is not inserted. Independently, in 1927, Georges LeMaitre, an astronomer and a Catholic priest (who is sometimes called the "father of the Big Bang Theory"), found that Einstein's equations supported an expanding universe, and he related his view to experimental observations. The idea that the universe may not be static, but is expanding based on solutions to Einstein's equations, was the first key discovery in the development of the Big Bang Theory. [4]

The second key discovery was an experimental one. Edwin Hubble found observational evidence for the expansion of the universe. In order to understand this discovery, we have to think through the following question: How do we know anything in astronomy? We have not visited the places that we see in the night sky (except for the moon). So, how do we know about these places? The answer is . . . light. What can we know from light? We can know the direction from which it came to us, the frequency or wavelength of it, the intensity of it, and something called the polarization of it. This may not sound like a lot of information, but from it we can determine all kinds of things—the distances to objects (some are more difficult to measure than others), the elements that are in an object, as well as the speeds of objects moving toward or away from us.

How do we know the speed of an object moving away from us by observing its light? We can measure the wavelength of the light that is being emitted from the object. Light has wave properties. For visible light, the wavelength corresponds to a specific color. In a wave you have crests (high-

est points) and troughs (lowest points). The wavelength is the distance between adjacent crests or the distance between adjacent troughs in a wave.
Red light has a wavelength of about 600 nanometers (nm). (One nanometer is
equal to 0.000000001 meters.) The number corresponds to a specific color of
red. Figure 2.3 shows a comparison between paint by numbers and the light
that is emitted by a star. In paint by numbers, the key at the bottom tells you
which colors to paint different objects so that a number stands for a particular
color. From a star, certain specific "colors" of light are emitted. Those colors
correspond to numbers that describe the wavelength of the light.

If we observe this wavelength of light to be larger than what it "should"
be, the object must be moving away from us. This is called a redshift. It is the
Doppler effect for light. The Doppler effect is the increased/decreased frequency that you observe when an object, emitting waves at a particular
frequency, moves toward you/away from you. We are more familiar with the
Doppler effect for sound. Just think of the decreased frequency (indicating a
longer wavelength) you hear when an ambulance is going away from you.

Once we observe the light, how do we know what the color of the light
"should" have been? The answer is that the colors that come out are a kind of
bar code for the elements that are contained within the object. For example,
hydrogen has a very specific set of colors that are emitted when it is heated.
We assume that those same colors are emitted from hydrogen on other stars/
planets, and so if the numbers (the frequencies) of those colors are lower than
those of the colors for hydrogen on earth (decreased frequencies), we say that
a redshift has occurred. The shift in frequency tells us the speed with which
the object is moving away from us. If you have ever been stopped by the

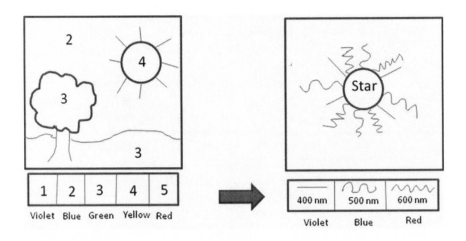

Figure 2.3.   Just as a number represents a color in paint by numbers, a number (frequency) represents a color of light emitted by a star.

police for speeding, you have experienced the Doppler effect for light, since the radar gun is an application of this effect.

In 1930, Hubble (an American astronomer and one of the most important cosmologists of the 20th century) and Milton Humason (another American astronomer whose observations greatly assisted Hubble) made great improvements to the observational measurements of the distances and radial velocities of galaxies. (The *radial* velocity is the speed of the object directly toward or away from the observer along the line of sight.) When Hubble plotted the radial velocities of galaxies versus their distances from us, he found a pattern. Figure 2.4 is the graph of his original data.[5]

A point on the graph represents a galaxy. On the horizontal axis of the graph is the distance to a galaxy. The vertical axis is the velocity of the galaxy. A positive velocity means that the galaxy is moving away from us. A negative velocity means that the galaxy is moving towards us.

The points tend to fall on a straight line which is shown on the graph. (LeMaitre noticed this relationship, too, albeit with less-conclusive data.) The graph expresses what is known as "Hubble's Law." What does this graph tell us? It tells us that other galaxies are all moving away from us at a rate that is proportional to each galaxy's distance from us. (With the im-

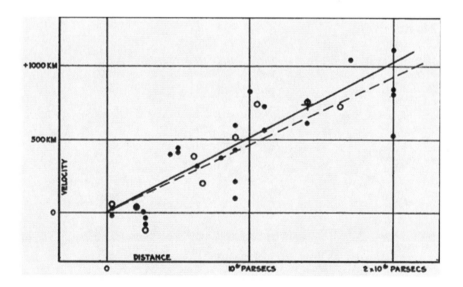

Figure 2.4. The original graph of Hubble showing the relationship that we call today "Hubble's law." Source: Edwin Hubble. "A Relation between Distance and Radial Velocity among Extra-Galactic Nebulae," Proceedings of the National Academy of Sciences of the United States of America 15, Issue 3 (1929): 172.

proved precision of today's instruments, the points fall much closer to the line.)[6]

In order to understand Hubble's law, try thinking about the following analogy: Suppose you are in a car parked on a road and there are other cars parked ahead of you and behind you at equal distances as shown in Figure 2.5. Then using the same relationship expressed in Hubble's law, the cars directly in front and behind you (marked as A in the figure) would move at one particular speed and the two cars in front/behind (marked as B in the figure) would move at double that speed since they are twice as far away.

This is a really curious result. Why should this be? Why are we at the center of it all? Why should it be that other galaxies want to get away from ours and that the ones farther away travel even faster to get away from us? It turns out that there is another interpretation of the data. You would also get this same graph if *space* itself was stretching. This interpretation is the one that was accepted at that time as supporting the idea that the universe is expanding.

Going back to the car analogy, imagine that the cars remain parked and the road underneath the cars is somehow stretching so that instead of one unit of distance between cars, after some time you have two units of distance

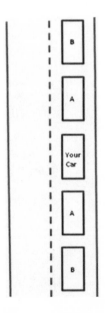

Figure 2.5. To understand Hubble's law, think of parked cars. While you remain parked, cars A start moving away from you at a particular speed while cars B move away from you at double that speed since car B is twice as far away as car A. This is an analogy of how other galaxies move compared to our galaxy.

between each car. Car A moved one unit of distance away in that time so you could say that it moved 1 unit distance/time interval. However, car B moved 2 units of distance away from you in the same amount of time since the distance between your car and car B doubled. You could say then that car B moved more quickly than car A since it moved 2 units of distance/time interval compared to the 1 unit distance/time interval of car A. In addition from the vantage point of car B, you get the same result. Someone in car B would say that *your* car is moving away from *theirs* at 2 units distance/time interval.

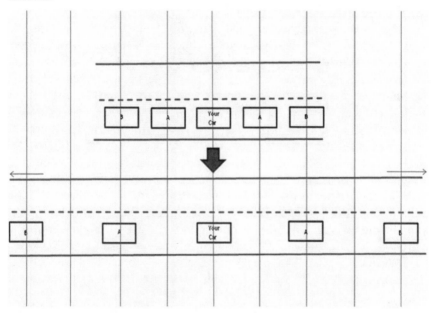

Figure 2.6.   In one time interval, the parked car scenario goes from the top picture to the bottom picture. The road stretches with all of the cars remaining stuck to the road in their respective parking places. Car A has moved 1 unit of distance in the time interval in which a unit of distance is indicated by adjacent vertical lines. Car B has moved 2 units of distance in the time interval so that its "speed" is twice as fast as Car A (2 units of distance/time interval versus 1 unit of distance/time interval).

From the previous paragraph, we can see that the stretching of space would support Hubble's law without requiring us (our galaxy) to be at the center of it all. However, would the same physical effect for light still occur? In other words, with the stretching of space, would you still get a redshift as you do when an object is truly moving away from you in space? The answer is yes. To get a feeling for how this can be, think about a wave drawn on a rubber band as in Figure 2.7. On the left is the color of light that you should see. We already know that it can be represented as a number value of wavelength. What happens to the wavelength when you stretch the rubber band?

The wavelength becomes longer, which is a redshift. Hubble's law is consistent with the idea that space itself is stretching or that the universe is expanding.

Figure 2.7.   To understand how the stretching of space can give a redshift for light, imagine stretching a rubber band on which you have drawn a wave. As you stretch the rubber band, the wavelength increases.

Take a look back at the original graph of Hubble's law in Figure 2.4. Recall that any straight line has a slope, which in this case is the change in the velocity over the change in the distance. The slope is called Hubble's constant and is represented by the letter H. Hubble's constant has a physical meaning. We know that distance equals velocity times time or d=vt. If we divide both sides of this equation by the velocity, we get d/v=t. Hubble's constant gives us v/d. Therefore, if we take the inverse of Hubble's constant, we have a time. What time is this? Well, take one galaxy. The time is the distance it is away from us divided by the speed with which it is moving away from us. This is the time it took for the galaxy to go from being at the same location as us to its present distance away from us. This time is the same for all of the galaxies. Therefore, this time is the age of the universe. The Hubble constant gives us an estimate for the age of the universe. The current measured value for H is 73.5 km/s/ Mpc (plus or minus 3.2 km/s/ Mpc), where Mpc stands for megaparsecs which is a large distance. With this value for H, the age of the universe would be between 12 and 14 billion years old.[7]

The Big Bang Theory was not accepted by many scientists at first. In fact, Fred Hoyle is the one who first called the theory the "big bang" theory in derision. He preferred the Steady State Theory. However, the two discoveries of the dynamic solutions of Einstein's General Relativity equations together with observational evidence that galaxies are moving away from us began to convince scientists that the Big Bang Theory should replace the Steady State Theory as the prominent theory to account for the universe. But what other observations support the Big Bang Theory? Our next topic will answer this question.[8]

MORE EVIDENCE FOR THE BIG BANG THEORY

In general, a theory needs to make predictions that can be tested, and the Big Bang Theory is no exception to this rule. If the Big Bang Theory is correct, then we expect to see _____ in our observations. We will fill in the blank with two important sets of observations that were predicted and then confirmed for the Big Bang Theory. The first is the abundance of light elements, and the second is the prediction of cosmic microwave background radiation.

Before discussing the first prediction, I would like to review with you some basic chemistry and physics. All matter can be broken down into elements. An atom of each element consists of a nucleus (consisting of neutrons and protons) and electrons outside of the nucleus. The protons are positively charged, neutrons have no charge, and electrons are negatively charged. See Figure 2.8.

How is an element defined? What makes it unique? In other words, what makes hydrogen hydrogen and what makes helium helium? The answer is the number of protons. No matter how many neutrons or electrons there are, if there are 2 protons, the element is helium. Therefore the element in Figure 2.8 must be helium. If an element has more or less neutrons than the most abundant form of the element, then you have an isotope of the element. (In other words, an isotope of an element has the same number of protons, but a different number of neutrons.) See Figure 2.9 which shows the first three and lightest elements.

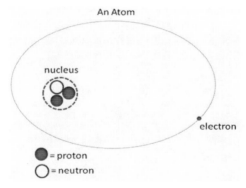

Figure 2.8.   An atom contains protons and neutrons in a nucleus with electrons outside.

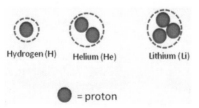

Figure 2.9.   An atom of an element is defined by its number of protons. The first three elements (the lightest) are shown.

You may have noticed that in principle you could create a helium atom by putting two hydrogen atoms together. Thus, the old dream of the alchemists would be fulfilled! (The alchemists tried to change lead into gold.) In principle, this is true, but there is a problem. Two protons do not want to get near each other. They repel because they are both positive and like charges repel. Then how are two protons able to stay together in a helium atom? It turns out that if you can somehow get two protons *really* close together, they will stick due to the "strong force." (The strong force is one of the four fundamental forces, the others being the electromagnetic force, gravity, and the weak force.) How can you get them close together? You can get them close together if you can get them moving very fast. When the temperature is very high in a region, this means that the atoms are moving fast. Therefore, in order to get them close together you need to heat them. When two lighter atoms come together to form heavier atoms, we have caused fusion, and energy is released. I have simplified the description of the process a bit, but this is the basic idea.

Now that we have reviewed some basic facts in chemistry and physics, we will return to one of the major predictions of the Big Bang Theory, the abundance of the light elements. In order to make predictions about the theory, scientists used the rules of physics that are true on earth and applied them to the problem of the early universe, moments after the universe began (cosmological principle). When all of the galaxies were in about the same location, there was a dense fireball. The temperature was very hot, and George Gamow in 1948 thought that perhaps all of the naturally occurring elements were fused and produced in this fireball. (The temperature one second after the universe began was around 10 billion degrees Kelvin/Celsius!) He sent his student, Ralph Alpher, to work on this problem. This work set off the two important predictions that we are discussing.[9]

Alpher and others found that only the lightest elements, hydrogen, helium, and lithium (and their isotopes) could have been formed in the early universe. (The heavier elements were formed later in the explosions of stars.) The forming of the lightest elements in the hot early universe is known as Big Bang nucleosynthesis. The abundance of the lightest elements can be predicted *if* the density of ordinary matter in the universe is known with the exception of one element, helium. The abundance of helium stays about the same for a wide range of densities of the universe and that amount is about 24%. Therefore, the prediction was that of all the known ordinary matter in the universe, about 24% of it should consist of helium. This prediction was verified. In addition, we currently have a special satellite called the WMAP (Wilkenson Microwave Anisotropy Probe), which is able to measure the density of ordinary matter in the known universe. With this value, we can also compare the measured abundances of the other light elements and compare them to predictions. Once again, the observations are in agreement with the predictions.[10]

The second prediction has to do with the cosmic microwave background. In order to understand this prediction better, it is helpful to go over two physical principles—the Plank spectrum and the electromagnetic spectrum. When an object gets really hot, it emits light. Think of embers burning in a fire. The hotter the fire, the bluer the light that is emitted. As the fire starts to die down, the embers glow red and are not as bright. Blue light, as we discussed earlier, has a shorter wavelength than red light. If you take a hot object and figure out all of the colors that are emitted, you will get a spectrum. A spectrum simply tells you the colors of light that you have and how much of each color you have. For a perfect absorber/emitter of light, you get what is called a Planck spectrum. This is best summarized in a graph, an example of which is shown in Figure 2.10.

The next physical principle is the electromagnetic spectrum. We have discussed already how each color in visible light corresponds to a wavelength. However, what is the origin of light? If we wanted to produce it from scratch, how would we? Light comes from charged particles that jostle around or oscillate. If the oscillation is very fast, the wavelength will be very small and the light will be more dangerous. What would happen if a charged particle were to oscillate faster than the frequency of violet light? Or slower than the frequency of red light? These oscillations do in fact occur, and we cannot see the light that results. However, we utilize these oscillations all of

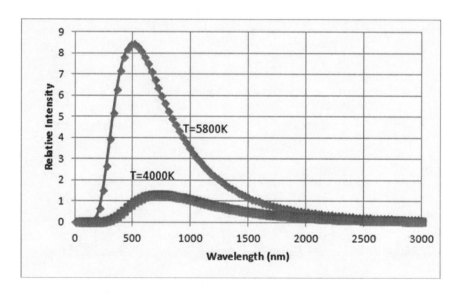

Figure 2.10. A typical Planck spectrum is shown for two different objects, one of which has a peak temperature of 5800 K and the other of which has a peak temperature of 4000 K. The horizontal axis is the wavelength of the light that is emitted from the object and the vertical axis describes the amount of light of each wavelength that is emitted from the object.

the time as they include radio waves, TV waves, microwaves, ultraviolet rays, and x-rays. All of these various waves are the same entity as visible light! We call these kinds of waves "electromagnetic radiation." The waves only differ in wavelength. Figure 2.11 shows the whole electromagnetic spectrum.

Returning to the second prediction in which we will need to know the two physical principles we have just covered, according to the Big Bang theory, when the universe was a few hundreds of thousands of years old, it would have cooled down from the 10 billion degrees mentioned earlier to a few thousand degrees Kelvin/Celsius. At this point in time, electromagnetic radiation, which was previously blocked from traveling in the universe, was set free as hydrogen atoms were formed. (Hydrogen atoms are not so good at blocking electromagnetic radiation.) This radiation would have had a Planck spectrum with a peak at a few thousand degrees Kelvin/Celsius. This temperature corresponds to a peak wavelength of about 1 micrometer. As the universe expanded since this time, that wavelength should have redshifted to a wavelength of about 1 millimeter. This wavelength is in the range of microwaves and corresponds to a peak temperature of a few degrees Kelvin/Celsius. Once this result was predicted, some scientists began to look for this radiation.[11]

In 1965, Arno Penzias and Robert Wilson were trying to eliminate noise in building a radio receiver. No matter what they did, they were not able to eliminate a weak microwave signal. In fact, they had found the cosmic microwave background radiation from the Big Bang, and they won the 1979 Nobel Prize for their discovery.[12]

The finding of Hubble's law, solutions to Einstein's equations, the cosmic background radiation, and abundances of the lightest elements all support the

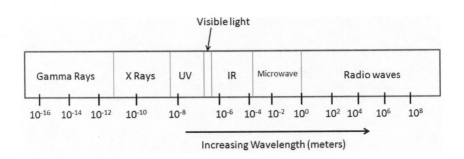

Figure 2.11. The electromagnetic spectrum includes radio waves, microwaves, infrared rays, ultraviolet rays, x-rays, gamma rays and visible light. All of the waves are electromagnetic radiation produced by oscillating charged particles. The waves differ only in wavelength, and our eyes can only see a small portion of the spectrum.

Big Bang Theory of the universe. But, were there any observations that did not support the theory?

THE BIG BANG THEORY TODAY

There were observations that did not support the theory, but they were not serious enough to cause scientists to discard the theory. Instead, the theory had to be modified. We will not go into too much detail on these problems. The first was that the universe was too flat. "Flat" means that the space in the universe does not have a lot of curvature (like a sphere) according to measurements. The second problem was that the cosmic microwave background radiation was too smooth. That is, it was constant in any direction that scientists looked. In the 1980's, Alan Guth, an American theoretical physicist, cosmologist, and professor at M.I.T., proposed an Inflationary Big Bang Theory in which these two problems are solved. This theory modifies the original Big Bang Theory a bit by asserting that there was a time of great inflation in the early universe in which the universe expanded faster than the speed of light. This inflation explains why the universe appears so flat and why the cosmic microwave background radiation is so smooth. This modified Big Bang Theory will be tested over the next years, and scientists will find out if it will be successfully defended. [13]

In addition to making modifications to the theory in order to explain as many observations as possible, scientists also use the current Big Bang Theory to predict the fate of our universe. The two main possibilities that are being considered are first, the universe will keep on expanding indefinitely, and second, the universe will eventually stop expanding and begin contracting. (The second possibility is known as the "Big Crunch"—after initially expanding, gravity will pull all of the matter back together in a big "crunch.") In order to determine which of these two possibilities is the more likely, scientists use experimentally determined variables, such as Hubble's constant (mentioned earlier) and the density of matter in the known universe. The fate of the universe is governed by a power struggle between the expansion pushing all matter outwards and gravity trying to pull all matter back together. If the density of matter is less than or equal to a "critical" density, the force of the expansion will win, and the universe will proceed to expand indefinitely according to the 2nd or 3rd lines from the top in Figure 2.12. However, if the density of matter is greater than the critical density, then gravity wins, and the universe will stop expanding and begin to contract and collapse on itself as in the fourth line from the top of Figure 2.12. [14]

An exciting development is that observations have indicated that the expansion of the universe is actually speeding up or accelerating. This result is very surprising. What could possibly cause the universe to speed up its

EXPANSION OF THE UNIVERSE

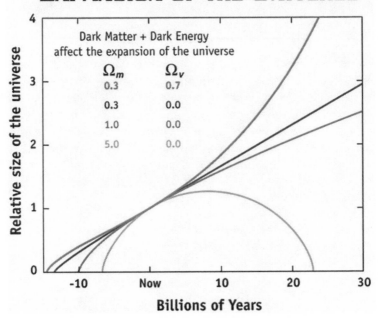

Figure 2.12. The following graph shows the fate of the universe for different values of the density of the universe as well as with and without the dark energy component. The top line shows that the universe will accelerate in its expansion and will expand indefinitely; this line results if the density is equal to the critical density *with* dark energy included as significant. The second/third lines from the top result when the density of the universe is less than/equal to the critical density without the dark energy included as significant. These lines indicate that the universe will also expand indefinitely. The fourth line from the top results when the density is greater than the critical density without the dark energy included as significant; this line indicates that the universe will stop expanding and will begin contracting back together, ending in the "Big Crunch." Image credit: NASA/WMAP Science Team.

expansion?! The answer is something scientists call dark energy. Dark energy is a hypothetical energy that has the effect of causing matter to repel matter (the opposite of the effect of gravity). Mathematically speaking, dark energy does what Einstein's cosmological constant (his greatest blunder) did. By observing the behavior of objects in space, dark energy has been indirectly observed. If the amount of dark energy is of a significant amount, then the universe will proceed according to the top line of Figure 2.12, in which case the universe will continue expanding indefinitely. [15]

Another interesting note is that most of the matter that is included in the measurements of the density of the universe discussed previously is called "dark matter." Ordinary matter includes all of the matter that we can directly observe (protons, neutrons, electrons, etc.). Dark matter has been indirectly observed by watching the behavior of objects in space and taking for granted that the same laws apply there as here (cosmological principle). Because of the observed behaviors of these objects, we infer that there is more matter present there than we are able to detect; this matter, which is inferred to be there, but escapes detection, is known as dark matter. Scientists believe that most of the matter that exists is in the form of dark matter! [16]

With our current measurements and calculations, the top line in Figure 2.12 (density equal to the critical density with dark energy playing a significant role) is emerging as the leading contender for the answer to the fate of the universe. [17]

In summary, the Big Bang Theory is the theory that the known universe was once a tiny, dense fireball, in which space expanded and continues to expand today. This theory came about due to new solutions of Einstein's General Relativity equations and new observations of other galaxies moving away from us. The theory is further supported by the abundance of elements in the universe as well as the existence of the cosmic microwave background radiation. However, no theory is considered as absolutely correct, which is why the Big Bang Theory is being tested today. It has had to be modified in order to account for other observations. Currently, mainstream science accepts the Inflationary Big Bang model, in which the universe underwent a very fast expansion in the beginning, as the theory which best explains the observational results that we have today. In addition, a universe that expands indefinitely with an accelerating expansion rate is emerging as the leading answer to the question of the fate of the universe. I hope you will keep yourself updated on the Big Bang Theory. With the influx of new observational and theoretical work, the theory could be modified, confirmed, or discarded in the future!

NOTES

1. "Universe 101: The Big Bang Theory: How Fast is Our Universe Expanding?," NASA/WMAP Science Team of the National Aeronautics and Space Administration, last modified December 21, 2012, http://map.gsfc.nasa.gov/universe/.

2. "Ideas of Cosmology," Center for the History of Physics, a division of the American Institute of Physics, last modified 2014, http://www.aip.org/history/cosmology/ideas/.

3. Hester and Bernstein, *21st Century Astronomy* (New York: W. W. Norton & Company, 2002), 419–423.

4. "Ideas of Cosmology," Center for the History of Physics, a division of the American Institute of Physics, last modified 2014, http://www.aip.org/history/cosmology/ideas/.

5. *Ibid.,* 172.

6. "LeMaitre, The Expanding Universe and the Primeval Atom," video, 55:45, lecture given by Prof. Helge Kragh at The University of Cambridge's Faraday Institute for Science and Religion on April 8, 2011, posted by The University of Cambridge on April 19, 2011, http://sms.cam.ac.uk/media/1132539.

7. "Universe 101: The Big Bang Theory," NASA/WMAP Science Team of the National Aeronautics and Space Administration, last modified December 21, 2012, http://map.gsfc.nasa.gov/universe/.

8. "Ideas of Cosmology," Center for the History of Physics, a division of the American Institute of Physics, last modified 2014, http://www.aip.org/history/cosmology/ideas/.

9. "Universe 101: The Big Bang Theory: How Fast is our Universe Expanding?," NASA/WMAP Science Team of the National Aeronautics and Space Administration, last modified December 21, 2012, http://map.gsfc.nasa.gov/universe/.

10. "Universe 101: The Big Bang Theory: Tests of the Big Bang Theory," NASA/WMAP Science Team of the National Aeronautics and Space Administration, last modified December 21, 2012, http://map.gsfc.nasa.gov/universe/.

11. Hester, *op. cit.,* 492–496.

12. Hester, *ibid.,* 492–496.

13. "Universe 101: The Big Bang Theory: Tests of the Big Bang Theory," NASA/WMAP Science Team of the National Aeronautics and Space Administration, last modified December 21, 2012, http://map.gsfc.nasa.gov/universe/.

14. "Universe 101: The Big Bang Theory: What is the Inflation Theory?," NASA/WMAP Science Team of the National Aeronautics and Space Administration, last modified December 21, 2012, http://map.gsfc.nasa.gov/universe/.

15. "Universe 101: The Big Bang Theory: What is the Ultimate Fate of the Universe?," NASA/WMAP Science Team of the National Aeronautics and Space Administration, last modified December 21, 2012, http://map.gsfc.nasa.gov/universe/.

16. "Universe 101: The Big Bang Theory: What is the Ultimate Fate of the Universe?," NASA/WMAP Science Team of the National Aeronautics and Space Administration, last modified December 21, 2012, http://map.gsfc.nasa.gov/universe/.

17. "Universe 101: The Big Bang Theory: What is the Ultimate Fate of the Universe?," NASA/WMAP Science Team of the National Aeronautics and Space Administration, last modified December 21, 2012, http://map.gsfc.nasa.gov/universe/.

Chapter Three

Cosmic Origins and Genesis

A Religious Response

Clifford Chalmers Cain

As Professor Stumpe has shown, the universe had a beginning, a beginning, so says astrophysics, accounted-for by the Big Bang theory. The universe had a beginning, so also says the Bible in its first book, Genesis, a beginning accounted-for by God.

Through "redshift," solutions to Einstein's relativity equations, Hubble's Law (that galaxies further away from us are moving faster than galaxies closer to us—"galaxies further from us recede at a rate of speed proportionate to their distance"), and background cosmic radiation (the work of Bell Laboratories scientists Arno Penzias and Robert Wilson), scientists have concluded that the universe had a starting point.

The Judaic-Christian-Islamic tradition also points to a starting point for the universe. In the Christian tradition, creation was constructed out-of-nothing (*creatio ex nihilo*). "In the beginning [*bereshit* in the original Hebrew], God created the heavens and the earth" (Genesis 1:1).

Of course, according to science, the creation of the universe took 12–15 billion years, with the earth taking 4.5 to 6 billion of those years. So, if one takes a literal interpretation of the Genesis texts, then science and religion are in unavoidable and irreconcilable conflict.

Galileo Galilei found himself in this jam in the seventeenth century. Employing the use of the newly-developed telescope, all of his scientific observations and conclusions forced him to place the sun at the center of the universe rather than the earth. This contradicted the worldview which the Church had embraced in and since the medieval period. It also contradicted the Bible, perhaps most notably the passage in the Hebrew Bible (Old Testament) Book of Joshua in which the sun stood still at God's command (Joshua

10:12–14). This implied that the sun moved around the earth, for only a moving object would then be ordered to stay fixed, immobile, in the sky.

Galileo, drawing on the hermeneutics of Augustine over a thousand years before him, posited that scripture should be allegorically interpreted when scientific findings and the Bible conflicted. Otherwise, a literal interpretation could stand.

So, the Conflict Model—a literal interpretation of Genesis as a seven-day process (with the seventh day a day of divine rest) opposed by a scientific explanation of cosmic origins as taking billions upon billions of years— forces one to choose between the two. If one chooses the religious option, then the scientific explanation must be denied. If one chooses the scientific option, then the religious account must be discarded. One cannot be religious and also scientific; one cannot be scientific and also religious.

But, clearly, the fifteen billion year time frame that represents the cosmic history of the universe does not jibe with the seven days' duration creation story in Genesis 1. If the Genesis 1 creation story (and the Genesis 2 story as well)[1] is literally interpreted, then there is no reconciliation possible between science and religion. God did it in 7 days, the universe itself did it in 15 billion years—one must choose between two utterly-opposing accounts. Science and religion conflict.

The Contrast Model—science talks about "how heaven goes," while religion talks about "how to get to heaven"—keeps each discipline in its respective domain. This model was also present in Galileo's time (in the "Letter to the Grand Duchess Christina," Galileo quoted approvingly Cardinal Baronio of the Roman Catholic Church, who said, "The intention of the Holy Ghost is to teach us how one goes to heaven, not how heaven goes.")[2]

Here, religion is concerned about humans' eternal destiny, while science is concerned about the origins of the world in which we live. "Theology and astrophysics are talking about two entirely different sets of truth . . ."[3] Theology affirms the religious claim or truth that the *cosmos* is "wholly dependent upon God for its existence,"[4] while astrophysics affirms the scientific theory or truth that the universe had a beginning, and then a subsequent 15 billion year history of chronological development. Religion deals with the fact of values, while science deals with the value of facts.

This alternate model—certainly not based on a literal reading of Genesis 1–2—circumvents the conflict by asserting that astrophysics tells us *how* the world came into being, and the Bible tells us *who* brought the world into being or *why* the world was brought into being. "How" is the purview of science, "Who" or "Why" is the purview of religion. So, God purposefully brought the world into being by initiating the process, and then natural processes alone ensued to complete it.

This affirms God as the Creator, an important doctrine in the Judeo-Christian-Islamic tradition. The universe had a beginning. God began it.

However, while this underscores the Doctrine of Creation, it does not preserve the Doctrine of Providence, which asserts that the God who creates, stays active in the world in order to fulfill God's purposes. In fact, even in the traditional Doctrine of Creation there is the affirmation or assumption that the God who first created, continuously creates in the world initially created. So, the contrast model preserves an initial Creation, but ends-up with a deistic conception of God (a God who started the process but then who watches from afar).

The Conversation Model brings the two fields to the same table for a conversation. Acknowledging that science asks questions about "how," while religion asks questions and provides answers about "why," the two fields can mutually-benefit from talking. Science can benefit religion by pointing to a beginning, before which the universe did not exist. An expanding universe presupposes a moment when the universe was a minute singularity which rapidly radiated outward. Before that, there was nothing.

This is in opposition to Fred Hoyle's "steady-state universe," the dominant cosmic worldview before the Big Bang. In that theory, the matter of the universe always "was." Hence, there was no beginning. In replacing this steady-state universe theory, the Big Bang theory has underscored an assertion held by religion—a cosmic beginning.

And religion can benefit science by affirming that, from a theological perspective, the universe also had a beginning. The notion of a "beginning" is foundational in both fields, in both Big Bang and in Genesis. Pope Pius XII said that the Big Bang theory supported the biblical idea of creation.[5] And astrophysicist Robert Jastrow contends:

> At this moment it seems as though science will never be able to raise the curtain on the mystery of creation. For the scientist who has lived by his faith in the power of reason, the story ends like a bad dream. He has scaled the mountains of ignorance; he is about to conquer the highest peak; as he pulls himself over the final rock, he is greeted by a band of theologians who have been sitting there for centuries.[6]

Beyond this, religion affirms the "anthropic principle": In their analysis and conclusions, astrophysicists have found that if some of the physical constants and other conditions as the universe began had been even slightly different, life would have been impossible. Stephen Hawking has said that if the expansion rate of the universe had not been what it was (and had varied "even one part in a hundred thousand million million"),[7] the universe would have collapsed before life could have formed.[8] "It is a remarkable fact of our universe that its physical constants are precisely right for the emergence of life and intelligence. If the strong nuclear force or the expansion rate, for example, had been even very slightly larger or smaller, organic life would have been impossible."[9] Peter Ward and Don Brownlee "point out that the factors which have enabled life to evolve on our planet are an almost incon-ceivable set of circumstances which are unlikely to occur elsewhere in the universe:"[10] They refer to a special set of circumstances—the earth's dis-tance from the sun which, like Goldilocks' porridge, is just right for life because water can exist in a liquid form; the size of our moon, which keeps the earth's axis tilted at exactly the right angle for the steadiness and stability needed for life; Jupiter's gravitational field absorbs asteroids and comets hurtling through the solar system, etc.—which they call "Rare Earth Factors" because they see as quite improbable these circumstances coming together in such a way as to create/allow/facilitate life.[11]

Physicist Freeman Dyson draws the following conclusion—"I conclude from the existence of these accidents of physics and astronomy that the universe is an unexpectedly hospitable place for living creatures to make their home."[12]

Dyson does *not* go on to indicate that this *proves* the existence of God, but rather that this acknowledges extremely critical values of various forces in the early universe, without which, that which came to be, would not have come to be.

The universe seems to have been "fine-tuned" for the possibility of life.[13] Again, this does not prove a divine "Tuner," but it leaves room for such. In this space, some theologians have placed a "designer," a force—God—that had a preferential interest in conscious life.

Stephen Hawking cautiously acknowledges, "The odds against a universe like ours emerging out of something like the Big Bang are enormous. I think there are clearly religious implications."[14] And as Ian Barbour adds, "The fine-tuning of the physical constants is just what one would expect if life and consciousness were among the goals of a rational and purposeful God."[15]

The anthropic principle, then, indicates that one almost infinitesimally small variation could have prohibited life at all. This theory, though it does not prove God, allows a possible *place* for God. Could God have started the Big Bang, and then guided it by persuading an alignment of all the variables for life? This divine involvement keeps God from being deistic (creating, but then no further activity), thereby preserving the notion of a divine *creatio continua*, a continuing creativity. Therefore, it is not necessary to jettison the Doctrine of Providence.

The dialogue or conversation model "explains" the possibility of God's involvement in initiating the process and then cultivating it—not by direct causation (why couldn't it have been done faster?), but by indirect causation, i.e., influencing the process (hence, longer). God's power in this model would be understood not as pure, unadulterated omnipotence (God can do everything—directly, immediately; God is the director, the dictator; God is meticulously in-charge; everything that happens is God's will), but as a persuasive force.

While science does not prove God's existence, it can supply nourishment for metaphorical models of God. Theology has repeatedly affirmed that "metaphorical" or "symbolic" or "analogical" language is the only language that we can use to talk about God.

"Univocal language" is language that has a 1:1 relationship. That is, the language that is used of God means *exactly* the same thing when it is used of human beings. That means that God's love, for example, is simply the same kind of love that is expressed by humans, only magnified or exponentially-enlarged. To proclaim, with the old hymn, that God "walks with me and talks with me and tells me I am His own," indicates that God literally walks with me and talks with me, just as a fellow human being might do.

By contrast, "equivocal language" is language that has no connection between its meaning when applied to humans and its meaning when applied to God. There is absolutely no correlation. Hence, God remains a complete mystery, and humans can say nothing at all about God.

Lastly, "symbolic language" is language that continues some degree of overlap. To say that God loves means that God's love is in a partial way the same as human love. Theologian Paul Tillich's distinction between a sign and a symbol is quite helpful here: A sign points to something, but a symbol participates in that to which it points.[16] The symbol does not fully exhaust the referent, but it *does* penetrate the reality of that referent. To say that God "walks" with me is to suggest that I sense God's presence in much the same way as I appreciate and enjoy the presence of a friend as we walk across my college's campus.

The world religion, Islam, is helpful here: In Islam, the affirmation of faith—*Allahu akbar*—begins and ends the five calls to prayer each day for Muslims. The phrase is typically translated as "God is great!," but actually should be (better) translated as "God is greater." That is, God is "greater than any conception of God, or any way of knowing God."[17] As Muslim scholar, Reza Aslan, sums this up, "God is greater than greatness."[18] In other words, God is greater than any conception of, or assertion about, God. In Paul Tillich's words, "Religiously speaking, God transcends his own name."[19]

Symbolic language, then, allows us to say *something* about God, and at the same time preserve God's transcendence, God's "greatness." As Tillich wrote, "God is our symbol for God . . . [and] literalism [univocal language] deprives God of his ultimacy, and religiously speaking, of his majesty."[20] That is, the conception we have of God is but a metaphor or an analogy for the way that God truly is. The reality of God always remains more than any portrayal and description of God can embody.

For a large portion of Christian theology and history of doctrine, God has been metaphorically pictured as a King. God is a King, and the earth is God's Kingdom. God is an absolute monarch who rules the earth the way a king rules a kingdom. And, human beings, who are created in God's image (Genesis 1:26–28), are to exercise this divine imprint by employing dominating power over nature the way God employs dominating power over the universe.

Ian Barbour suggests that science may instruct or inspire theology to think of other metaphorical models for God. As an example, Barbour shares the image of God as a Gardener.[21] God is a divine Nurturer, One who contributes to growth, to creativity, rather than an Omnipotent Potentate who rules over the earth with irresistible power.

That is, God is one influence among many, as the Contributor to growth (destiny) rather than as the sole Determinator of what happens (fate). Destiny implies that God supplies a creative impulse—which may be chosen and embodied, or not—but God does not dictate the outcome. The choice is real; the decision is free. God's will (God's attempt to direct the creation in a certain way) may be thwarted or averted, ignored or rejected.

The dialogue or conversational model can also help religion to embrace the deeper, more theological, and more pastoral message of the Genesis 1–2 creation stories. Both creation stories—Genesis 1:1–2:4a and Genesis 2:4b–25—state that *God* created. So, part of the "message" of the stories is to affirm that "in the beginning," it was God that created.

This is in contrast to Marduk, the Babylonian creation deity. The context of Genesis 1 is during the Babylonian exile of the Israelites.[22] In 586 BCE, the final exile of a conquered people to Babylon occurred at the hands King Nebuchadnezzar. While in Babylon, the exiles were not imprisoned, but allowed to live within the society. Within this freedom, some Israelites rose to positions of success, even prominence.

However, there was a powerful temptation—the temptation to assimilate, to become "Babylonian," not only in terms of culture, but also in terms of religion. Since the ancient world believed that military battles pitted not only respective countries' armies against one another, but also respective peoples' gods, perhaps the gods of the Babylonians were superior to the God of Israel. After all, the Babylonians won the war. And visually, despite the beauty of the Temple in Jerusalem (razed to the ground by the Babylonian army), the grandiose, impressive ziggurat temples in Babylon made the Jewish sacred site grow pale by comparison.

So, Genesis 1 designates God (*Elohim*) as the creator, not the god recognized as creator by the Babylonians—Marduk. Thus, the theology of Genesis 1 is that God, not Marduk, created.

While the theological message is to identify the true, divine Creator, the pastoral message of the passage is for the people not to give-up hope. As a defeated people, God had not given-up on them: Though they feared they were nobodies, they were, in fact, somebodies. Hence, the declaration is made that they were created in God's image (Genesis 1:26–28), and to have dominion and to subdue—grounds for hope for a people who themselves had been dominated and subjugated.

The Genesis creation stories, therefore, are not cosmic blueprints for the creation of the universe, but instead, bearers of a theological message and a pastoral message for a people in dire spiritual straits on the brink of losing their faith. Science can help religion in recognizing this. Science can deflect religion from seeing the Genesis stories as competing accounts of how the universe came to be and can guide religion to appreciate the deeper theological and pastoral meanings of the creation accounts. And, at the same time, the Genesis stories both assert that God is the Creator, that God played a role in causing that which is, to come to be.

And in dialogue/conversation, religion can help science. As previously mentioned, at the heart of the Judeo-Christian-Islamic tradition is the Doctrine of Creation, which not only claims a Creator who began it all, but also makes claims about the creation that was made:

Among those claims is the assertion that the Creation is good. That is, at every point in the Genesis 1 creation story, God pronounces the creation "good." Six times the creation is so proclaimed, and at the end of creation, God proclaims the whole entity "*very* good" (Genesis 1:31). The Hebrew word that is translated "good" is *tov*. And because *tov* is used before the arrival of humanity 28 verses after the initial "In the beginning, God created the heavens and earth" (Genesis 1:1), that would imply that the creation is intrinsically good. That is, the creation is not good because it is of use to humans, because humans have not yet been created. No, the creation is good-in-and-of-itself, intrinsically good.

Thus, while "extrinsic good" means that the creation is good because of what it provides as a benefit to humanity, "intrinsic good" means that the creation is good simply in itself. Thus, the world is innately good.

A good world invites exploration, while an evil world deters exploration. The affirmation that the world is good sometimes became forgotten in certain periods of history. When the Plague broke-out with severe and far-reaching impact on several occasions—and especially in the fourteenth century— it was believed that nature was the domain of the Devil. More seriously, nature was not only hazardous to one's physical health, it was also dangerous for one's soul.

It would take scientific investigation into the Plague to discover its cause. Francis Bacon— echoing Galileo Galilei's belief (and Augustine's before him by 1300 years) that nature was a "second Bible"—believed that examining nature would enable her to "yield her secrets." By exploring and investigating nature—by facing it and not fleeing it—science was able to determine that fleas on rats had caused the bubonic Plague, not God (as punishment for the sins of the people) nor the Demonic or the Devil (as the Evil One who is responsible for all malevolence).

And nature/creation is not only good, it is knowable. That is, there is a correlation between the structure of the universe and the structure of one's mind—this correlation is such that one can come to knowledge of the physical world. So, physicists are currently seeking a Grand Unified Theory (GUT) or a Theory of Everything (TOE) which would bring together various theories into one inclusive picture, one "supersymmetry theory." Some physicists suggest "string theory" as the most likely candidate.

Regardless of which theory is the most cogent consideration, the notion that such a theory *can be found*—or that the plethora of theories that must be accommodated into such a general theory were able to be confidently promulgated—depends on the assumption that the *cosmos* is rationally intelligible. "Einstein said that the only thing that is incomprehensible about the world is that it is comprehensible."[23] The rationality of the world, he continued, is central to science: "A conviction, akin to religious feeling, of the rationality or intelligibility of the world lies behind all scientific work of a high order . . . [there is] a deep faith in the rationality of the world."[24]

As Ian Barbour has pointed out, this assumption, this trust, has scriptural roots.[25] The rationality of the universe—and the universe's contingency—lie at the center of the Judeo-Christian-Islamic (the Abrahamic traditions') doctrine of creation: If/since God is rational, the universe/world is orderly [the *Logos*—the rational structure of the universe—is the Word and the Word became flesh (John 1:1f)]; and if/since God is free, the universe/world did not have to be the particular way it is. It is therefore contingent upon the freedom or choice of God.

The world can therefore be understood by observing it.[26] This presupposition lies at the heart of the scientific method. Science trusts that the world is real, that it is potentially knowable, and that it can in fact be known through the application of our observational and logical skills.

> Science as a cosmology is based upon the assumption that there is, in Alfred North Whitehead's words, *an Order of Things*, and, in particular, an *Order of Nature*. . . . [This is] our faith that order exists in nature.[27]

Religion affirms this basic, fundamental "faith" assumption of science.

British physicist and Anglican priest, John Polkinghorne, underscores this "fit" between the rationality in the structure of our minds and the rationality in the structure of the world. He says that God is the "common ground of rationality" in our minds and in the world. He maintains that the theist can therefore account theologically for the intelligibility that the scientist and the scientific method assume.[28] This assertion does not suddenly revolutionize science. However, it undergirds the epistemological assumption of science— that the world is real and knowable, and that the scientific method can be trusted in that its results correspond to the way the world truly is.

NOTES

1. Scholars have long acknowledged two creation stories in Genesis—1:1–2:4a and 2:4b–25. The first dates from the 6th century BC/BCE Babylonian captivity, while the second is from the 10th century BC/BCE reign of King Solomon.

2. Galileo Galilei, "Letter to the Grand Duchess Christina (1615)," in *The Essential Galileo*, trans. and ed. by Maurice Finocchiaro (Indianapolis: Hackett Publishing Co., 2008), 109–145.

3. John Haught, *Science and Religion* (New York: Paulist Press, 1995), 109.

4. Keith Ward, "God as a Principle of Cosmological Explanation," in Robert Russell, Nancy Murphy, and C. J. Isham, eds., *Quantum Cosmology and the Laws of Nature* (Notre Dame: Vatican Observatory and U. of Notre Dame Press, 1993), 249.

5. Pope Pius XII, "Modern Science and the Existence of God," in *The Catholic Mind* (March 1952), 182–192.

6. Robert Jastrow, *God and the Astronomers* (New York: Norton, 1978), 116.

7. Stephen Hawking, *A Brief History of Time* (New York: Bantam Books, 1988), 121.

8. *Ibid.*, 291.

9. Ian Barbour, *When Science Meets Religions* (New York: HarperCollins, 2000), 42.

10. James R. Curry, *Children of God, Children of Earth* (Bloomington, IN: AuthorHouse, 2008), 187.

11. Cf. Peter D. Ward and Don Brownlee, *Rare Earth: Why Complex Life is Uncommon in the Universe* (New York: Springer-Verlag, 2000).

12. Freeman Dyson, *Disturbing the Universe* (New York: Harper and Row, 1979), 251; quoted in Ian Barbour, *op. cit.*, 29–30.

13. Ian Barbour, *op. cit.*, 29.

14. Stephen Hawking, *Stephen Hawking's Universe* (New York: Morrow, 1985), 121.

15. Ian Barbour, *op. cit.*, 59.

16. Paul Tillich, *Dynamics of Faith* (New York: Harper and Row, 1957), 42–43; cf. David Tracy, *Blessed Rage for Order* (New York: Seabury Press, 1975), 103.

17. James Carroll, *Jerusalem, Jerusalem* (Boston, New York: Houghton, Mifflin, Harcourt, 2011), 120.

18. Reza Aslan, *No god but God* (New York: Random House, 2006), 150.

19. Tillich, *op. cit.*, 45.

20. *Ibid.*, 52.

21. Ian Barbour, *op. cit.*, 59–60; cf. Sallie McFague, *Models of God* (Minneapolis: Fortress Press, 1987), and her article, "The World as God's Body," *Christian Century* (July 20–27, 1998), 671–673, and her book, *The Body of God: An Ecological Theology* (Minneapolis: Augsburg Press, 1993); and Grace Jantzen, *God's World, God's Body* (Philadelphia: Westminster Press, 1984).

22. For more details, see Clifford Chalmers Cain, "Stewardship as a Work of Art," in *Many Heavens, One Earth*, ed. by Clifford Chalmers Cain (Lanham, MD: Lexington Books, 2012), 51–61.

23. Ian Barbour, *op. cit.*, 52.

24. Albert Einstein, *Ideas and Opinions* (London, Souvenir Press, 1973), 262; cf. Frederick Ferre, "Einstein on Religion and Science," *American Journal of Theology and Philosophy*, Vol. I, 1980), 21–28.

25. Ian Barbour, *loc. cit.*

26. Cf. Michael Foster, "The Christian Doctrine of Creation and the Rise of Modern Science," in *Creation: The Impact of an Idea*, ed. by Daniel O'Connor and Francis Oakley (New York: Scribner, 1969).

27. Quoted in James R. Curry, *op. cit.*, 16.

28. John Polkinghorne, *One World: The Interaction of Science and Theology* (Princeton, NJ: Princeton University Press, 1987), 45, 63, 98.

Chapter Four

Seeing the Reality of Evolution

Gabe McNett

INTRODUCTION

Imagine a room utterly devoid of light. It is completely dark. An apple sits on a table in front of you. Would you be able to see it? An interviewer asked this of a middle school student, Karen, to assess her understanding of vision.[1] Karen believed the apple would be visible, but of a different color. She believed we could never create conditions where sight is impossible; our eyes would always adjust. When asked about the source of her knowledge, Karen replied, "[It's] given from experience. . . . You just know because of stuff you put together in your head, and, I've never even thought about these questions before, but my answers make sense to me." Researchers then completely darkened the room to make sight impossible and continued the interview. After several minutes of being unable to see, Karen still insisted her eyes would adjust so she could see in complete darkness. "It might even take a couple years!" she said.

Karen's understanding of vision makes sense. Some of you reading this chapter may have agreed with her. Few of us have ever experienced complete darkness, so typically we can see at least something. But scientifically we know that vision is impossible in the absence of light. Vision comes from light-sensitive cells that react to light reflected from objects in our environment. Even small amounts of light allow the perception of at least something. Often these cells are part of an "eye," which may consist of only one or two light-sensitive cells, as in algae, flatworms, or a jellyfish larva,[2] or eyes may be more complex with a lens that refracts and focuses light onto retinal tissue, where light-sensitive cells are found. Animals such as humans and octopuses have this arrangement. Whether a microscopic speck or the size of a soccer ball,[3] most eyes, generally-speaking, function in a similar manner.

45

We know how vision works not just because it is "obvious given our experience," or just because "it makes sense." We know this based on the logic and reason of scientific inquiry—observation, making predictions, testing hypotheses, experimentation, and always being open to refining our understanding as we gain new information. As Dr. Laura Stumpe mentioned in Chapter Two, the methods of scientific inquiry represent a systematic, trusted, verifiable way to apprehend reality, and it works. Moreover, it works despite our minds being susceptible to illusions, misconceptions, myths, logical fallacies, and superstition. Anyone can make any variety of claims, but to know what is really true about our world we need to test empirically-derived explanations, and only accept these when there is sufficient evidence to support them.

Science also shows us how complex eyes originated. They were not created suddenly but evolved over long time periods through successive, intermediate stages. Consider mollusks, organisms that include snails, squids and octopuses. Mollusks have eye arrangements that range from simple to complex, and these differences are reflected in their genes, development, and physiology.[4] When we place mollusks in the order they evolved, we see a beautiful arrangement of intermediate steps toward more complex eyes. More-recently-evolved eye arrangements represent modifications of those found in older groups. For example, take limpets, an older group of snail-like mollusks. Limpets have eyes that are a simple flat layer of light-sensitive cells. Closely-related organisms have a similar cell layer, but with an indentation to form a cup, which provides better directional sense. Still other mollusks have an indented cup with a viscous blob that acts as a simple refractive lens. More-recently-evolved groups such as octopuses have eyes with a lens, iris, cornea, layer of retinal tissue, and an optic nerve that transmits signals to the brain. From a simple cellular arrangement to a complex eye, each mollusk species shows an eye arrangement that is a modification of another previously-existing arrangement. The complex eye found in vertebrates (i.e., animals with a backbone, including humans) arose through a similar series of tiny, successive modifications over hundreds of millions of years.[5]

The story about Karen is illustrative for two reasons. First, Karen's beliefs were based on personal experience, which may not reflect what is necessarily true. Second, her misunderstandings were resilient; they persisted in spite of her being shown the reality. For Karen, the conflict between personal beliefs and scientific reality is a reflection of innocent, youthful naiveté. A mismatch between professional and public understanding becomes more problematic when it characterizes an entire scientific field, as is the case with evolutionary biology. Further mix-in public apprehension, fear, and a generally-negative perception, and you have much of the public's current relationship with evolutionary theory, one of the most profound, well-supported theories in the history of science. My goal in this chapter is to help the reader see the scientific reality of evolutionary theory, and why it is important. I will first explain what evolution is and then focus on misconceptions to clarify what it is not. I will then discuss some of the benefits of understanding evolutionary theory, and finally how it is perceived by the general public. My hope is that the reader will not just better understand the importance and reality of evolutionary theory, but also appreciate how it can provide beauty, awe, and wisdom about our world. As Darwin[6] noted at the very end of *The Origin of Species*, "there is grandeur in this view of life."

WHAT EVOLUTION IS

The publication of *On the Origin of Species* in 1859 by Charles Darwin marked a moment that forever changed how we view the world and our place in it. Darwin's revolutionary idea was two-fold: First, he recognized that populations change over time, and that every living organism on earth is descended from previously-existing species. This means that all living things share a common ancestry far back in time. Second, he also described the primary mechanism for how this process occurred and is still occurring to-day—natural selection. Interestingly, the first part of Darwin's idea was not entirely new, as even Darwin's grandfather, Erasmus Darwin, had suggested in his own writings that species share a common descent and change over time. Charles Darwin's brilliance was bringing these two ideas together and marshaling a spectacular amount of evidence to support them.

Darwin inferred natural selection because he was both a brilliant natural-ist who meticulously observed the world around him, and a brilliant thinker who synthesized ideas from widely different disciplines (Figure 4.1; mod-ified from[7]). His observations represent simple, indisputable facts about nat-ural populations and living organisms. Populations have the potential for explosive growth, but they are limited in size due to a lack of resources such as food, water, space, and shelter. Darwin also realized that individuals vary in many ways, not just in their anatomy, but also in their behavior and physiology, and much of this variation is passed from parent to offspring. So, there is the potential for explosive growth, but populations are limited and not all individuals are the same. From these observations, Darwin inferred the process of natural selection—that there must be inequities among individ-uals in their abilities to survive and reproduce. As generations pass, since some individuals reproduce more than others and many traits are heritable, populations will inevitably evolve and change as a consequence. But this process requires context. It depends on the population's *current* ecological and environmental conditions. Each population experiences its own unique conditions and pressures, and that experience is "recorded" by those who pass on more of their genes. Think of a population over time as a genetic lineage. Evolution by natural selection is the process whereby a subset of individuals passes on more of their genes, and populations "track" the inevitable change in their respective environment, generation after generation. Over time, populations may split, with each "daughter population" experiencing its own unique pressures, thereby accumulating genetic differences from each other and their ancestors. Some lineages go extinct, some persist. Continuing this whole process for billions of years yields spectacular organismal diversity.

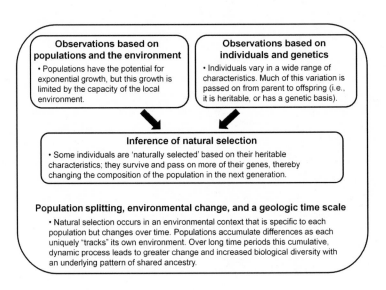

Figure 4.1.

EVOLUTION AS A PROCESS

Evolution may be viewed as both a process and a pattern: *Processes* such as natural selection cause populations to change over time and diverge (split) genetically, yielding a *pattern* of common ancestry analogous to a family tree. First, let us consider evolution as a process using a simple, common example (Figure 4.2). Imagine a small population of bacteria in a Petri dish. Individuals vary in many traits, but let us consider a single genetically-based trait—antibiotic resistance. Individuals vary in their level of resistance, and each bacterium produces offspring with a similar sensitivity (i.e., it is a heritable trait). With plenty of space and nutrients, the population will first increase at a near-exponential rate, but eventually stabilize at a size permitted by the local conditions. When an antibiotic is introduced, it causes sensitive individuals to produce fewer offspring. More-resistant individuals survive and reproduce more successfully, filling the void created by sensitive individuals. As a result, the composition of the population changes in subsequent generations (i.e., it evolves). This simple example describes what many refer to as "microevolution," or relatively small-scale change within a population. Even most critics of evolutionary theory do not dispute this simple example. Two points are worth stressing here: First, genetically-based variation for antibiotic resistance existed *before* the antibiotic was introduced (see Misconception 5). The antibiotic did not cause the beneficial mutation to arise, it merely established the limiting environmental conditions in which individuals had to survive and reproduce. Second, individual bacteria do not evolve (also see Misconception 7). Each individual's sensitivity remained the same. Individuals were "naturally selected" based on their genetically-inherited characteristics, and the *population* evolved as the environment changed.

Real-world pathogens like methicillin-resistant *Staphylococcus aureus* ("MRSA") or multi-drug-resistant tuberculosis ("MDR-TB") add relevance to our example, but it was deliberately simplistic for the purpose of illustration. We followed a single trait (antibiotic resistance) in a simple environment (Petri dish) for only a single generation, and natural selection was the

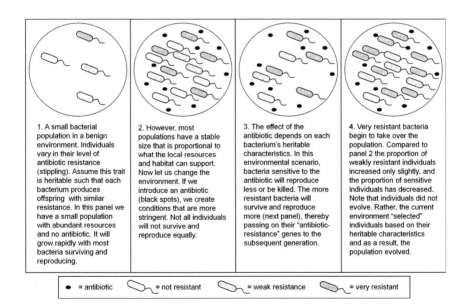

1. A small bacterial population in a benign environment. Individuals vary in their level of antibiotic resistance (stippling). Assume this trait is heritable such that each bacterium produces offspring with similar resistance. In this panel we have a small population with abundant resources and no antibiotic. It will grow rapidly with most bacteria surviving and reproducing.

2. However, most populations have a stable size that is proportional to what the local resources and habitat can support. Now let us change the environment. If we introduce an antibiotic (black spots), we create conditions that are more stringent. Not all individuals will not survive and reproduce equally.

3. The effect of the antibiotic depends on each bacterium's heritable characteristics. In this environmental scenario, bacteria sensitive to the antibiotic will reproduce less or be killed. The more resistant bacteria will survive and reproduce more (next panel), thereby passing on their "antibiotic-resistance" genes to the subsequent generation.

4. Very resistant bacteria begin to take over the population. Compared to panel 2 the proportion of weakly resistant individuals increased only slightly, and the proportion of sensitive individuals has decreased. Note that individuals did not evolve. Rather, the current environment "selected" individuals based on their heritable characteristics and as a result, the population evolved.

● = antibiotic   = not resistant   = weak resistance   = very resistant

Figure 4.2.

only mechanism for evolutionary change, analogous to how a lever (mechanism) might lift an object (result). Hence the common phrase, "evolution *by* natural selection." Other processes ("mechanisms") can cause evolution, such as genetic mutation, migration, and even chance events (genetic drift). However, natural selection is widely considered the most significant mechanism.

Overall, we might summarize this discussion on processes as follows. Environmental changes act as a "filter," or sieve, on existing genetically-based variation. Populations "pass through" this environmental filter when individuals vary in their reproductive output. A subset of individuals has relatively greater success because they happened to possess characteristics advantageous in that particular environment (but which may be detrimental in the future). The composition of the population changes over time as a result.

EVOLUTION AS A PATTERN

Now let us consider the idea of evolution as a pattern (e.g., common descent, transitions to new "kinds," evolutionary relatedness, biogeographic distributions). In general, evolutionary patterns highlight what many refer to as "macroevolution." For many, this is also the part of evolutionary theory in which they claim disbelief. At this point, a hypothetical critic might say, "Sure, bacteria evolve antibiotic resistance, but we've never seen a bacteria turn into another kind of organism!" This and similar critiques will be dealt with in the next section and in Misconceptions 10–12.

First, we should be clear with what is meant by "macroevolution." Most scientists use this term to refer to the evolution of a new species, a process called "speciation." Two populations are different species if they do not regularly interbreed and produce viable, fertile offspring. This concept can be confusing because species-level differences often have less to do with appearances and more to do with genetics (or at least how genetic differences, whether large or small, are manifested). For example, two distinct fly species may look identical, but be unable to interbreed, but a Chihuahua and a Great Dane represent the same species. More often, however, people use the term macroevolution to refer to the evolution of higher taxonomic groups, which some laypersons refer to as "kinds," such as birds from a reptilian ancestor, humans from a chimp/human ancestor, or whales from land-dwelling vertebrates. I assume here that critics of evolution, in particular macroevolution, claim disbelief based on these higher-level transitions.

Belief in microevolution but not macroevolution is scientifically untenable. The fundamental processes involved in micro- and macroevolution are exactly the same, in particular natural selection. The key difference between the two is merely how long those processes have been operating (and of course, any ecological/environmental changes that may occur over that time period). Admittedly, scientists do debate how additional factors affect macroevolution, such as the evolution of novel characteristics or geological and climate-related changes,[8] but both concepts involve precisely the same processes. Finally, lack of acceptance of macroevolution is often based on unrealistic expectations, such as wanting to directly see millions of years of evolution (see Misconception 10). We cannot expect scientists to recreate millions of years of evolution in a test tube any more than we expect them to hold the universe in their hands.

How does macroevolution occur? To better understand this, we need first to acknowledge that nature is vastly more complex than bacteria in a Petri dish. Macroevolution can occur in many ways, but most commonly it starts with a population splitting, or two populations becoming somewhat isolated by a reproductive barrier (e.g., behavioral, spatial, ecological, or geographic). With a barrier to reproduction, two populations no longer exchange genes, and then they are likely to accrue genetic differences. To better understand how macroevolution proceeds, we will consider three additional factors— *variation in population structure*, *environmental change*, and *geologic time*.

Natural populations are not uniform across their range. Often they are composed of smaller sub-populations that might vary in size, extent of isolation, genetic constitution, and the environmental/ecological conditions each experiences. Imagine our Petri dish like a tiny world all on its own. There are bacterial clusters of varying size and isolation. Imagine further that the concentration of antibiotic varies across the dish, perhaps even being absent from some regions. Recall that evolution requires an environmental context. *Antibiotic-sensitive* bacteria might benefit from having a higher reproductive rate when antibiotics are absent,[9] but struggle to reproduce when an antibiotic is present. As a result, populations in our little "Petri dish microcosm" are pushed and pulled in different directions, and these variable forces will manifest themselves in genetic differences between populations. The second factor is environmental change. Natural selection is cumulative, and the environment changes over time. Populations change as a consequence, but they will not accumulate change in the same manner, any more than two pinballs released side-by-side in a pinball game will travel the same path. Individuals comprising each population will accumulate change in their DNA, and therefore also in their anatomy, behavior, physiology, and molecular constitution.

Evolution of a group of organisms is often represented with a branching tree-like pattern, scientifically-derived using genetic, molecular, physical, and/or behavioral data. (Note: Some groups are better represented as a tree with vines draped across its lower branches,[10] but a basic tree is a useful starting point). A population split into two "daughter populations" is depicted as a fork in the tree, with each branch (genetic lineage or population) following its own unique evolutionary path. The fork itself is the ancestral population that split, and from which each lineage arose. Extant (currently existing) populations are the branch tips. Think of the two "daughter populations" as siblings; both came from the same parental population. More distantly related populations—those separated for a longer period of time and that have accumulated greater genetic differences—are those separated by additional forks deeper in the tree. These might be analogous to distant cousins or greater. The longer two lineages are genetically separated, the greater the differences that accumulate between them, and the more forks that separate them.

Now let us add our third factor—geologic or evolutionary time, a very non-intuitive concept. Consider the following metaphor. If we take the earth's age of about 4.5 billion years and pretend it is a day (24 hours), we can ask how much time constitutes the evolutionary history of a particular group. Life does not even appear for the first few hours of our metaphorical day. Mammals do not even appear until about twenty minutes before midnight! What about our own species, *Homo sapiens*? Our entire history—including all human civilizations and even the time since *H. sapiens* split from some of our most recent common ancestors, such as the Denisovans or *H. neanderthalensis*—occupies less time (< 10 seconds) than it takes to read this sentence. The entire evolutionary history of our own species occupies less than the last ten seconds of a twenty-four hour period! The key point here is that evolution has been occurring over a time period that is difficult for the human mind to comprehend. Immense time can result in immense diversification and evolutionary change; it can nurture the growth of the most incredible "family tree."

A thought experiment may help to reinforce evolution as a pattern. Imagine you tracked your own family's genealogy to create a family tree. Metaphorically speaking, you are situated at one of the branch tips. Imagine you could walk down the branch, like walking back in time. If you went back several generations, you would meet your great, great, great grandparents. Those individuals are no longer around, but the branch you are traversing represents their lineage, which remains. You are one of their descendants. Continue walking back through dozens of generations more, and you will have gone back hundreds of years. Perhaps you are excited to find somewhere, in a nearby cluster of branches, some medieval royalty. Soon all written documentation of your genealogy ends, but you can keep walking. Your lineage did not end. In fact, a wealth of archaeological evidence shows you can easily continue your journey for hundreds or thousands of generations more, through the advent of industry, agriculture, and our hunter/gatherer culture. But why stop there? Another 100–150,000 generations, or a few million years, and you would meet the ancestors of some of your nearest evolutionary cousins who are now extinct, *Homo neanderthalensis*, *Homo erectus*, or the Australopithecines. Being extinct, they would be represented metaphorically as nearby branches that are "broken." They do not extend as far to the "top" of the tree as your own branch. Some more traveling, and you would come to the fork represented by the ancestor we humans share with chimpanzees, orangutans, and gorillas (themselves being just a slightly more distant branch). All are the living descendants of that ancestral population. Continue walking and you would come to the fork that represents the ancestor of all mammals, then the ancestor of all vertebrates, and later the ancestor of all multicellular organisms. (Note: We are assuming you have dramatically increased your rate of travel. Remember the immensity of geological time with our metaphorical day!) If you continued on this evolutionary journey all the way to the base of the tree, you would have traveled back approximately 3.5 billion years, and you would have traversed the most amazing "family tree." It is the "family tree" representing the diversity of all of life. The pattern of evolution and common descent shows us that you are related to all living things, from your parents, siblings, cousins, great-great-great grandparents, to your pet and your houseplants. Relatedness is just a matter of degree. If you back far enough, you will find that you share a common ancestor (a "fork" in the tree) with any other organism on the planet. Organisms from more recently-diverged populations are genetically more similar, like siblings. Greater genetic differences reflect more distant relationships. Seeing the reality of evolution and its giant family tree is like discovering millions of family members you never knew you had! It connects the diversity of all living things that have ever lived.

There truly is grandeur in this view of life.

HOW DO WE KNOW?

We have established that critics of evolutionary theory generally accept the fundamental process of evolution—natural selection—but many claim disbelief with large-scale change (see Misconceptions 10–12). The generally-slow pace of evolution makes such change difficult to intuit, a bit like trying to grasp an epic story when you are confined to a single page. Despite the fact that one human does not even live through a tick on the evolutionary clock, evidence for the "epic story" of evolution is abundant. Reviewing all the evidence for major evolutionary transitions is outside the scope of this chapter, but I will highlight two examples to give the reader a glimpse of just a fraction of this evidence. (If interested, I highly encourage the reader to pursue this topic further on his or her own.)[11]

Cetaceans—whales and dolphins—are among the most beautifully-adapted sea-dwellers. It is clear they are not fish. Their spine moves by vertical undulation like a terrestrial mammal, and some even have hidden, vestigial hind legs embedded in their flesh, disarticulated from the spine. It is also clear they are mammals. They breathe using lungs, have hair (though not much), bear live young, and nurse them with mammary glands. The evolutionary explanation of these facts is that whales evolved from four-legged terrestrial ancestors. Yet for years, cetaceans were widely celebrated by evolution critics as evidence the theory was false. Why? Their criticism was imbedded in the question, where were the fossils that showed this supposed transition from four legs and feet to fins, flippers, and flukes? Even scientists were puzzled by the lack of fossils. Darwin famously speculated in the first edition of *The Origin of Species* that perhaps the closest terrestrial cousin to whales was a bear! (Current evidence shows the closest living relative is the partly-aquatic hippopotamus). Darwin later omitted his brief discussion in subsequent editions. Now, in a fascinating bit of historical irony, the terrestrial ungulate-to-whale transition is now one of the best documented macroevolutionary transitions. Over the last 20–30 years, scientists have found a beautiful array of intermediate fossils. These fossils document nearly every aspect of the amazing transition, with a small terrestrial mammal gradually becoming larger and more aquatic, with hind legs first moving out to the side to be used like paddles and supports (kind of like a seal), then getting smaller and disarticulating from the spine. Eventually, the hind legs disappear, nostrils migrate to the top of the head and fuse to form a single blowhole, and the inner ear becomes modified to support echolocation. All these changes are recorded in the fossils, but evidence is not restricted to the appearance of the fossils. Independent dating of the fossils puts them in precisely the correct temporal order. We even see evidence in the phenomenon called "atavism," or "atavistic traits."[12] Atavistic traits often represent a genetic disruption, or reawakening, of a "hidden" developmental pathway whose genes have been switched off. Atavistic traits occur via genetic mutation and reveal ancestral body plans. These are not ridiculous, nonsensical mutants, like a mammal sprouting leaves from its head or a plant growing fish-like scales. Atavisms *always* reflect the correct evolutionary ancestor-descendant relationship—chickens with reptilian, crocodile-like teeth;[13] horses with toes;[14] humans with tails;[15] or dolphins and snakes with hind legs.[16] Overwhelming evidence supports the fact that cetaceans evolved from a four-legged terrestrial mammal (specifically, an "even-toed" ungulate, or artiodactyl).

One of the more contentious macroevolutionary transitions is that of our own species—humans evolving from a species of ancestral social primate. Many have heard chimpanzees and humans share anywhere from 98–99% of their genetic makeup, but they also share a very peculiar *difference* with respect to their chromosomal make-up. Chromosomes are chunks of DNA that in most organisms superficially resemble old-fashioned bundles of yarn. A variable number of chromosomes comprises the totality of a particular organism's genetic make-up, or its genome. The human genome has 46 chromosomes, or 23 pairs, whereas all of our nearest primate relatives (e.g., chimpanzees, gorillas, orangutans) have 48, or 24 pairs. We have two fewer chromosomes than our closest relatives, as though we are missing a pair. Where did they go? The answer to this question came when scientists conducted a detailed analysis of human chromosome #2,[17] one of our largest chromosomes. Chromosomes are marked with clear "ends" (called "telomeres") and a clear middle ("centromere"). If we look at our chromosome #2, we see something quite unusual. It has *two* "middles," one about a quarter along the chromosome's length, and the other at about three-quarters length. It also has four "ends," two of which are found where they do not belong, in the center of the chromosome! The most logical way to create such a pattern would be to fuse two "normal" chromosomes end-to-end. Is there evidence this happened? Yes, there is: When we compare the DNA sequence of chromosome #2 to chimpanzee chromosomes, it turns out that our chromosome #2 has a nearly-identical genetic sequence to *two* chimpanzee chromosomes. The only way our "two fewer chromosome quirk" makes sense is that our chromosome #2 originated from the head-to-head fusion of two ancestral chromosomes, and this occurred after humans and chimpanzees split from a common ancestor. This is the only plausible scientific explanation for this curious difference. It is difficult to reconcile this with a simple "we were created that way" explanation. In addition to this quirk and much like the whale fossils, there also exists a fascinating array of transitional fossils that show macroevolutionary trends toward becoming more "human," and less like an ancestral primate. For example, we see an increase in braincase capacity; decrease in jaw extension; a trend toward walking upright with corresponding changes to feet, fingers, and toes; changes in thumb anatomy; and an increase in height. Fossils and other paleontological and archaeological evidence also show an increase in tool use, the advent of language, and the use of fire and development of cooking. The transition from social primate to human is beautifully documented and continuously being updated.

I focused on whales and humans for the sake of demonstration, but there are many, many other macroevolutionary transitions. These are not just fanciful, hypothetical conjectures, but well-supported events in the history of the evolution of life's diversity. We know amphibians evolved from fish-like ancestors, mammals from reptilian ancestors, plants from algal-like ancestors, and birds from theropod dinosaurs. For example, the evolution of birds from theropod dinosaurs is now supported by such a vast diversity of fossils of feathered dinosaurs, we cannot in good conscience use "feathers" as a defining characteristic of birds. Evolutionary theory helps make sense of anatomical quirks, non-functional traits, and wonderfully-adapted features. It also shows us how one "kind" of organism evolves into another "kind" to create the diversity of life we see.

Having discussed what evolution *is*, I will now turn to what evolution is *not*.

WHAT EVOLUTION IS NOT:
TWELVE COMMON MISCONCEPTIONS

Misconception 1: "Evolution is just a theory."

The irony with this misconception is that technically, it is true! Evolution is a theory. Authoritative use of a weighty term like "theory" brings the imperative to know its precise meaning. Common usage implies an untested, speculative idea. Many use "theory" this way, despite that being technically incorrect. Critics of evolution use the word in this way to imply evolutionary theory lacks supporting evidence. However, the proper scientific meaning of theory goes far beyond even a well-supported hypothesis. A true theory represents a broadly-unifying set of statements based on abundant evidence and reason. It provides a more comprehensive understanding of nature and has no credible evidence against it, much like "atomic theory," "Big Bang Theory," "cell theory," or "germ theory." So ironically, yes, evolution is a theory, despite the flippant implication of the word "just."

Misconception 2: "If we evolved from apes, why are apes still around?"

At first read, this misconception seems very reasonable, like our middle school student, Karen, who thought her ideas just "made sense." To start, part of the confusion here stems from misunderstanding of what is meant by "apes." Technically, it refers to several extant species of primate, but here I will assume that most associate it with one of the two species of chimpanzee, the common chimpanzee (*Pan troglodytes*) or the bonobo (*P. paniscus*). When used in this sense, we did not evolve from apes. Why? Because this argument confuses extant apes with our ancestors. Recall our discussion of a family tree: This is like confusing a nearby branch tip with a fork from which it arose. Humans and chimpanzees (both branch tips) arose from a common ancestor (a fork) that is neither fully ape nor fully human. In evolutionary terms, chimpanzees are our cousins. In genealogical terms, this misconception would be akin to confusing a first cousin with a deceased great-grandparent. So, we should not expect apes to "disappear" because humans evolved, any more than we should expect our cousins to "disappear" when we were born. To be sure, some of our close evolutionary relatives have gone extinct, such as the Neanderthals or the Australopithecines. Think of these as nearby tree branches that broke off or died. But just as you and your cousin share a common ancestor in your grandparents, chimpanzees and humans share a common ancestor that is neither ape nor human, but a distinct organism that no longer exists.

Misconception 3: "Evolution is guided or involves perfection."

Evolution is nothing more than a natural process. It requires no supernatural guidance or great cosmic direction for its operation. It cares not a whit for our destiny, hopes, or salvation, any more than the process of cell division "hopes" we grow up healthy and avoid cancer. Moreover, with evolution come not only remarkable adaptations, but also imperfection, caprice, waste, and even apparent good and evil.

Evolution creates workable, not perfect solutions. Imperfection is due to several factors. First, the environment constantly changes, so what benefits the current generation could be a liability in future generations. Evolution is a dynamic process, but one that lacks foresight and is always one generation behind. In our bacterial example, adding an antibiotic immediately changed the environmental conditions. Now imagine discontinuing its use for a subsequent generation. Since antibiotic resistance comes with a developmental cost, resistant bacteria are now at a relative disadvantage, despite just having an advantage the generation prior. There is no greater trend toward perfection, but simply a "tracking" of environmental changes. Second, imperfection can come from genetic correlations or genes that affect more than one characteristic, a genetic phenomenon called pleiotropy. Consider an example from a breeding experiment, which is an analog for natural selection where someone chooses which individuals (and their desired traits) have the reproductive advantage. Just over fifty years ago, Russian scientist Dmitri Belyaev started a breeding experiment to create a tame fox that could be more easily-hunted. He selected breeding individuals based on a single behavioral trait—tameness. Foxes certainly became tamer, just as we see in the evolution of the domestic dog. In subsequent generations, however, the tame foxes in the population also developed curly tails and colored patches of fur on their heads.[18] Why would this be when he only selected for tameness? Genes associated with tameness also affected anatomical features.

Imperfection also comes from constraints and compromises. Consider choking.[19] How can evolution explain a leading cause of death that can come from such a fundamental activity as eating? This hardly constitutes a perfect, much less, intelligent design. The answer comes from the fact that our anatomy reflects a long evolutionary legacy inherited from distant aquatic relatives. Deep in our evolutionary tree, the common ancestor of all vertebrates was a sea-dwelling organism that used the same tube for breathing and feeding. Water entered the front, food and oxygen were filtered out, and anything leftover would exit the other end. Pockets later evolved off this one-way tube and served as back-up respiratory organs to gills. Our fish-like ancestors swallowed air to service these pockets. Eventually, these evolved into "proto-lungs," and eventually modern lungs. As vertebrates evolved to colonize land, lost their gills, and breathed air, genetic and developmental processes were constrained by the underlying basic body plan. If you had a backbone, you necessarily had two connected pathways—an esophagus for food and a trachea for air. But the evolutionary history of our basic body plan only partially explains why we choke. Despite this "bad" design, humans and most other vertebrates evolved a reflexive mechanism with the epiglottis, a structure which helps prevent choking. It blocks our trachea when we swallow. This "fix" works, but is itself imperfect. In humans the epiglottis is lower than in most other animals. Our lower epiglottis is really what makes us prone to choking. Why is our epiglottis lower? It turns out that a lower epiglottis benefits humans by providing us with more flexible speech. The evolutionary process was constrained by the genetic and developmental mechanisms we inherited from our ancestors, and it produced a workable, but not perfect, solution.

We have described evolution as populations passing through a sieve, or filter. In thinking of imperfection, perhaps panning for gold might be a useful extension of this analogy. Just because you favor gold, you still get plenty of "dirt."

Misconception 4: "I don't believe we came from a random process."

Evolution may be unguided and imperfect, but this does not imply randomness. "Selection" of individuals based on how well they reproduce in their current environment, by definition, is the opposite of random. The bacteria in our Petri dish were selected not by random lottery, but according to their degree of antibiotic resistance. Evolution does have random components, however. Genetic mutations are mostly random in the sense that they can occur virtually anywhere in an individual's genome, and regardless of whether they are beneficial or costly. Genetic drift is another random component, which involves a sampling error of individuals. Imagine a natural disaster that kills most individuals of a small isolated population. The remaining individuals could never represent the genetic diversity of the original population, any more than a handful of cards could ever represent the "diversity" of the entire deck. That is, the genetic composition of the population changed. It evolved. Despite random components, the main mechanism of evolution—natural selection—is distinctly non-random.

The quintessentially non-random feature of natural selection leads to another fascinating result—the *appearance* of conscious, intentional design. We often think of the word "adaptation" when the form of a feature so beautifully fits its function, or features that seem so intricate and complex. It is tempting to see the work of an artificer in something like an insect that is indistinguishable from a leaf. But like ripples on a sandy beach or the capti-vating motion of a murmuration of starlings, such apparent "design" is the result of purely natural processes. How can this be? Natural selection is a cumulative, not one-step process. It is not like a tornado whipping through a junkyard to form a functional jet airliner. It is more like the unintentional, natural process of a water droplet freezing on a dust particle, with additional crystals constrained to form only where other crystals have are already formed, but the end result is the apparent intentional beauty of a snowflake. Similarly, a mantid insect that mimics a flower to kill its prey is not the result of some diabolical predatory creation. Its ancestors evolved small beneficial mutations that conferred slightly greater concealment, eventually "creating" a mantid that appears as a flower. It should not be forgotten that should the mimicked flower go extinct, the mantid's apparent "design" would now be more like a gaudy circus clown attempting to blend into a common crowd.

Misconception 5: "If something is beneficial, it will evolve."

Common statements such as, "the moth evolved dark coloration because it *needed* to blend-in with the environment," give an erroneous impression of how evolution works. Evolution is not a conscious process that works to-wards a predetermined goal; it does not involve effort, trying, or wanting (also see Misconception 3). Recall again our simple bacterial example (Fig-ure 4.2). The current environment, determined by the presence/absence of an antibiotic, "selected" among the genetically-based variation that already ex-isted in the population. The composition of the population changed, not individual bacteria, and it would be an ambitious statement to say it hap-pened because each bacterium "wanted" or "needed" it. This would imply that the effectiveness of the antibiotic was determined by the "personal" desires of each bacterium. Rather, the effectiveness of the antibiotic was determined by whatever genetic variation for antibiotic resistance the popula-tion happened to possess. Had there been no genetic variation for resistance to that particular antibiotic, the population would have gone extinct locally.

Misconception 6: "Evolution is all about selfishness and immorality."

"Survival of the fittest" is a somewhat unfortunate phrase. At the extreme, it has been grossly and perversely misconstrued to support various past notions of "social Darwinism," ideas that suggest we might achieve social progress by deterring the survival and reproduction of certain individuals inappropri-ately deemed "less fit." This is certainly not what evolution is about. More often, this phrase simply misleads people into believing that only brutal, selfish, and immoral individuals succeed. This belief is encapsulated in simple phrases such as, "if we believe we're just animals, we'll act like animals." Many behaviors we see in nature certainly appear callous and ruthless when viewed through the lens of our cultural standards. Admittedly, for a trait to evolve by natural selection it does need to benefit the bearer, but this ignores the fact that "selfish" behaviors can benefit others. There are many ways that evolution favors helpful, cooperative, or altruistic behaviors. Two individuals might benefit directly, such as predators that cooperate to catch prey that neither could capture alone, and they might even share their catch. Many helpful behaviors are directed toward relatives. One example is a young bird that helps to rear its siblings instead of reproducing on its own. How can natural selection favor such behaviors if the helper does not reproduce? The concept of "kin selection" shows us that helping our relatives is the genetic equivalent to having our own offspring. In effect, an individual passes on a copy of his or her genes indirectly by aiding in the success of a close relative. Evolution also helps us understand why we might be helpful to a non-relative, even a stranger, under a variety of scenarios.[20] Our recent ancestors likely spent much of their time in small social groups where they interacted repeatedly. In such a scenario helpful behaviors can evolve via direct reciprocity, whereby helpful individuals are successful because generous deeds can be repaid. This would be similar to you giving a friend a ride to the airport. Subconsciously, you expect your good deed to be reciprocated in the future. To put it another way, you are less likely to help a friend who never repays your good deeds. Helpful behaviors can even evolve in a one-shot interaction toward a complete stranger.

Animals that live in social groups succeed when they cooperate, even though such behavior may be viewed as "selfish" when viewed through the perspective of the individual performing the helpful act. It is easy to envision our ancestors cooperating when hunting, being vigilant, or birthing a child, for example, but what benefits the recipient can also benefit the helper. As a result, we have inherited a "psychological blueprint" skewed toward cooperative and generous behaviors. The helpful individual need not even be consciously aware of why they are being helpful; it is simply a product of the genes and the environment of our ancestors. Indeed, we even see the very roots of morality in some of our closest living relatives (e.g., monkeys, chimpanzees), such as cooperation, empathy, a sense of fairness, and helping non-relatives.[21] To summarize, evolution is not inherently selfish, brutal, or immoral. Rather, cooperative, pro-social behaviors, including restraint from violent or lethal behavior, have evolved repeatedly in countless species from microbes and insects, to salamanders, fish, and humans.

Misconception 7: "Individuals evolve."

Evolution by natural selection proceeds by passing heritable variation to the next generation, not through variation accrued within an individual's lifetime. Suppose you are an athlete. You will not necessarily have a "muscular" baby with incredible strength and endurance. Your child may inherit a genetic disposition favorable to acquiring such traits, but he or she will still have to weight-train and exercise to achieve comparable results. These are developmental changes acquired within the lifespan of a single individual. Such traits are also known as "Lamarckian traits," after Jean-Baptiste Lamark, the scientist who first suggested they form the basis for evolutionary change. However, they do not. Recall our bacterial example (Figure 4.2): Individual bacteria did not change, only the composition of the population changed. The physical traits of individuals are merely the most common "target" of natural selection—beak size, feather color, speed, behavioral predispositions, and so on.

The heritable variation that forms the basis of natural selection comes from direct alteration of the sequence of "letters" that make up our DNA sequence, the so-called A's, T's, G's, and C's. These "letters" represent the sugar molecules adenine, thymine, guanine, and cytosine. However, recent developments in the field of epigenetics are adding some fascinating twists to this basic model of inheritance. Imagine inheriting some sort of genetic imprint of your grandmother's harrowing childhood, your mother's difficult pregnancy, or your father's parenting struggles. Epigenetics involves modifications to the DNA that are separate from changes in the DNA sequence itself. It comes from the Greek language where "epi" means "outer," "over," or "above." Changes might include the addition of a small group of organic atoms, such as a methyl or acetyl group, to a portion of our DNA strand. Another change might be the compaction of a chromosome such that it is less accessible for the creation of a protein product. The fascinating part is that these changes are affected by the organism's *current* environment (i.e., within an individual's lifetime), and we are now learning that some of these changes can be inherited to affect the behavior or appearance of future generations![22] Geneticists have called this "transgenerational epigenetics." It seems to have a minimal role in the overall evolutionary process, however. There is no evidence of transgenerational epigenetics leading to adaptation, for example, much less affecting a macroevolutionary transition. Nevertheless, it will be exciting to follow developments in this field.

Misconception 8: "Evolution explains the origin of life."

In his book, Darwin used the phrase, "On the Origin of Species," not "On the Origin of Life." Evolution explains how life diversified into millions of species once it originated, but not how it originated. Scientific research on the origin of life constitutes another scientific field, often called abiogenesis. This is currently an exciting field of inquiry that is constantly revealing new information about the nature of the conditions of early earth and how life may have started. Questions on the origin of life are better answered by a biochemist, not an evolutionary biologist.

Misconception 9: "Humans are no longer evolving."

Some regard evolution as the study of past events, as though its scientific purview is restricted to dinosaurs and fossils. Populations, including human populations, are currently evolving. Whenever a breeding population possesses heritable variation that leads to disparities in reproductive output, it will evolve. The primary misunderstanding with this misconception comes from unreasonable expectations regarding the speed of evolution. First, consider that humans and chimpanzees split from a common population a little more than five million years ago, yet both remain strikingly similar in their anatomy, genetics, and physiology. We are clearly different in some ways, to be sure, but these relatively subtle differences have taken over five million years to evolve. Second, reproductive disparities can be affected by culture, such as contraceptives that can limit the spread of disease and prevent child-bearing, or fertility treatments that can facilitate a couple's reproductive output. Third, the speed of evolution itself depends in large part on generation time. Recall that evolution results when a non-random subset of individuals passes on their genes to the *next generation*. A bacterial population might experience 70–80,000 generations in a single human generation. Consequently, bacteria evolve more rapidly in absolute time than humans or whales. Despite these qualifications, several instances of recent human evolution have been documented. For example, humans evolved lactose tolerance as our culture became more pastoral within the last 10,000 years.[23] Tibetan populations evolved the ability to persist in high altitude, low oxygen, environments over thousands of years.[24] These are evolutionary changes, not acquired traits (see Misconception 7), and they are relatively fast considering human generation time.

The perceived success of humans as a species also likely contributes to this misconception. One might suggest our medical and technological success means we are no longer "struggling to survive and reproduce." At first this makes sense because natural selection on humans may be less intense in some respects, such as the reduction in offspring mortality in developing nations over the last 100 years. Alternatively, one might reasonably argue that natural selection has become *more* intense in other respects. For example, as we saturate our environment with antibiotics and pollutants, we may be enhancing the ability of pathogens to evolve resistance.[25] Also, the novel chemicals we are introducing into our environment may affect us in unknown ways. Add to these facts our ability to travel around the globe, and we have the ability to share these pathogens and novelties with relative ease.

Misconception 10: "We have never observed one kind evolving into another."

I remember once when I was stuck in traffic in front of an elementary school, and I noticed that in the front lawn a reader board sign read, "elcome back! First day of school August 30th." A capital "W" lay in the grass in front of the sign. I was reminded of the common "You were not there" arguments used by evolution critics. The argument in a nutshell is that, since we have never *directly* observed one "kind" change into another "kind," there is no evidence for evolution. Often critics fail to define precisely what they mean by "kind." If they mean species, this has been observed directly in the lab. Scientists have used natural selection to generate new species of fruit flies in only thirty-five generations.[26] Long-term lab experiments on bacteria have also generated genetically-distinct lineages with entirely new metabolic capabilities.[27] However, generally, critics refer to "kind" to imply a designation above the species level, such as transitions that involve humans evolving from social primates, or birds from theropod dinosaurs. Since we cannot observe these large-scale changes directly, critics suggest there is no evidence they happened. Similarly, I was not present to see whether the "W" in the grass had, in fact, been displaced from the reader board sign. Maybe the wind blew the letter from elsewhere, a plausible though unlikely hypothesis. Maybe an extraterrestrial or omnipotent being placed it there to deliberately fool me. I presume most would agree this is decidedly less-likely. If I was to infer that the "W" had simply fallen from that particular sign, despite not being there to see it, no reasonable person would question my inference. Given the evidence, and until other evidence suggests this hypothesis is wrong, my inference is not just reasonable, logical, and plausible, it is highly probable. I did not need to be present to currently accept this as reality. Moreover, if additional evidence did suggest otherwise, I would modify my inference to accommodate this new development.

I give this simple example to illustrate a basic point: Evidence in science and many other fields may be direct or indirect. Inferences may involve either form of evidence. It would be hard to convict a criminal if we always required *direct* observation of his or her unlawful deed. Or, how could historians accept the reality of the Revolutionary War since no living person was alive to observe it directly? How could we study archaeology? Geology? The problem with this misconception is that it rests on the incorrect assumption that events must be directly witnessed to be credible. Nobody would seriously entertain the notion that atomic theory is false because we have never seen an atom, particularly when we can build rather wicked bombs based on what we have inferred to be true. Similarly, evolution is not falsified because we do not live millions of years to view major evolutionary transitions. We infer major transitions, be it birds from theropod dinosaurs or humans from ape-like ancestors, based on abundant evidence from multiple scientific fields. Observations can be direct or indirect, and science uses both in conjunction with reason, empiricism, and a willingness to try new ideas when current explanations lose explanatory power.

Misconception 11: "Evolution is not science because it is not testable."

Related to the previous misconception that evolution is not observable are claims that evolution is not science because it is not testable. Here, the basic principles of evolution by natural selection are *directly* testable (Figure 4.1). We can measure whether a population has heritable variation. We can test whether that variation affects individuals' abilities to pass on their genes. If these conditions are met, evolution by natural selection is an indisputable, inevitable consequence. Macroevolution also makes testable predictions. There are a number of observations that, should they occur repeatedly and be confirmed, would render evolutionary theory false. One example would be finding fossils in the "wrong place." For example, the first "proto-mammals" evolved approximately 150–200 million years ago. If we consistently found fossilized mammals in rock strata that dated to 500 million years ago, or if we found fossils consistently out of temporal order more generally, it would put evolutionary theory in jeopardy. This has not happened. Evolution is science because it is empirically based and falsifiable; it makes testable predictions that are subject to disproof.

Misconception 12: "There are no transitional fossils."

Transitional fossils refer to the "intermediate forms," or so-called "missing links," that reveal an intermediate state between an ancestral form and that of its descendants. They are distinct organisms with an amalgam of features. The famous *Archaeopteryx* has bird-like features such as feathers, a "wishbone," an opposable big toe, and a bird-like hipbone. It also has reptilian characteristics such as the lack of a true bill (particularly the horny covering called the rhamphotheca), unfused vertebrae, claws, teeth, and a long bony tail. It represents an ancestral form of the "bird lineage," a "proto-bird" that is neither fully avian nor reptilian. It is transitional. The whale fossils discussed earlier reveal various stages of anatomical transitions—nostrils that move rear-ward and progressively merge, or legs that progressively disappear. There are numerous transitional fossils that reflect major evolutionary transitions. In fact, you can think of any organism alive today as a transitional form; we just do not know its descendants, much less their appearance.

This misconception is rooted in several factors, many of them simply based on erroneous or unrealistic expectations. First, many misunderstand the concept of a transitional form. Evolution critics often posit ridiculous hypothetical creatures that are better placed in a book on mythology than biology (e.g., the "crocoduck" of internet fame). Further, their critique is made more ridiculous by assuming the nonexistence of such mythical creatures disproves evolution. Second, many expect a transitional form to appear suddenly, like a bird emerging from a reptilian egg. Third, many expect well-preserved fossils to be abundant and widespread, despite the conditions under which fossils are formed being stringent and restrictive. The fact that so many of the major evolutionary transitions are so well-documented is a testament to the hard work of paleontologists. Fourth, many people have the false, preconceived expectation of there being discrete boundaries between different "kinds" of organisms, such as "reptile," "bird," "fish," or "human." In reality, any biologist who has studied the diversity of life will tell you these boundaries are artificial, man-made, and better viewed as a continuum, rather than a discrete boundary. Extant organisms themselves show a diverse continuum of features (recall the various "eyes" in the introduction). The fossil record is no different.

BENEFITS OF UNDERSTANDING EVOLUTIONARY THEORY

The goal of science is to learn what is real about the natural world and in some cases, apply that knowledge, as we see in medicine or technology. Evolutionary theory provides us with an abundance of practical insight.[28] Scholars from dozens of academic disciplines have applied the concepts of natural selection to their respective fields. These disciplines range from genetics, pediatrics, physiology, and psychology, to history, computer science, anthropology, and dozens more.[29] Evolutionary theory and its principles can be used to identify a pathogen, track the progress of disease,[30] or infer its source or criminal transmission.[31] We can use it to create computer algorithms, which themselves might be used to devise military tactical plans[32] or optimize communication networks.[33] Insight from evolutionary theory can even be used to develop new drugs,[34] improve crop yield,[35] or save endangered species.[36] Even those who deny evolutionary theory reap the benefits when they get an annual flu vaccine, which is annual precisely because the virus evolves so rapidly. It should seem clear that a world devoid of all the aforementioned applications would be a different world indeed.

In addition to practical benefits, evolutionary theory can help us answer profound questions. We gain considerable insight about the origin of life's diversity and also our own history. Humans most recently diverged from social human-ape ancestors. We diverged more distantly from amphibian-like ancestors, and more distantly still from fish-like ancestors. Our genome bears the signature of having been passed through this history. We inherited an anatomy, neural mechanisms, behavior, and physiology that while unique and beautiful in their own way, are far from perfect. We were built from a long history of workable solutions, imperfections, and compromise, not supremely designed. Acknowledging these facts helps us understand much more than our predisposition to choking. We gain insight into why we might suffer from back pain and allergies, addictions to sugar and fatty foods, why we will always live in an environment with pathogens, and why we might benefit from being judicious in our use of antibiotics or fever-reducing medicine.[37] The insight we gain is difficult to overemphasize. We learn how reputation, cooperative behaviors, laughter, or gossip might have evolved in a small social network of highly cognitive organisms (see Misconception #6). Even though some of our behaviors are no longer adaptive in today's environment, our evolved psychology lingers. Gossip is our propensity to discuss other's actions, particularly in their absence. In small social groups, such behavior may have functioned to mediate the social network, sharing who might be helpful or trustworthy and policing against cheats and "free riders."[38] Laughter and humor likely functioned as reliable communication signals of non-aggressive intentions and facilitated playful behavior.[39] We even see the roots of laughter in our closest relatives, chimpanzees and gorillas. Or consider murder.[40] An evolutionary view of animal behavior shows us that countless animal species engage in risk-prone behavior, even killing members of their own species, when resources are limited and/or when individuals perceive limiting prospects for future reproduction. Put another way, individuals with adequate resources who perceive favorable prospects for future reproduction are less likely to engage in high-risk behavior, including killing others of the same species. But an honest discussion on evolutionary influences on murder rates, much less any other aspect of human behavior, is difficult when "evolution" is such a taboo topic and a theory that many in the general public do not accept.

PUBLIC PERCEPTION AND ACCEPTANCE
OF EVOLUTIONARY THEORY

Evolutionary theory is one of the most important scientific advances in human history. It explains the origin of life's diversity, unifies a vast array of academic disciplines, and provides immense insight and benefit. For 150 years, it has withstood some of the most rigorous scrutiny only to make gains in its explanatory power. Scientists do debate its subtleties and are constantly making refinements, as required in any scientific field, but there is no mistaking the reality and overwhelming validity of evolution in the scientific community. Unfortunately, most of the American public has difficulty seeing the reality of evolution. In a widely-cited study of public acceptance of evolutionary theory across thirty-four countries, the United States ranked 33rd, ahead of only Turkey and behind Cyprus.[41] Approximately 40% of the American public accepts evolutionary theory. This has been further supported by a wide range of opinion polls conducted over the last thirty years. The discrepancy between the scientific and public sectors has even been true since Darwin's publication, when much of the scientific community immediately accepted Darwin's ideas, yet Darwin himself knew they would detonate a cultural bombshell among the general public. He waited two decades to publish his book partly for this reason.

Why is there such strong aversion to evolutionary theory among the American public? Partly this may be the fact that evolution is a deceptively simple idea that becomes less intuitive with greater study, leading many to believe they understand it when in fact, they do not. Accordingly, misconceptions and misunderstandings abound. Studies have shown several factors can be associated with a person's conception and acceptance, including geographical region, sex, age, and educational experience.[42] Despite these factors, studies regularly show what Darwin anticipated 150 years ago. The most significant source of resistance to evolutionary theory is the nature and strength of one's religious background.[43]

Why do people's religiosity often conflict with their acceptance of evolutionary theory? Evolution shows us that species are mutable, that humans fit neatly into an enormous family tree, and that we are "merely animals." These notions are anathema to religious doctrines that see humans as being specially created, with their own special place in the universe. There also exists a well-funded vocal minority that takes these perceived affronts even further by making the illogical and false equation between acceptance of evolutionary theory and a life devoid of morality, meaning, and beauty. As a result, they directly combat evolution by perpetuating misconceptions and attempting to influence public opinion and policy, most notably in how evolution and science are taught in our schools. Evolution is also frequently equated with materialistic and naturalistic philosophies, which suggest that the physical world is all that exists. While many proponents of evolution may ascribe to these philosophies to varying degrees, they are separate from evolutionary theory. Science is wedded only to discovering what is really true about our world. Finally, evolution is science, which itself has had a contentious history with religious belief. Consider the fact that when asked what they would do if a scientific finding disproved a tenet of their religious beliefs, most people (64%) say they would continue to believe what their religion teaches rather than accept the scientific finding.[44] When the majority of the populace willfully refuses to accept scientific facts, and do so with the strongest conviction, such fervor can be an impediment to social progress. [45]

So what can be done? Defending evolutionary theory is about defending science. We know science works. We all use it on a daily basis. It overcomes our natural tendencies toward illusion, fallacies, superstitions, and myths to show us what is really true about our world. It shows us evolution is true, the same as it shows we have a spherical globe, a heliocentric ("sun-centered") solar system, germs cause disease, and that gravity acts on objects with mass. Our scientific feats are truly impressive. We have learned so much about our world, yet it is up to each of us, including scientists, to reap the fruit of this labor. Scientists can do a better job of communicating and demystifying their enterprise. For example, when some treat evolution as a fearful doctrine, presenting it with caution or hesitation, they potentially introduce apprehension in those who want to learn more. Perhaps the most important efforts come from the reader and the general public. Skepticism, critical discussion, curiosity, openness to new ideas, and awareness and honesty of our ignorance all form the core of the scientific enterprise. These should also form the core of our public discourse. We should question and criticize false claims to knowledge. Where science falls short, we should be grounded by our ignorance but compelled by our curiosity. Yet when science shows us something is true about our world, we need to be open to new ideas. Considering how American students consistently rate behind many other nations in scientific literacy,[46] we can only make progress when ideology, fear, myth, and misconception no longer override what is true. Facts do not go away because we do not like them. For some, seeing the reality of evolution might require reconciliation with conflicting beliefs and philosophies. It also means seeing the world as it really is. It means appreciating life and the origin of its diversity, viewing all organisms as unique, not just humans. It means gaining a better understanding of an almost bewildering array of phenomena, from antibiotic resistance and disease to gossip and murder. We can choose to see this reality in all its grandeur—its benefits, insight, and applications. Or, we can choose to view it through a lens clouded by apprehension, fear, myth, ignorance, and misconception. As long as we refuse to accept scientific realities, we will find ourselves in complete darkness, hoping and waiting for our eyes to adjust, when what we really need is the world to be illuminated with scientific literacy.

NOTES

1. Harvard-Smithsonian Center for Astrophysics. *Minds of Our Own, Part I: Can We Believe Our Eyes?* Science Education Department, Science Media Group. 1997.

2. Detlev Arendt and Joachim Wittbrodt, "Reconstructing the eyes of Urbilateria," *Philosophical Transactions of the Royal Society of London: B* 356 (2001): 1545–1563.

3. Dan-Eric Nilsson, Eric J. Warrant, Sönke Johnsen, et al., "A unique advantage for giant eyes in giant squid," *Current Biology* 22 (2012): 683–688.

4. Todd H. Oakley and M. Sabrina Pankey, "Opening the 'Black Box': The genetic and biochemical basis of eye evolution," *Evolution: Education and Outreach* 1, no.4 (2008): 390–402; Luitfried von Salvini-Plawen and Ernst Mayr, *On the Evolution of Photoreceptors and Eyes* (New York: Plenum, 1977).

5. Trevor D. Lamb, Edward N. Pugh Jr, and Shaun P. Collin, "The origin of the vertebrate eye," *Evolution: Education and Outreach* 1, no.4 (2008): 415–426.

6. Charles Darwin, *On the Origin of Species by Means of Natural Selection, or the Preservation of Favoured Races in the Struggle for Life* (London: John Murray, 1859).

7. Ernst Mayr, *The Growth of Biological Thought* (Cambridge, MA: Harvard University Press, 1982); T. Ryan Gregory, "Understanding natural selection: Essential concepts and common misconceptions," *Evolution: Education and Outreach* 2 (2009): 156–175.

8. Douglas H. Erwin, "Macroevolution is more than repeated rounds of microevolution," Evolution and Development 2, no.2 (2000):78–84.

9. Richard E. Lenski, "Bacterial evolution and the cost of antibiotic resistance," *International Microbiology* 1 (1998):265–270.

10. W. Ford Doolittle, "Phylogenetic classification and the universal tree," *Science* 284 (1999): 2124–2128.

11. Jerry A. Coyne, *Why Evolution is True* (New York: Viking Press, 2009)

12. Brian K. Hall, "Atavisms and atavistic mutations," *Nature Genetics* 10 (1995): 126–127.

13. Matthew P. Harris, Sean M. Hasso, Mark W.J. Ferguson, et al, "The development of Archosaurian first-generation teeth in a chicken mutant," *Current Biology* 16, no.4 (2006)371–377.

14. Gould, Stephen J. *Hen's Teeth and Horse's Toes* (New York: W.W. Norton and Company, 1983).

15. Anh H. Dao and Martin G. Netsky, "Human tails and pseudotails," *Human Pathology* 15 (1984): 449–453.

16. Brian K. Hall, "Developmental mechanisms underlying the formation of atavisms," *Biological Reviews* 59 (1984): 89–124.

17. LaDeana W. Hillier, Tina A. Graves, Robert S. Fulton, et al, "Generation and annotation of the DNA sequences of human chromosomes 2 and 4," *Nature* 434 (2005):724–731.

18. Lyudmila N. Trut, "Early Canid domestication: The Farm Fox Experiment," *American Scientist* 87 (1999): 160–169.

19. Randolph M. Nesse and George C. Williams. *Why We Get Sick: The New Science of Darwinian Medicine* (New York: Times Books, 1996).

20. Andrew W. Delton, Max.M. Krasnow, Leda Cosmides, et al, "Evolution of direct reciprocity under uncertainty can explain human generosity in one-shot encounters," *Proceedings of the National Academy of Sciences USA.* 108, no.32 (2011): 13335 –13340; Martin A. Nowak and Karl Sigmund, "Tit for tat in heterogenous populations," *Nature* 355 (1992): 250–253; Martin A. Nowak and Karl Sigmund, "Evolution of indirect reciprocity." *Nature* 437 (2005): 1291–1298.

21. Franz de Waal, *The Bonobo and the Atheist: In Search of Humanism Among the Primates* (New York: W.W. Norton & Company, 2013).

22. Eva Jablonka and Gal Raz, "Transgenerational epigenetic inheritance: Prevalence, mechanisms, and implications for study of heredity and evolution," *Quarterly Review of Biology* 84 (2009): 131–176.

23. Nabil S. Enattah, Timo Sahi, Erkki Savilahti, et al, "Identification of a variant associated with adult-type hypolactasia," *Nature Genetics* 30, no.2 (2002): 233–7; Joachim Burger, Martina Kirchner, Barbara Bramanti, et al, "Absence of the lactase-persistence-associated allele in early Neolithic Europeans," *Proceedings of the National Academy of Sciences USA* 104, no.10 (2007):3736–3741; Sarah A. Tishkoff, Floyd A. Reed, Alessia Ranciaro, et al, "Convergent adaptation of human lactase persistence in Africa and Europe," *Nature Genetics* 39 (2007): 31–40.

24. Tatum Simonson, Yingzhong Yang, Chad D. Huff, Haixia Yun, Ga Qin, David J. Witherspoon, Zhenzhong Bai, et al. "Genetic evidence for high-altitude adaptation in Tibet," *Science* 329, no.5987 (2010): 72–75.

25. Michael R. Gillings and Hatch W. Stokes, "Are humans increasing bacterial evolvability?" *Trends in Ecology and Evolution*, 27 (2012):346–352.

26. William R. Rice, and George W. Salt, "The evolution of reproductive isolation as a correlated character under sympatric conditions: experimental evidence," *Evolution* 44, no.5 (1990): 1140–1152.

27. Zachary D. Blount, Christina Z. Borland, and Richard E. Lenski, "Historical contingency and the evolution of a key innovation in an experimental population of Escherichia coli, " Proceedings of the National Academy of Science USA. 105, no.23 (2008): 7899 –7906.

28. James J. Bull and Holly A. Wichman, "Applied evolution," Annual Review of Ecology, Evolution, and Systematics 32 (2001):183 –217.

29. Mark Pagel, "Natural selection 150 years on," *Nature* 457 (2009): 808–811.

30. Lauren M. F. Merlo, John W. Pepper, Brian J. Reid, et al, "Cancer as an evolutionary and ecological process," *Nature Reviews Cancer* 6 (2006):924–935.

31. Diane I. Scaduto, Jeremy M. Brown, Wade C. Haaland, et al, "Source identification in two criminal cases using phylogenetic analysis of HIV-1 DNA sequences," *Proceedings of the National Academy of Sciences USA* 107 (2010): 21242–21247.

32. Robert Kewley and Mark Embrechts, "Computational military tactical planning system," IEEE Transactions on Systems, Man and Cybernetics, Part C - Applications and Reviews 32, no.2 (2002): 161–171.

33. Liwen He and Neil Mort, "Hybrid genetic algorithms for telecommunications network back-up routing," BT Technology Journal 18, no.4 (2000): 42–50.

34. Charles Karan and Benjamin L. Miller, "Dynamic diversity in drug discovery: Putting small-molecule evolution to work," *Drug Discovery Today* 5, no.2 (2000): 67–75.

35. Lloyd T. Evans, *Crop Evolution, Adaptation and Yield* (Cambridge, England: Cambridge University Press, 1996).

36. John C. Avise, "A role for molecular genetics in the recognition and conservation of endangered species," *Trends in Ecology and Evolution* 4, no.9 (1989): 279–281.

37. Randolph M. Nesse and George C. Williams. *Why We Get Sick: The New Science of Darwinian Medicine* (New York: Times Books, 1996).

38. Robin I.M. Dunbar, "Gossip in an evolutionary perspective," Review of General Psychology 8 (2004): 100–110.

39. Matthew M. Gervais and David S. Wilson, "The evolution and function of laughter and humor: A synthetic approach," *Quarterly Review of Biology* 80 (2005):395–430.

40. David M. Buss, *The murderer next door: Why the mind is designed to kill* (New York: The Penguin Press, 2005); Martin Daly and Margo Wilson, *Homicide* (New York: Aldine de Gruyter, 1988).

41. Jon D. Miller, Eugenie C. Scott, and Shinji Okamoto, "Public acceptance of evolution," *Science* 313 (2006):765–766.

42. Alan J. Almquist and John E. Cronin, "Fact, fancy, and myth on human evolution," *Current Anthropology* 29 (1988):520–522; Susan Carol Losh and Brandon Nzekwe, "Creatures in the Classroom: Preservice Teacher Beliefs About Fantastic Beasts, Magic, Extraterrestrials, Evolution and Creationism," *Science & Education* 20 (2011): 473–489; Tony B Yates and Edmund A. Marek, "Teachers teaching misconceptions: a study of factors contributing to high school biology students' acquisition of biological evolution-related misconceptions," Evolution: Education and Outreach 7 (2014): 1–18.

43. Jerry A. Coyne, "Science, religion, and society: the problem of evolution in America," *Evolution* 66, no.8 (2012): 2654–2663.

44. David Masci, "How the public resolves conflicts between faith and science." Pew Forum on Religion and Public Life, http://pewforum.org/Science-and-Bioethics/How-the-Public-Resolves-Conflicts-Between-Faith-and-Science.aspx. 2007.

45. Jerry A. Coyne, "Science, religion, and society: the problem of evolution in America," *Evolution* 66, no.8 (2012): 2654–2663.

46. National Center for Education Statistics. Digest of Education Statistics. Data available at http://nces.ed.gov/programs/digest/d10/tables/dt10_411.asp. 2011.

Chapter Five

Evolution and Divine Providence

A Religious Response

Clifford Chalmers Cain

In the previous chapter, biologist Gabe McNett's presentation and description of evolution, and common misconceptions of it, raise a number of challenging points for religion and theology. Among these challenges are the conclusions that "evolution is nothing more than a natural process"; that this evolutionary process has involved, and involves, an extraordinary lengthy period of time, "a time period that is difficult for the human mind to comprehend"; and that the status of humans in the world is interconnected with the rest of living things and not unique ("[Evolution] forever changed how we view the world and our place in it.").

Regarding the first challenge, it may be necessary for religion and theology to alter the way it conceives of God and God's activity in the world, since from a scientific point-of-view there is no necessity of invoking God or divine activity in order to explain the mechanism and process of evolution.

> In this civilization of science and technology, it is no longer necessary to label every natural phenomenon as an act of God. In fact, just the opposite is true. We tend to consider every other explanation for the significant events of life. Wars are the result of geopolitical conflicts among nations and empires; crime rates reflect underlying societal pressures; the rate of unemployment is tied to policies of giant bureaucracies; the innermost feelings of the individual are understood in scientific perspective as events in the chemical and electrical circuitry of the brain. Increasingly we see our lives as being shaped by forces that are entirely within the sphere of science. . . . [This] situation requires *a new way of thinking about God* [emphasis mine] commensurate to the challenge presented by a culture of science and technology. [1]

Though evolution may not intentionally point us in the direction of the Divine and a divine source or blueprint for how life came to be on planet earth and how that life developed, it may be helpful in inspiring the re-conception, the re-visioning, of how God's power is understood: Though evolution, for understandable reasons, would not invoke the necessity of an omnipotent God controlling the details of evolutionary history and achieving whatever goals were desired, and in a near-instantaneous fashion, it may be nevertheless possible to affirm a God who is present in the midst of the process and who works through indirect, influential action.

And in terms of the length of time required to account for evolutionary development, the scriptural literalist must choose between the account re-vealed in the Bible and the account provided by science. For in Genesis 1, humanity is suddenly and instantaneously created (vs. 26–28) at the apex of the process of creation and as unique living beings. In Genesis 2, the genders are created as bookends of the process—the male is created first, then all other living things (which are unable to provide a suitable partner for the male); and finally, as the summit of creation, the female is created (from a rib from the ribcage of the male, thus symbolizing their close interrelationship and intimacy). In either created order—Genesis 1 or Genesis 2—humans are specially created by God, in completed form, "intact." *Homo sapiens sapiens* are today what we were "back then." There is no lengthy process leading to their simultaneous emergence in Genesis 1 or their sequential emergence in Genesis 2.

Given this literal biblical understanding, no reconciliation can be effected here between the biblical story and the theory provided by evolutionary biology. The two points-of-view are at-odds with one another, and a person must choose one or the other. This is the conflict model.

Another alternative is to embrace Deism—the theological idea that God started the evolutionary process, but then let it run on its own. In this concept, God is, indeed, the First Cause or the Prime Mover. One could argue that without God the process would not have been begun. However, God is not subsequently involved in the process that God began.

Along these lines, one might argue that the "laws" that govern the process were established by God, just as a general or a coach puts together a battle strategy or a game plan, or as a teacher or professor gives a homework assignment. But unlike a general who continues to send orders to the troops, or a coach who is involved in the game as it is played, or a teacher who may be called-upon for help along the way, God remains silently off the battle-field, inactively on the sidelines, and *incommunicado* away from the kitchen table where the homework is being completed.

Save for the introduction of miracles—when God intervenes when things have moved too far off-course—God is not involved. And miracles—at their *best*, conceptually and biblically—are occasional, very infrequent, "interruptions of natural process." So, nearly-always, God is not involved.

Theologian Ted Peters offers the story of his cuckoo clock in his dining room as a metaphor: His cuckoo clock runs entirely on its own, if as Dr. Peters recounts, he remembers to wind it up. But once wound, the clock operates without any maintenance and involvement on his part. Of course, occasionally he has to intervene to correct the time if it has fallen behind or run ahead; but aside from this unusual interference in the operation of things, he is unnecessary.[2]

So it is with God, according to Deism. God wound-up the universe, and now it runs on its own. God kick-started evolution, and ever since, it has proceeded according to its own mechanisms. No maintenance external to the process is necessary, all causes-and-effects are internal to the operation. However, this does not rule out the occasional "miracle," when God must intervene to set things right when they have gone (too far) awry (this would be "sporadic" or "occasional" divine providence).

As was noted in the "cosmic origins" response chapter (Chapter 3), this theological model preserves God's creative act, but reduces it to "bumping things" into motion or jump-starting a process in which God then no longer participates, to which God makes no further contribution. The Doctrine of Creation is preserved, but at the expense of the Doctrine of Providence (God's working in the world): God was involved at the start of evolutionary process, but since then, it has run on its own. This is the contrast model: God fires the starting pistol, and then natural laws/evolutionary process run the race.

Based on the biblical witness to a God who acts in the world, and addressing the desire for a concept of God that is related to everyday life in the world and relevant to Christian liturgical practice (worship) and devotional practice (prayer, for example), theology must recover somehow the concept of a God who acted/acts in the world. In terms of evolutionary process, this means specifying how divine agency could be involved. Science can help theology to attempt this. It cannot tell theology *how* to do that, but it can provide some insights and challenges that will guide theology in this task:

If God's involvement is to be asserted and then described in evolutionary history, it must be done in such a way that the natural explanations of that history are preserved. How does one affirm both that natural factors/explanations and God's involvement are affirmed? How can/do the natural and the supernatural come together here? In short, what difference did/does/can God make?

As mentioned before, a conversation with science could help in the re-thinking and the re-formulation of the understanding of God's power. Clearly, an omnipotent God who wills everything that happens to happen and wills everything that does not happen not to happen, will not fit with evolutionary theory.

Process theology is a theological model that has much to commend it in this task.[3] Process theology is a brand of theology emanating from the United States, and promotes a view of the world that involves change, development, novelty, and organic unity. It also posits a concept of God as having two natures. As in classical theism, God has a transcendent aspect and also an immanent aspect. Technically, these aspects are called God's "primordial nature" and God's "consequent nature," respectively.

God's primordial nature is the unchanging "side" of God, a divine dimension that lies beyond the change that characterizes all human reality and experience in the world. To influence the creation, God the Creator provides an impetus for action, a possibility for actualization, to each living thing in the creation. This is God's suggestion for the development of those living things. It is what is "best" for that creature at that moment in its existence. However, God does not cause or force the living thing to adopt this suggestion, for that is up to the free will of the creature. But it is presented as a lure for adoption.

But God is not just a provider of these suggestions, these ideals for actualization. God also receives from the creation the results of living things' previous choices. These are taken into the divine Reality through God's receptive or "consequent" nature. Based on what has been adopted/accepted in the past, God presents a new possibility correlated to that past. Not all things would be necessarily possible, so God chooses the best thing out of what would still be possible as God's "will" for that creature.

God, then, is immanent in the process, the development, the becoming, of the individual living thing. But God's suggestion is not irresistible (God's will is not inviolable). Instead, it is one of several influences available to, and having a bearing on, the single creature. God is involved as a provider of these lures; though God determines what the divine lure is at that moment in time, God does not/cannot determine what influence the creature chooses.

The transcendent God—the God who is "beyond" or "greater"—is then involved immanently in the world. God is not the God of Deism who is transcendent but is not immanent, a God who created but is no longer involved in the day-to-day goings-on in the world. Rather, God is extensively, meticulously, intimately connected, as one influence among others, attempting to direct the creation to more complete rather than lesser fulfillment, to higher rather than lower actualization, to greater rather than reduced beauty, to richer rather than poorer novelty.

But the immanent God who provides such lures toward actualization is not only present, not completely "here." God is not the God of pantheism (a conceptualization in which God is identical to, and contained fully within, the world) whose presence has been accented at the expense of God's transcendence. For God is "there" as well as "here," transcendent as well as immanent, "beyond" as well as "with." The world is metaphorically, symbolically, God's "body." Just as humans are more than their bodies, but are intimately connected to such physicality, so the physical world is God's body, but God is more than this body.[4]

Process theology's notion of "divine lure" points to a God who profoundly, pervasively, and inclusively influences, but who does not determine fully, any single or corporate action. God works within the creative process, perhaps as an author whose characters' scripts are not written from the beginning, but a story which depends on the characters' choices and self-development as well. Indeed, not everything that emerges is necessarily what God would have preferred or intended. Evolution's unproductive directions and dead-ends—evolution's "waste" of life and suffering and extinction—do not reflect an omnipotent God who causes *every* thing to occur as it did/does, but rather a God who lovingly tends the process—providing initial aims as internal influences/causes and not as a determinative, irresistible external cause. Thus, God's power is a secondary cause, not a primary cause.

The notion that God has a role to play in the world—that God acts in history and nature—is crucial to the Christian tradition (and, of course, to the entire Judeo-Christian-Islamic tradition). "Whether it be considered a theme or a presupposition, the notion that God is active in the world . . . is central to the Biblical tradition."[5] The Bible consistently and repeatedly speaks of the mighty deeds of *Theos*. In fact, biblical theology is, in the thought of one scholar, a recital of "the acts of God."[6] Therefore, Deism won't do! And Schubert Ogden argues that theologians *must* speak of God's action in the world—in history and in nature—for a theology without such an active God is impossible.[7]

So, *that* God acts is a non-negotiable assertion by theology. But, then, *how* does God act? Is there any space for reference to God's acts in the world in a modern scientific view? "God and God's mighty acts" appear logically inconsistent and devoid of an experiential reference."[8] Or, as German physicist Harald Fritzsch has put it, "Is there room for God in a world that seemingly can dispense with His intervention in the processes of the universe?"[9]

Scientist Norman F. Hall and writer Lucia K. B. Hall believe that science and religion *cannot* be reconciled on this point because religion

> makes the assumption that the universe and its inhabitants have been designed and created—and, in many cases, are guided—by "forces" or beings which transcend the material world. . . . Science, on the other hand, assumes that there are no transcendent, immaterial forces and that all forces which do exist within the universe behave in an ultimately objectively or random fashion. . . . The Universe as a whole is assumed to be neutral to human concerns.[10]

As Ralph A. Alpher adds, "Surely if a necessity for a God-concept in the universe ever turns up, that necessity will become evident to the scientist."[11]

The notion that everything that happens in the world, is God's will, and the result of God's direct action through a thorough, coercive, meticulous providence, is no longer tenable in a world where all natural events and processes are understood through the scientific method to proceed from natural causes and lead to natural effects. The theory of evolution depends on such naturalistic causes, not supernatural ones.

Beyond this, "meticulous providence" evaporates human freedom: As Albert Einstein noted almost sixty years ago:

> Nobody, certainly, will deny that the idea of the existence of an omnipotent, just, and omnibeneficent, personal God is able to accord man solace, help, and guidance; also, by virtue of its simplicity, it is accessible to the most undeveloped mind. But, on the other hand, there are decisive weaknesses attached to this idea in itself, which have been painfully felt since the beginning of history. That is, if this being is omnipotent, then every occurrence, including every human action, every human thought, and every human feeling and aspiration is also His work; how is it possible to think of holding men responsible for their deeds and thoughts before such an almighty Being? In giving out punishment and rewards, He would to a certain extent be passing judgment on Himself. How can this be combined with the goodness and righteousness ascribed to Him?[12]

So, does evolutionary theory rule-out God in terms of nature's being God's creation, and life on earth being the direct result of God's action? And does the sheer expanse of evolutionary history contradict the notion of a quick(er) creation story (Genesis 1's "seven days") and the special creation of *Homo sapiens sapiens* as a species intact, fully-formed, and complete "all at once" in a given moment in either biblical or cosmological time?

Is God necessary to account for what is (in terms of evolutionary history)? "All natural events are understood to proceed from natural causes and to lead to natural effects; in no case is it necessary to invoke the special action of God to account for such occurrences."[13] Einstein's voice adds:

> The more a man is imbued with the ordered regularity of all events, the firmer becomes his conviction that there is no room left by the side of this ordered regularity for causes of a different nature. For him, neither the rule of human or the rule of divine will exists as an independent cause of natural events. To be sure, the doctrine of a personal God interfering with natural events could never be *refuted*, in the real sense, by science, for this doctrine can always take refuge in those domains in which scientific knowledge has not yet been able to set foot. But I am persuaded that such behavior on the part of the representatives of religion would not only be unworthy but also fatal. For a doctrine which is able to maintain itself not in clear light but only the dark, will of necessity lose its effect on mankind, with incalculable harm to human

progress. In their struggle for the ethical good, teachers of religion must have the stature to give up the doctrine of a personal God, that is, give up that source of fear and hope which in the past placed such vast power in the hands of priests.[14]

Though "few any longer are disposed to explain the occurrence of particular events by referring them directly to God's intervention in the natural order . . . , this is completely inconsistent with the supposedly authoritative biblical conception of God as one who continuously *acts* in and upon nature as its Lord."[15]

Since the Renaissance and the Enlightenment, the belief has evolved that there are no events which happen without natural causes. And taking this one step further, if an event can be totally explained in terms of natural forces (i.e., these forces provide a "sufficient cause" for it), what justification is there for introducing the idea of another perspective, the unnecessary action of an additional agent? Occam's razor (the simplest explanation is the preferred and only necessary explanation) and LaPlace's "I have no need of that hypothesis" (no additional explanation is needed) apply. Thus, no extra-worldly reference nor any super-natural referent is necessary. God as a transcendent agent invoked to explain what has occurred is no longer tenable or essential.

The Western notion of God has been informed by the metaphor of a supreme Agent who intervenes from the outside into the causal nexus of natural and historical events. The Bible emphasizes a God who acts, the Lord of history and nature who injects from beyond into and upon the realm of human historical and natural processes.

Thus, the concept of a God who *acts* is in grave danger. As New Testament biblical scholar, Rudolf Bultmann, once said, "There remains no room for God's working."[16]

If one cannot affirm the traditional understanding of *how* God acts, but wishes to affirm *that* God does act (thus to avoid placing "God" in serious jeopardy with no job description), then a radical reinterpretation of the concept of "act of God" must be attempted and therein offered an alternative description of *how* God acts. Since "not all the ways in which [the] fathers in the faith have spoken of God's action are relevant possibilities for . . . today,"[17] a way which *is* a relevant possibility must be presented.

> What we desperately need is a theological ontology [description of reality] that will put intelligible and credible meanings into our analogical categories of divine deeds and of divine self-manifestation through events. . . . Only an ontology of events specifying what God's relation to ordinary events is like, and thus what [God's] relation to special events might be, could fill the now empty analogy of mighty acts.[18]

Science can be helpful here in that it emphasizes that cause-and-effect must lie within a naturalistic framework. Only internal causes qualify as necessary explanations. No appeal to an external cause is warranted or acceptable to science. So, again, Deism won't work here—with no divine activity save the initial act to start the process processing—as a solution to the theological problem: Deism preserves *creation ex nihilo*, but sacrifices divine providence, God's activity, since the moment of the creation's initial blossoming.

And ruling-out God entirely—while palatable to atheists and agnostics such as Richard Dawkins, the late Stephen Jay Gould, the late Christopher Hitchings, and Sam Harris, *et.al.*—will not do for theists and Christian theists who regard God as the central foundation of their *Weltenschauung*, their worldview.

For a growing number of persons both in the theological circle and in the life of the Church, process theology "offers a way of recovering the conviction that God acts in the world"[19] that can preserve a role for God in the network of cause-and-effect of things *and* be reconciled or amenable to science's insights and conclusions. God furnishes the initial direction, but the becoming entity is responsible for its own actualization. Genuine freedom is involved here: The emerging entity (Whitehead called it an "actual occasion") may choose to actualize the divine-supplied "aim" or direction, or it may elect to choose from among other possibilities in its context. Because God cannot control the creature's self-actualization, God seeks to persuade each entity to actualize the possibility that is best for it. Insofar as the entity's choice is in-line with what God thinks best, the divine persuasion has been effective and "God's will" has been done. God's continuing creation (God's *creatio continua*, God's acts in the world) are manifested in God's creating "by persuading the world to create itself."[20]

Thus, God contributes to the evolutionary process, but God does not determine it. God is one influence among many other influences. This can explain the lengthy, almost unfathomable reaches of evolutionary time and the seemingly "blind alleys," the regressions and tangents, and the vast waste that are all a part of evolutionary process.

One of the most interesting, marvelous, and helpful of recent inventions has been GPS ("Global Positioning System"). When one makes a change in direction that is not in keeping with what the GPS would prefer, a female voice comes-on and announces that the system is "recalculating." GPS does not force the driver to follow it, to accept its suggestion of the fastest and best way of getting to one's destination. But at every turn, GPS enters back into the process, once again suggesting how to alter course and get back to what it has deduced is the proper or "best" way to proceed.

God's providence provides the same sort of suggestions. God offers the suggestion that is best for the "actual occasion" (the individual entity, whether human or non-human). The entity elects within its respective parameter of freedom what factor or influence to follow. This choice is genuine freedom, for there is no coercion from God. But God is faithful to the process, and once whatever choice that is made is decided, God returns to the entity with the best course for the entity to follow now. Once again, the entity responds freely, and God stands ready in response to the outcome. When the entity's decision is to accept God's influence, then God's will "is done"—is accomplished, is made actual.

It is important to emphasize that God is not omnipotent, but God *does* have power. However, that power is not coercive, vertical, nor top-down, but rather persuasive, horizontal, and social. Power may be understood as the capacity to influence the outcome of any process of actualization.[21] This "capacity to influence" allows both persuasive and coercive power. Coercive power directly affects the outcome, for the process must conform to its control. Persuasive power operates more indirectly, for it is effective in determining the outcome only to the extent that the process appropriates (thus conforming to) the direction/aims presented in the persuasion. "Coercive power and control are commensurate, while persuasive power introduces the additional variable of acceptance by the process in actualization."[22]

Based on this understanding, God has no coercive power at all. God's influence "is always persuasive."[23] And this inevitably involves risk. "Each divine creative impulse is adventurous, in that God does not know what the result will be."[24] God is *not* the all-powerful Monarch ruling the earth and its inhabitants with coercive, dictatorial power.

Therefore, divine cause-and-effect is not like billiard balls bouncing off one another, as if cause was entirely independent and external to the effect, and effect was independent and external to the cause. Though billiard balls are related to each other and produce changes in each, the relations and the resulting changes do not enter into the essence of the billiard balls (they are purely "accidental").[25] No, divine cause-and-effect is by means of "incarnation of the other."[26] Efficient causation (that which initiates or brings-about change) is by means of the incarnation of the other through the entities influencing each other—and God as an entity influences all other entities, by means of the incarnation of the other, an entering into, a taking into, of each other. A "final cause" (purposeful cause or the determinator of the outcome) results from each entity's determination of the final outcome—i.e., how to actualize itself. Every thing—everything—becomes what it decides to be.

As a result, God functions as efficient cause, but not as final cause. God functions as "that actual entity from which each temporal concrescence receives that initial aim from which self-causation starts."[27] That is, each entity creates itself by realizing an aim/direction internal to it (the aim comes from an external source—God—but in the entity's taking note of it, it becomes internal). God initiates the move toward a definite outcome from an indeterminate situation, but the entity itself completes the process which God only initiates. God is powerful—horizontally influential—but not omnipotent—vertically deterministic:

> The image of God as cosmic watchmaker [or as cosmic tyrant] must be abandoned; and be replaced by the image of God as gardener in the vineyard, fostering and nurturing its growth; or by the image of God as companion and friend who inspires us to achieve the very best that is within us. [28]

God acts, then, by "being felt by [God's] creatures." [29] That is, God acts by influencing, by being "felt," by being considered. God acts by being.

There is evidence of this in the Bible: Whereas most of the biblical materials portray God as a coercive, power-wielding Lord and controller of all the events of nature and history, some biblical texts suggest a God who is touched by the world and who suffers over and with the sins of God's people. In these particular materials, God's power is assumed, but the extent of that power is not unlimited. [30] For example, in Genesis 6:6, "God repented that God had made humankind, and it grieved God to his heart." In the prophetic books— Hosea and Jeremiah—Israel remembers God's suffering and anguish over God's chosen people. Two striking examples are:

> How can I give you up, Ephraim? How can I hand you over, O Israel? How can I make you like Admah? How can I treat you like Zeboiim? My heart recoils with me; my compassion grows warm and tender. (Hosea 11:8)

> Is Ephraim my dear son? Is he the child I delight in? As often as I speak against him, I still remember him. Therefore I am deeply moved for him; I will surely have mercy on him, says the Lord. (Jeremiah 31:20)

Rabbi Abraham Joshua Heschel raises this theme in his famous book, *The Prophets*:

> The fundamental feature of divine reality, present in the prophets' consciousness . . . [is] pathos. Concern and involvement characterize God's relation to the world. God is always concerned. God is personally affected . . . God is a God of pathos. The idea of divine pathos has also anthropological significance. It is humanity's being relevant to God. To the biblical mind, the denial of humanity's relevance to God is as inconceivable as the denial of God's relevance to humanity. This principle leads to the basic affirmation of God's participation in human history, to the certainty that events in the world concern God and arouse God's reaction. It finds its deepest expression in the fact that God can actually suffer. [31]

Christian theologian Kazo Kitamori bases his religious emphasis on "the pain of God" on biblical texts which suggest God's being impacted by the world in God's attempt to influence that world (and not God's absolute control and coercive power over the world)—Psalm 103:8–14; Psalm 145:9; Isaiah 54:7–8:[32]

> For as the heavens are high above the earth, so great is God's steadfast love toward those who fear him. . . . As a father has compassion for his children, so the Lord has compassion for those who fear him. (Psalm 103:11, 13)

> The Lord is good to all, and God's compassion is over all that he has made. (Psalm 145:9)

> With everlasting love, I will have compassion on you, says the Lord, our Redeemer. (Isaiah 54:8b)

And the second installment of Jurgen Moltmann's trilogy—*The Crucified God*—focuses on the crucifixion of Jesus as the foundation of Christian theology and thus illuminative of God's reality.[33] God is a God who suffers with, and for, humanity.

And while God is more often portrayed as a God whose power is unlimited, there *are* instances when/where God struggles: God struggles with the watery chaos in creation (Genesis 1:1—God must overcome the *tohu wa bohu*—the "formless void," the "watery chaos"); Exodus 6–15—God struggles through Moses with a Pharaoh who will not initially let the people go and then reneges when he has released them; Genesis 32—God wrestles with an ethically-insensitive Jacob.

Charles Darwin began his cruise as a religious man when he sailed on *The Beagle*. Indeed, he had considered becoming a "country parson." Undoubtedly schooled in the popular and regularly-used early-nineteenth century textbook by William Paley—*Natural Theology: Evidences of the Existence and Attributes of the Deity, Collected from the Appearances of Nature*[34] —his theological worldview was that of God the world-maker, based on Paley's argument from design and the watch-maker: If one were to come upon a watch lying on the ground and notice the harmony, complexity, beauty, and coordination of the parts, the investigator would understandably and justifiably conclude that there had been a watch-maker who created this timekeeper. By analogy, when one looked upon the world and noticed the harmony, complexity, beauty, and coordination of the parts, the investigator would understandably and justifiably conclude that there had been a world-maker who created this planet and life upon it.

But on the voyage, Darwin was unsettled by the brutality and barbarism of the tribe the sailors encountered at Tierra del Fuego. Violence was common-place, and life was cheap, illustrated by the example of the child who was killed by bashing his head against a wall in punishment for some ever-so-mild wrongdoing.

Darwin also noted nature "red in tooth and claw." The fox hunted, killed, and devoured the rabbit. A wasp laid eggs in a caterpillar, and the larvae lived by feeding on the flesh of the host. Ninety-nine per cent of all species which had ever lived on earth had gone extinct. Beyond this, there were terrible waste and suffering in evolutionary history, with dead ends, blind alleys, and a process which was not very well orchestrated, if "designed" at all (e.g., the laryngeal nerve in giraffes and humans is unduly, inefficiently, and unnecessarily long).

Lastly and perhaps most prominently, the death of Darwin's beloved daughter, Annie, was devastating for him. How could the death of such a young, beautiful, and brilliant young child be reconciled with a God who ruled the world with irresistible power, controlled everything that happened, and had carefully designed nature? How could such a God be thought as loving and judged good?

How *can* an omnipresent, omnibenevolent, and omnipotent God be reconciled with these sights and observations? In this way, science can help sharpen theology's "answers" to this perennial and perplexing question of *theodicy*. Here are the customary options, which were initially and partially listed in Chapter One in connection with the example of the suffering of Job (this topic will be further discussed and developed in Chapter Ten, especially in the context of the Holocaust):

A first option is that God is not good; rather, God is evil. So, suffering exists because God is malevolent. This option certainly preserves God's power, but it sacrifices God's goodness.

A second option is that God causes or permits suffering in order to test our faith and/or develop our character. "Soul-strengthening" can be the consequence of such experience and is what God intends.

A third option is that there are two cosmic powers who contend with each other, God, who is good, and the Devil (or the Demonic), who is evil. As a result, pain and suffering are caused by the Devil, not by God. God's goodness is thereby preserved, but God's power is mitigated, in that God shares power in this "cosmic dualism" with the Devil.

A fourth option is that human freedom is the source of evil, for human choice is responsible for pain and suffering. Humans in their freedom sometimes choose what is moral, sometimes what is immoral. When they abuse this free will, evil is the result. In the process of human moral choice, God's limits God's absolute power so that human freedom is genuine and not an illusion. Horrendous historical events such as the Holocaust are traced to the immoral choices of Adolf Hitler and the Nazis, not to God. This "explains" moral evil, but not natural evil such as that resulting from earthquakes, tsunamis, spontaneous fires, and disease.

A fifth option is that we simply do not know why/how God permits or causes suffering. We cannot know: For God is a transcendent God, far beyond us and majestic and unfathomable, while we are mere mortals. As limited, finite creatures, we cannot grasp such elusive mystery. This view preserves God's goodness and power, but at the expense of humans' capacity to reason and to know.

A sixth option is to regard the good things that happen as rewards for virtuous behavior and the bad things that happen as punishments for wrong-doing and vices. In this view, God causes everything to occur that occurs, and suffering is God's punishment for human sin. This model preserves God's goodness and power, but this sense of justice (you get what you deserve, and you deserve what you get) fails when the innocent suffer (for example, the figure "Job" in the Hebrew Bible or Old Testament).

A seventh option is that God is not all-powerful. God has the power to influence the world, but God does not have the power to determine every-thing that happens and the outcome of everything that occurs. This view preserves God's goodness, God's omnibenevolence, but not God's power, God's omnipotence. God may be a good God, but, compared to the image of God as all-powerful, here God is anemic.

Again, science's presentation of the reality of life in the world through its observations and its insights could help theology sharpen its "answer" to the question of evil, the issue of theodicy.

The first challenge posed by evolutionary to religion and theology was that evolution is understood to involve nothing more than a natural process. The second challenge was the tremendous length of time involved in evolu-tionary process and the suddenness of creation in the biblical account. The third challenge is the understanding of the place of humans in the world as set-forth in evolutionary theory.

Evolution points to us humans as deeply and organically connected to the rest of life. Indeed, according to evolutionary theory, all life is traceable to common ancestry. By contrast, religion and theology present humans as a "special" creation, different from and seemingly disassociated with, the rest of life. What are we to make of this difference, this discrepancy, between the two fields of science and religion?

Perhaps a conversation with science could help with the understanding of what it means for *Homo sapiens sapiens* to be special or distinctive among the species, to be uniquely "made in God's image": Three thousand years ago, the psalmist asked, "What is man?" (Psalm 8:4). Today, one might ask as well, "What is so special/distinctive about humans, and what is their place and role in the rest of the natural world?"

A traditional theological approach to these questions leads one to the first chapter of Genesis, where "man" is the only species made "in the image of God":

> Then God said, "Let us make humankind in our image, according to our likeness . . ." So God created humankind in his image, in the image of God he created them; male and female he created them. (Genesis 1:26–27)

In this Genesis 1 account, no other species is created "in the image of God." Therefore, in this special act of God, humans are created last as the summation and apex of creation, placed "apart from" nature, to enjoy kingship over all other things. Here nature is made for human beings, and therefore humanity's role in the natural world, and humans' relationship to nature, is to dominate and conquer it (vs. 26, 28, 27).

Historically, some very prominent theologians have interpreted the "image of God" in ways that underscored this separateness and superiority of humankind:

For instance, Paul Tillich said being made in God's image meant that human beings uniquely had the capacity to reason. Critical thinking and abstract thought were what made *Homo sapiens sapiens* special, and these capabilities reflected God, because God had created the universe with rational structures, thus allowing knowledge to be gained from it by humans who were rational. God was rational; so was the species made in God's image.[35]

Joining Tillich, Swiss theologian Karl Barth asserted being made in God's image meant that human beings were "rational animals." Barth indicated that humans, in contrast to all other living things, were endowed with the capacity to think and to know. But he added that this, by itself, was not enough to distinguish humankind sufficiently from other species.

So Barth also posited that being made in God's image meant human beings were free to choose and therefore were responsible for their actions. Moral action and moral responsibility were what made *Homo sapiens sapiens* special and separate, and these reflected God, because God was independent and not coerced in God's actions. God was free; so was the species made in God's image.[36]

Similarly, Dutch theologian Hendrikus Berkhof indicated that being made in God's image meant humans were created to have *dominion* over creation. In fact, "dominion" also occurs in Genesis 1:26 and adjacent verses as well. Berkhof proclaimed that having lordship over the rest of the created order was what made *Homo sapiens sapiens* special and distinct, and this reflected God, because God was Lord over God's whole creation. God was sovereign over all; so was the species made in God's image.[37]

Regardless of the particular differences among them, these thinkers come together in their affirmation that "human beings made in God's image" grants human beings a unique status which separates them from, and sets them over, the rest of the created order. Thus positioned, and then instructed to "dominate and subdue," that is exactly what human beings have done. And so, one would inclusively and succinctly observe:

Acid rain is falling down, and garbage dumps are filling up.
The ozone layer is thinning, and pollution is thickening.
Human populations are burgeoning, and endangered species are going extinct.
Global temperatures are expanding, and the rain forest is shrinking.
Oil spills are spreading everywhere, and toxic waste is headed anywhere that will take it!

By contrast, science clearly points out that biologically and genetically humans are "kin" to other species. At one point in his notes, Charles Darwin writes, "We are all netted together . . ." and at another juncture, "[It's] more humble and I believe true to see us created from animals."[38]

Theological ethicist Paul Jersild makes the point that historically persons of faith have reacted defensively to their biological, evolutionary, and genetic connection with the rest of life. "We are so used to stressing our uniqueness as human beings that any reminder of our connectedness with the animal world is often regarded as a threat."[39]

Sigmund Freud adds his voice,

> Humanity has in the course of time had to endure from the hands of science two great outrages upon its naive self-love: The first was when it realized that our earth was not the center of the universe. . . . The second was when biological research robbed man of his particular privilege of having been specially created, and relegated him to a descent from the animal world.[40]

However, if *Homo sapiens sapiens'* uniqueness/distinctiveness is interpreted and understood as "ontological" (a descriptor of our nature, i.e., who we are), then this distinctiveness *is* threatened by humans' kinship with the community of life. But if human uniqueness is interpreted and understood as "axiological" (a descriptor of our behavior, our values—i.e., how humans choose to act), then humans' distinctiveness is confirmed by human relationship with the community of life. *Homo sapiens sapiens* are responsible for this community's well-being and care. Without it, the human species cannot act upon, and act out, its God-given responsibility. Humans' being made in God's image is not a status, but a verb—it's what *Homo sapiens sapiens do.*

This scientific emphasis on the connectedness of humans with other creatures can inform humans and enable them to adjust their understanding of human beings and their role in the natural world. It also could encourage humans to take into consideration the "humbler, more modest" account of the creation of man in Genesis 2:

The commonality with other creatures which Darwin noted and detailed, and which science proclaims, is echoed in the *second* chapter of Genesis. In *its* account of creation, *'adam* is made from the dust of the earth, just like all the non-human living species (in the original Hebrew, *'adam* from *'adamah,* "man" from the "dust"). Here man's kinship is emphasized over man's kingship.

Several thinkers reflect this "alternative" imagery for human identity and function:

Biblical scholar Walter Brueggemann said that being made in God's image meant that humans were created to rule over creation *in the way that God ruled over creation*. Creatively using power to invite, evoke, and permit was what made *Homo sapiens sapiens* special and a reflection of God, because this is the way that God exercised God's power. God ruled as a servant-king, but not as a dictator-tyrant; so should the species made in God's image. [41]

Physicist and theologian Ian Barbour suggested that being made in God's image meant that humans were created to be responsible for creation in the way that God was responsible for creation. Having created the earth, God now takes care of it. So, being entrusted with responsibility for the creation and for caring for it well was what made *Homo sapiens sapiens* special and a reflection of God, because that is what God does. God was responsible for what God made; so should be the species made in God's image. [42]

Theologian Marjorie Suchocki asserted that being made in God's image meant that humans were created in interrelationship with all living things, just as God exists in relationship with all that is. Being consciously in relationship with all life on earth—human and non-human—was what made *Homo sapiens sapiens* special and a reflection of God, because God intentionally and intimately relates to all that God has made. God exists in loving relationship with all living things in the creation; so should the species made in God's image. [43]

But, of course, Genesis 1 underscores a distinctiveness, a specialness, for human beings. So, in light of science and in light of Genesis 2, and in response to the insights of Brueggemann, Barbour, and Suchocki, what might it mean for human beings to have been created in the image of God of Genesis 1? What might it mean for humans to have been *uniquely* created in God's image? What is special and distinctive about *Homo sapiens sapiens*?

It is not *long life*—the tortoise lives far longer; it is not *strength*—a chimpanzee is eight-to-ten times as strong as a human; it is not *sight*—the eagle recognizes things from a much greater distance away; it is not the *ability to reason*—other mammals (such as the great apes, killer whales, and dolphins) have been shown to think and be reflective and solve problems by a process that cannot be distinguished from rationality; it is not *smell*—a dog can pick-up odors that humans cannot discern; it is not *speed*—a Thompson's gazelle or a cheetah runs at a much faster velocity; it is not *hearing*—a bat can hear sounds that humans fail to detect; it is not *language*—recent studies have shown that chimpanzees communicate using something akin to language, and whales communicate with one another over hundreds of miles; it is not *technology*—other species use "tools," such as the finch that uses twigs to extricate ants from a hole in the ground or insects from a tree, and other primates that use sticks and branches and stones to accomplish tasks and achieve goals, and bats and dolphins that use sonar or echolocation (and these are "built-in" or "hard-wired" technologies!); it's not *olfactory receptors and the sense of smell*—a white-tailed deer has 250 million olfactory receptors in its maze of nasal passages, while humans have just 5 million. Deer use this "keen sense of smell to detect predators, find food, and learn the whereabouts and reproductive status of other deer."[44] What, then, is special—distinctive—about human beings?

In short, humans are made uniquely in the image of God for a special *function*, a vast *responsibility*, and not for a superior *status*. That is, human beings are God's representatives on earth, charged with caring-for and looking-out- for the entirety of planetary life. In Genesis 2:15, human beings are charged to serve and to preserve the Garden. This notion of serving and preserving provides a creative tension, a counterbalance, and a restraint for Genesis 1:28 where human beings are to have dominion over and subdue the natural world. Given what science has illustrated about the intimate connection between humans and the rest of life on earth, this must be interpreted as using the power of the position to care-for and serve, to protect and preserve.

If we inform our understanding of Genesis 1's "image of God" with science and with Genesis 2, then only humans are in a position to formulate a biocentric ethic (a life-centered ethic that takes into consideration the situations and rights of all living things—human and non-human). As a result, only *humans* sin by not living-up to the moral demands of such an ethic. As environmental theologian Jay McDaniel has put it, "To be made in God's image is not to leave our earthiness behind; rather it is to become fully human by realizing our potential for wisdom and compassion."[45] This wisdom and compassion are not to be reserved for our relations with fellow humans, but are to be properly extended to the whole of life. As a result, humans have a responsibility for the rest of creation and are held accountable by God for how this responsibility is discharged—humans are morally blameworthy or morally praiseworthy depending on how they fulfill this obligation.

Concerning this notion of the image of God, Canadian theologian Douglas John Hall has written perceptively and persuasively: The image of God, he declares, is not something which humankind *has*, but rather something which humankind *does*. "Humans made in the image of God," then, does not refer to one particular trait or one set of characteristics which humans possess, but instead refers to something which humans act-out. The image of God is not "substantial" (a part of humans' essence or being or *ontology*), but "relational" (a part of humans' behavior or actions).[46]

Being made in God's image, then, lays an ethical responsibility on humans based on kinship—a connectional model emphasized by science and by

Genesis 2—rather than on arrogance based on kingship—a monarchical model. The "image of God" is more a verb than a noun, a function not a status. Intrinsic to this is the affirmation that humans are a part of, not apart from, nature. Man was made for nature; nature was not made for man. Nature is not a commodity to own; nature is a community to serve.

Science and Darwin's theory of evolution—emphasizing humans' connectedness to the rest of nature, creation—can help people of faith understand more fully what it means to be created in the divine image and to grasp more deeply and more completely the meaning of the creation of humans in Genesis 1 and 2. Theologian Phil Hefner's phrase "created co-creators" points to this vision of human creativity and action as an essential dimension of humans' being created in God's image:[47] We are to rule-over (exercise our power) and care-for (serve and service) the world in ways that fulfill this destiny. The world to which we are related—and other species with whom we are interconnected—are all bound together in sustainable well-being and by the goal of survival. "Human destiny cannot be divorced from the larger world in which that destiny plays out."[48]

And as a result, science and religion might join forces here to work on solving the environmental crisis which besets the planet. Science could provide the ecological consciousness—the knowledge of the environmental problems that challenge us and the knowledge of how to begin to provide answers to them. Religion could provide the ecological conscience—the inspiration to take that knowledge and apply it. Science would provide the means, religious would provide the motivation.

Both fields are needed: For the environmental problems are at their base spiritual problems. They arise from non-sustainable values that direct and influence our behavior. If humans believe that nature is an object which is "there" for them to manipulate, take, and "use" to satisfy their every want, then they will recklessly and rapaciously tap nature as a vast storehouse of natural resources from which they can make incessant and insensitive withdrawals. Humans' greed, materialism and consumerism, short-sightedness and selfishness are values which fuel their use and abuse of nature.

So, *Homo sapiens sapiens* must replace those values with values that are healthy and sustainable—restraint vs. the current greed, spiritual orientation vs. the obsession with materialism and insatiable consumerism, long-term consequences vs. short-term gain, other-directedness (altruism) vs. selfishness and egocentrism.

Religion, which at its best, draws humans out from ourselves to consider the "other," and reminds them of our responsibility for that which is greater than ourselves, is crucial for the solving of our environmental problems.

Religion reminds science that the environmental problems humans face are but symptoms of an underlying disease. Ecological issues are the visible consequences of the values-dilemma which lies invisibly at the heart of the matter.

And science reminds religion that the environmental problems humans face will not be successfully addressed without understanding them as the result of violating the patterns and rhythms ("laws") of nature. Unless humans understand how nature works, then even the best of their intentions may be counter-productive.[49]

Thus, science can provide religion with the information which can guide its compassionate response to a pressing situation—science can provide an "ecological consciousness." And religion can provide science with the motivation to take this knowledge and use it for the solution of the problem and the healing of the world—an "ecological conscience."

NOTES

1. Charles F. Henderson, Jr., *God and Science: The Death and Rebirth of Theism* (Atlanta: John Knox Press, 1986).

2. Ted Peters, *The Cosmic Self* (New York: HarperCollins, 1991), 136–137.

3. Process theology is based on the philosophical outlook and worldview of mathematician and philosopher, Alfred North Whitehead. Writing in the first-half of the twentieth century, his many books are anchored by his *Process and Reality* (New York: Macmillan, 1929). Notable theologians who have drawn from his thought for both inspiration and content include John B. Cobb, Jr., David Ray Griffin, Schubert Ogden, Pierre Teilhard de Chardin, Clark Williamson, Sallie McFague, Charles Hartshorne, Marjorie Suchocki, Daniel Day Williams, Norman Pittenger, Philip Clayton, and Jay McDaniel, among many others. I, myself, am deeply indebted to Whitehead and to several of the others listed, in my own theological development. These thinkers and their writings are commended to the reader.For a very helpful overview and brief introduction to process theology, see Philip Clayton, "God Beyond Orthodoxy: Process Theology for the Twenty-first Century," a paper delivered at the Center for Process Studies at Claremont School of Theology on September 9th, 2008 (clayton.ctr4process.org/files/papers/ Godandorthodoxy-r3.pdf).

4. Sallie McFague, "The World as God's Body" (*The Christian Century*, July 20–27, 1998), 671–673; Sallie McFague, *The Body of God: An Ecological Theology* (Minneapolis: Augsburg Press, 1993); Grace Jantzen, *God's World, God's Body* (Philadelphia: Westminster Press, 1984.)

5. John B. Cobb, Jr., and David Ray Griffin, *Process Theology: An Introductory Exposition* (Louisville: Westminster John Knox Press, 1976), 48.

6. George E. Wright, *God Who Acts* (London: SCM Press, 1952), *passim.*

7. Schubert M. Ogden, *The Reality of God* (New York: Harper and Row, 1966), 14–15.

8. Clifford Chalmers Cain, "God's Providence and Pastoral Care" (unpublished doctoral dissertation, Vanderbilt University, 1981), 10.

9. Harald Fritzsch, *The Creation of Matter: The Universe from Beginning to End* (Basic Books, Inc., 1984).

10. Norman F. Hall and Lucia K. B. Hall, *The Humanist* (May/June 1986).

11. Quoted in Delos McKown, "Science vs. Religion in Future Constitutional Conflicts" (*Free Inquiry*, Summer, 1984).

12. Albert Einstein, *Out of My Later Years* (The Einstein Estate, 1956).

13. Gordon Kaufman, *God the Problem* (Cambridge, MA: Harvard University Press, 1972), 120.

14. Albert Einstein, *loc. cit.*

15. Gordon Kaufman, *op. cit.,* 121.

16. Rudolf Bultmann, *Jesus Christ and Mythology* (New York: Charles Scribner's Sons, 1958), 65.

17. Schubert Ogden, *The Reality of God* (New York: Harper and Row, 1966), 164.

18. Langdon Gilkey, "Cosmology, Ontology, and the Travail of Biblical Language" (*Journal of Religion*, Vol. 41, No. 203, 1961), 200.

19. John B. Cobb, Jr., and David Ray Griffin, *op.cit.,* 51.

20. Lewis Ford, "Divine Persuasion and the Triumph of Good," *The Christian Scholar*, (Vol. L, No. 3, Fall, 1967), 237.

21. Clifford Chalmers Cain, *op. cit.,* 82.

22. Delwin Brown, Ralph James, and Gene Reeves, eds., *Process Philosophy and Christian Thought* (Indianapolis: Bobbs-Merrill Publishing Co., 1971), 288.

23. Alfred North Whitehead, *The Adventures of Ideas* (New York: Macmillan Co., 1933), 189.

24. John B. Cobb, Jr., and David Ray Griffin, *op. cit.,* 51.

25. *Ibid.*, 23.

26. Clifford Chalmers Cain, *op. cit.,* 84.

27. Alfred North Whitehead, *Process and Reality* (New York: Macmillan Co., 1929), 374.

28. Delwin Brown, Ralph James, and Gene Reeves, eds., *op. cit.,* 289. This image of God as "gardener" I mentioned in the previous chapter's religious response, noting Ian Barbour's use of it in *When Science Meets Religion* (New York: HarperCollins, 2000), 60; it is also biblical, though rare—Genesis 2:8, for example.

29. Daniel Day Williams, "How Does God Act?: An Essay in Whitehead's Metaphysics," in William L. Reese and Eugene Freeman, eds., *Process and Divinity* (La Salle, IL: Open Court Publishing Co., 1964), 170.

30. Clifford Chalmers Cain, *op. cit.,* 91.

31. Abraham Joshua Heschel, *The Prophets*, Vol. II (NewYork: Harper and Row, 1962), 87, 15, 64, 39.

32. Kazo Kitamori, *Theology of the Pain of God* (Richmond: John Knox Press, 1965), *passim.*

33. Jurgen Moltmann, *The Crucified God*, (New York: Harper and Row, 1974); *The Theology of Hope* (Minneapolis: Augsburg Press, 1967) and *The Church in the Power of the Spirit* (Philadelphia: Fortress Press, 1977) are the other two installments of the trilogy.

34. William Paley, *Natural Theology; or, Evidences of the Existence and Attributes of the Deity, Collected from the Appearances of Nature* (London: J. Faulder, 1802).

35. Paul Tillich, *Systematic Theology*, Vol. I (Chicago: University of Chicago Press, 1951), 157.

36. Karl Barth, *Church Dogmatics*, Vol. III.2 (Edinburgh: T. and T. Clark, 1936–1961), 76, 77, 83, 323–324)

37. Hendrikus Berkhof, "God in Nature and History," *New Directions in Faith and Order* (Geneva: World Council of Churches, 1968), 18.

38. "Evolution and Wonder: Understanding Charles Darwin," interview of James Moore by Krista Tippet on National Public Radio's *Speaking of Faith*, February 5th, 2009; http://speakingoffaith.publicradio.org/programs/2009/Darwin/transcript.shtml, 8.

39. Paul Jersild, *The Nature of Our Humanity* (Minneapolis: Fortress Press, 2009), 21.

40. Sigmund Freud quoted in Delos B. McKown, "Science vs. Religion in Future Constitutional Conflicts," *Free Inquiry*, (Summer, 1984).

41. Walter Brueggemann, *Genesis* (Atlanta: John Knox Press, 1982), 32; Steven Bouma-Prediger agrees with Brueggemann's claim that humans are called to rule creation the way God rules creation—lovingly. Therefore, human beings are morally accountable for their rule, the only species to be so [*For the Beauty of the Earth* (Grand Rapids, MI: Baker Book House, 2001), 123].

42. Ian Barbour, *Earth Might Be Fair* (Englewood Cliffs, NJ: Prentice-Hall Publishing Co., 1972), 149.

43. Marjorie Suchocki, Public Lecture, Franklin College, Franklin, Indiana (May, 1989).

44. Missouri Department of Conservation, *Conservation* magazine, 2013.

45. Jay B. McDaniel, "Red Grace and Green Grace," in *With Roots and Wings* (Maryknoll, New York: Orbis Books, 1995), 57.

46. Douglas John Hall, *Imaging God: Dominion as Stewardship* (Grand Rapids, MI: Eerdmans Publishing Co., 1986), 111f. Of course, *all* species have unique/distinctive roles to play in ecosystems. As one species among many, human beings have as their distinctive role the caring-for and serving of the entire ecosystem of which they are a part.

47. Philip Hefner, *The Human Factor: Evolution, Culture, and Religion* (Minneapolis: Augsburg Press, 1993), 27f.

48. Susan B. Thistlethwaite, ed., *Adam, Eve, and the Genome* (Minneapolis: Fortress Press, 2003), 109f.

49. For example, human population growth is arguably one of the most pressing environmental concerns, exacerbating depletion of natural resources, hastening climate change, multiplying waste, accelerating species extinction, driving deforestation, multiplying world hunger, etc. The desire of religious persons to help solve this problem by compassionately providing food for the world's hungry people is noble. But unless the provision of food is accompanied by the advocacy and availability of safe, effective, available, cheap birth control, then this loving and merciful action makes the problem worse: For a number of scientific studies have shown that reproduction increases with nutrition; there is a correlation between health and reproductive rate. Plus, more people living and procreating draws even more heavily on food resources. And this does not even take into consideration additional factors such as economic and social pressures like the need for more hands for manual, agricultural labor; infant mortality rates which increase the number of births to end-up with the needed or desired number of children for this labor and for parents' security later in life; cultural preference for large families, and a preference for male children.

Chapter Six

The Complex Relationship between Nature and Nurture

Jane Kenney-Hunt

Are talents and abilities predetermined? What about physical appearance? Are we destined by our biology to be tall or short, thin or heavy, athletic or clumsy, cigarette smokers or abstainers, accountants or entertainers? What are the roles of our experiences and the environments in which we grow up? In short, what is it that makes us who we are?

The relative roles of nature, or inherited traits, and nurture, or the environment, are an area of intense interest for scientists and non-scientists alike. In the public sphere, discussion of nature and nurture and their relative roles can resemble a debate about free will versus predestination. "Nature versus nurture," however, is a false dichotomy. Our traits are not determined by either inheritance or the environment, but by their interaction.

Genetics is the study of heredity, the way in which traits are passed from one generation to the next. Inheritance can be observed by comparing children with their parents. Children often resemble one or both of their parents very closely in some respects, but not in others. For example, a baby may inherit the blue eyes of his parents, but have blond hair while both parents have brown. The child of a musician may be tone deaf, and the child of professional basketball players might turn out quite tall but not as agile or athletic as her parents. Why are children both similar to and different from their parents?

As scientific knowledge has advanced, we have begun to understand more about the complex interaction between genes and the environment. Environment can refer to physical surroundings, like temperature, but it may also refer to chemical exposure, dietary nutrition, or the environment of the womb in which a fetus develops. The effect of the environment on an organism differs depending on its genes. The inheritance of traits is much more complicated, and much more interesting, than is generally appreciated.

To begin to understand inheritance, we will first look within the cell at the molecule that contains the genetic instructions that are passed from parent to offspring. This molecule is DNA.

WHAT IS DNA?

Deoxyribonucleic acid, or DNA for short, is a molecule made up of two long chains, or strands, wrapping around each other in a double helix shape. Each strand includes repeating units called nitrogenous bases. The two strands of the DNA double helix are connected to each other through chemical bonds between the bases. There are only four bases in DNA, and they bond to each other according to strict rules. Adenine (A) always binds with thymine (T) and cytosine (C) always binds with guanine (G). This structure was first published in 1953 by James Watson and Francis Crick.[1] The DNA double helix can be visualized as a spiral staircase, with the sides of the staircase as the DNA strands and the steps of the stairs as the chemical bonds between the bases holding the strands together. The order of the bases within the DNA molecule forms the genetic code, which provides operating instructions to every living organism. DNA is also the molecule of inheritance, used to pass those instructions from one generation to the next. All known living cellular organisms, from the smallest bacterium to the largest whale, use DNA as the molecule of inheritance. There are some differences in the details of genetic processes, especially between simple single-celled and complicated multicellular organisms. For the sake of simplicity, this chapter is mainly concerned with genetics in humans.

All cells contain DNA, which is a stable and relatively durable molecule. It is possible to extract DNA from the cells of long-dead organisms, such as extinct wooly mammoths preserved in permafrost for tens of thousands of years.[2] Cells are found not only in tissues like muscle, but also in body fluids like blood, and in follicles at the roots of strands of hair. Because of this, DNA can often, but not always, be collected at a crime scene for identification of a victim or perpetrator (DNA fingerprinting, see below).

DNA within a cell is divided into pieces called chromosomes. Sexually-reproducing organisms normally have two copies of each and every chromosome in every cell of the body. One chromosome in each pair is inherited paternally, from the father, and the other chromosome is inherited maternally, from the mother. The exception in humans is that men have one X and one Y chromosome. The X chromosome in men is inherited maternally and the Y is inherited paternally. Women have two X chromosomes, one from each parent, but no Y chromosome.

A genome is the collective term for all of the DNA possessed by an organism. Once it became technologically possible to establish the sequence, or order of bases within a particular DNA molecule, geneticists began to investigate the sequences of the genomes of many species including humans. The goal of the Human Genome Project, begun in 1990 and completed in 2003, was to determine the sequence of all the DNA found in a human cell. The human genome has about three billion base pairs, and 20,000–25,000 genes.[3] The Human Genome Project and related studies have driven major technological and computational advances in genetic analysis, and by 2014, over two thousand genes and genetic loci that have effects on human diseases and other traits had been identified.[4]

WHAT IS A GENE?

On the molecular level, genes are portions of DNA that provide instructions to the cell, describing how to produce specific proteins or ribonucleic acid (RNA) molecules. The classical genetics concept of a gene, however, is that of a unit of inheritance, in which a gene controls a particular trait. This idea is most commonly introduced to biology students through the work of Gregor Mendel. Mendel was born in 1822 in what is now part of the Czech Republic and performed his research in a monastery, beginning in the 1850's. Mendel studied the pea plant, which has simple, easily measured binary traits like yellow or green pea coloration. Mendel investigated traits including plant height, seed color, pod color, and seed texture. While Mendel was not alone in investigating the inheritance of traits in the nineteenth century, it was he who first demonstrated that instructions for a trait pass from one generation to the next as discrete units inherited individually, one from each parent.[5] For example, if a plant with green peas was crossed to a plant with yellow peas, the offspring plant would receive one green pea version of the pea color gene from one parent, and one yellow pea version of the gene from the other parent. The offspring plant would then pass either the green version or the yellow version of the gene to its offspring. We now know this is because the offspring plants inherit one copy of each chromosome (and thus one copy of each gene) from each parent.

In the early twentieth century, Mendel's work was rediscovered and these observations were combined with the growing body of knowledge about the molecular nature of inheritance, leading to the concept of the gene we have today.

How does DNA code for proteins? Proteins are composed of amino acids. The order of amino acids within a protein is determined by the order of nitrogenous bases within a gene. It is strong evidence for the common evolutionary origin of life that the same genetic code (with a few small evolved differences in certain organisms) is used by all cellular life to assemble amino acids into proteins from the instructions carried in molecules of DNA.[6]

The production of proteins from genes can be "turned on" (expressed) or "turned off" (unexpressed), depending on the needs of the organism. Most, if not all, cells in a multicellular organism are specialists, producing only certain proteins in order to perform particular functions. Because all cells contain the entire genome, it is through turning genes on and off during development that cells specialize into skin, stomach, bone, and brain cells and produce specific molecules to fill those roles.

Cells express genes at different rates and at different times through complex, regulated processes. For example, when a wound is healing, gene products that aid in replacement and repair of tissue are expressed, and the length of time in which those genes are expressed depends in part on the size of the wound and how long it takes to heal. Other genes are expressed only in certain tissues at certain times during embryonic development. Knowing which protein is encoded by a gene still doesn't provide all the information about the function of the gene, or how and when it is expressed within an organism.

WHAT IS GENETIC MUTATION?

All cells derive from existing cells. In order to grow or to replace dead cells, the cells of our body divide in two. When a body cell is preparing to divide and produce a daughter cell, its entire genome must be replicated through a process called "mitosis" so the new cell may have its own copy. Genomes are vast, containing as many as several billion bases depending on the species. During DNA replication, the cell proofreads the genetic code to look for incorrectly added nitrogenous bases, missing bases, and other errors. Cells make copy errors in new DNA molecules at the rate of only about of 3×10^{-8} (0.00000003) per base per generation.[7] DNA sequence can also be altered through exposure to ultraviolet (UV) light, X-rays, and chemicals called "mutagens." When the order of bases in the DNA molecule changes, whatever the reason, it is called a "mutation." Mutation may involve something as simple as a substitution of one base for another, or as profound as the deletion of large segments of DNA or a piece of a chromosome. Mutations can result in new and different gene products if they fall within a gene by changing the sequence of the bases in the genetic code. A mutation may also disrupt a gene so that the sequence no longer provides instructions the cell can read, even though the rest of the gene is still there.

A mutation that occurs only in a body (or somatic) cell might affect the organism, but it has no impact on the next generation. For a person to pass a mutation to his or her children, the mutation must exist in the DNA in a germ cell, which gives rise to the sperm or egg. For example, exposure to UV light can cause mutations in the DNA of skin cells, and result in skin cancer, but these mutations do not affect the sperm or egg cells. The mutation, and the skin cancer, are not inherited.

Mutation is the cause of genetic disease, so the word carries a negative connotation, but mutation is not necessarily negative. It is also the source of the variation in DNA sequences that results in some people being short and some tall, some blond and some redheaded. Without mutation, we would not have both red and white roses. Mutation can lead to new and advantageous traits. If a mutation has a strong effect on survival or reproduction, such as causing a person to be more resistant to contracting a serious disease, that person is more likely to survive to have more children than the average. Those children that inherit the mutation for disease resistance will also tend to have more children, and so on, until the mutation becomes common.

Mutation will not give anyone the ability to control magnetic forces or read minds, but past mutations have provided several human populations with the ability to easily digest lactose, and thus consume dairy products as adults. In most humans and other mammals, this ability declines shortly after weaning. The enzyme that allows the digestion of lactose is called "lactase," and several different mutations that allow lactase to be produced into adulthood have evolved in human populations in the last 2,000–20,000 years.[8] A mutation that provides the ability to enjoy ice cream and cheese is not quite as dramatic as the mutations of science fiction, but it is a useful mutation in an environment with access to nutrition from milk products. Those that were lucky enough to inherit these mutations thrived, and passed them to their offspring, which is why lactase function in adults is reasonably common today.

Changes in genetic sequence over billions of years have led to the diversity of life on earth. Ultimately, mutation provides the heritable variation that is the material for evolutionary change (see chapter 4).

WHAT IS AN ALLELE?

Mutation in the DNA sequence of a gene results in an alternative version of a gene, called an "allele." The relationship between DNA sequence, genes, and alleles is illustrated in Figure 6.1. If the instructions in DNA are like a blueprint for a house, then alleles are like different options for wall paint in the living room or a choice of stove in the kitchen. Mendel's pea plants (see above) had yellow and green peas because they had different alleles of the pea color gene.

All humans have the same genes. It is our alleles that make us genetically different. These differences in alleles can be partly responsible for differences between people in height or weight, and in likelihood to develop cancer or obesity. At the molecular level, alleles may result in differences in traits by causing genes to express different proteins or different amounts of the same protein.

Confusion about the difference between genes and alleles is common. When it is reported in the media that "the gene" for a certain trait has been identified, what this usually means is that a particular allele of a gene has been identified as having an effect on the trait. For example, the "breast cancer gene" BRCA1 is not a breast cancer gene at all. BRCA1 has a role in important cell regulatory processes and normally has a tumor-suppressing function.[9] Unfortunately, mutations in BRCA1 have led to alleles that no longer have this function. It is therefore correct to say that someone has "the allele" for breast cancer rather than to say that someone has "the gene" for the disease.

Every person has a maximum of two alleles of any gene because they have two copies of each gene, one inherited from each parent, except for the genes on the X and Y chromosomes in men (see above). It is possible to inherit the same allele from both parents, resulting in two copies of the same allele. Many genetic diseases, such as cystic fibrosis, result from inheriting two damaged or non-functional alleles of a gene. These are sometimes called "recessive diseases."

Several alleles of a gene may exist in a population, resulting from more than one mutation event. Even so, one person can still have only two alleles. A familiar example of multiple alleles is the gene for ABO blood groups in humans.[10] This gene affects the molecules on the outside of red blood cells. These molecules, called "antigens," are recognized by the immune system. If someone receives a transfusion of blood with an antigen the immune system identifies as foreign, it will respond against the new blood. This is why doctors carefully select the type of donated blood for blood transfusion, based on the patient's own type.

There are three alleles that determine which ABO blood type a person will have. These alleles are called I^A, I^B, and i. These three alleles lead to four different blood groups—A, B, AB, and O. Alleles can act together to influence a trait, or the presence of one allele can hide the presence of the other. The alleles I^A and I^B act together, and a person with both those alleles has blood of type AB. When the I^A or I^B allele is found with the i allele, however, it masks the presence of the i allele. People with type A blood have either two I^A alleles or one I^A and one i allele. People with type B blood have two I^B alleles or one I^B allele and one i allele. People with type O blood have two i alleles. The immune system of a person with type A blood will identify the type B blood cells as foreign, and the immune system of those with type

B blood will do the same with type A blood cells. People with type O blood lack any antigens at all, with important implications for blood donation. Blood from people with type O blood can be safely *donated* to people with type O, A, B, or AB blood, because there are no antigens for the blood recipient's immune system to detect and attack. This is why type O is called the "universal donor." People with type O blood can only *receive* type O blood, because they will have an immune response to type A and B blood cells.

As discussed above, every person inherits two copies of each gene, one from each parent. While all body cells have both copies of each gene, the sperm and egg cells through which DNA is passed to the next generation are different. Each sperm or egg cell has only one chromosome of each pair and so only one copy of each gene. When a sperm or egg cell is formed, it receives at random either a maternally-inherited or paternally-inherited copy of each chromosome, resulting in a unique combination of alleles. When a sperm fertilizes an egg to form an embryo, the new embryo has two copies of each chromosome, one inherited from each parent. This is a key concept in genetics: New allele combinations, or genotypes, are formed each generation in sexually-reproducing organisms.

Using the example of alleles of the gene for ABO blood type discussed above, let us take a closer look at how the inheritance of alleles leads to genotypes. Imagine a woman has type A blood because she has one I^A allele and one i allele. Her male partner has type B blood, with one I^B allele and one i allele. The woman's egg cells each have just one of her alleles, either I^A or i. The man's sperm cells also have just one of the man's alleles, either I^B or i. What blood groups are possible in their children? Eggs carrying allele I^A may be fertilized by sperm carrying either I^B or i alleles. Eggs carrying allele i may also be fertilized by sperm carrying I^B or i alleles. Thus, it is possible for a child to inherit one I^A and one I^B allele (resulting in blood type AB), one I^A and one i allele (type A), one i and one I^B allele (type B), or two i alleles (type O). This example demonstrates how children can have very different traits—blood types—than their parents, simply by inheriting different pairs of alleles. When multiple genes and the environment have an effect on a trait, as they often do, the inheritance of traits becomes even more difficult to predict.

GENES AND TRAITS

A "phenotype" is an observable trait or traits possessed by an individual. This may include a physical characteristic, such as body weight, or a behavior, such as hours spent sleeping per day. Phenotypes result from the interaction of genes and environment.

Phenotypes controlled mainly by a single gene with insignificant environmental contributions are the easiest to study and understand, and thus were among the first traits to be explained by genetics. They also make the easiest examples to explore in the classroom, so single-gene traits, such as those in Mendel's pea plants or ABO blood groups (see above), are the traits most often familiar to non-scientists.

Human phenotypes known to be affected by a single gene include the presence or absence of a cleft chin. There are also a number of known human diseases, such as Tay-Sachs, that are caused by a mutation in a single gene. Alternatively, some genes have alleles that are known to be associated with a disease, but these alleles are not the sole cause of the disease. Breast and ovarian cancers are associated with specific mutations in the genes BRCA1 and BRCA2, and women with these alleles are very likely to develop cancer, but most breast cancer patients have normal alleles of the BRCA1 and BRCA2 genes.[11]

Most traits, however, are affected by many genes. Complex traits result from the interaction of multiple genes and the environment. These include body height and weight, skin color, most cancers, type II diabetes, heart disease, longevity, fertility, and so on. Nutrition, chemical exposure, or stress may play a role in the development of some of these phenotypes, as well as the genotype of the individual. The expression of a complex trait is like the result of a complicated construction project, involving many individuals with different jobs working together. The dynamics of the group and the materials available contribute to the completed building, analogous to the way in which many genes and gene products work together in a variety of ways, within the context of the environment, to produce complex phenotypes.

In discussing the relationship between genes and traits, or genotype and phenotype, we approach the important concept of "heritability." Put simply, heritability is a measure of the importance of genetic factors, rather than the environment, in determining a particular phenotype.[12] A trait such as eye color is strongly heritable, while a trait like body weight, which is strongly influenced by the dietary environment, is less heritable.

Heritability is very difficult to calculate in humans. The environmental effects on important health-related phenotypes can include diet, exposure to disease, place of birth, maternal nutrition during fetal development, and psychological stress. These environmental effects complicate efforts to disentangle genotype and phenotype. Factor-in multiple alleles, interaction among genes, and the large number of genes in the genome, and separating genetic and environmental contributions to phenotype becomes extraordinarily difficult.

Genetic Variation

There are about 20,000 genes in the human genome,[13] and many of these genes have two or more alleles. There are also stretches of DNA between human genes which are highly variable. All this variation makes possible the identification of individuals by their unique DNA sequences, called "DNA fingerprinting." Geneticists have identified regions of the human genome where there are several possible alleles, and through extensive data collection, the relative frequency of these alleles is known. The statistical probability of a particular combination of alleles can then be calculated. If enough locations in the genome are tested, a DNA sample can be matched to an individual person with a very high degree of confidence. One use of DNA fingerprinting is paternity testing. A child inherits one allele from each parent, so the child will share one allele with his or her father at every location in the genome (barring the very rare mutation). If a putative (assumed) father's DNA fingerprint matches the child's, and only one man in 10 million would have that same DNA fingerprint, the judge will likely conclude that the evidence for paternity is overwhelming. A putative father can also be definitely eliminated if the child does not share one of his alleles at each tested location. DNA fingerprinting can also be used to identify perpetrators in criminal cases if usable DNA is left behind for comparison to a suspect's DNA. DNA fingerprinting can also be used to positively identify human remains. The DNA of a person expected to be closely-related to the deceased (such as a sibling, parent, or child) can be fingerprinted and compared to the DNA of the remains. DNA fingerprinting has also been used to identify the relationships among ancient Egyptian royal mummies.[14] As DNA fingerprinting technology becomes less expensive, it has also begun to be used by genealogists to help identify distant relatives. The same technology can be applied in wildlife conservation and management. By extracting DNA from discarded hair or scat (excrement), the number of unique individual genomes, and thus individual animals, in a population can be estimated without capturing each animal[15] —a a great advantage with widely dispersed, dangerous, or timid animals. The fact that more closely-related individuals will share more alleles than more distantly-related individuals can be applied even more broadly by looking at different regions of the genome to determine the evolutionary relationship between species.

Yet while we can identify individuals by their unique combination of alleles, this information may not tell us very much about the traits of the organism. The fingerprint gives us a genetic, but not physical, description, though a few traits can currently be discerned from genome sequencing, such as ABO blood group and likely eye color.[16] The presence of a genetic disease can also be determined from an individual's genome sequence, if the gene variant (allele) that causes the disease has already been identified.

We can see the results of human genetic variation as we look around us. People vary in many phenotypes, including height, hair color, body shape, facial features, and the shape of fingers and toes. They also have variation in ways that are less easy to observe, such as susceptibility to the common cold. New genotypes appear constantly, but rather slowly, through mutation. A genotype might produce a phenotype that is deleterious in one environment, but very favorable in a new one, so what was once a rare genotype can become more common over generations.

An example of a human genotype that is favorable in one environment but not another involves a molecule called "hemoglobin." The purpose of hemoglobin is to transport oxygen molecules in the blood. Sickle cell disease is a dangerous condition in which red blood cells, which are normally round, form a hard crescent or sickle shape due to a mutation in the gene for the beta subunit of hemoglobin.[17] Sickle cells break down more quickly than normal blood cells, resulting in anemia. They can also get stuck in the small blood vessels of the body, causing pain and damage. Two of the gene's alleles are Hb^A, which codes for normal beta hemoglobin, and Hb^S, which causes blood cells to sickle. Individuals who have two normal alleles (genotype $Hb^A Hb^A$) have normal blood cells. Individuals with one of each ($Hb^A Hb^S$) have what is called sickle cell trait and have mostly normal function, but can suffer from sickness in low oxygen environments or when engaging in intense physical activity. Those who inherit two copies of the sickling allele ($Hb^S Hb^S$) have sickle cell anemia. Despite this, the Hb^S allele is in high frequency in some parts of the world, particularly in sub-Saharan Africa. Why would such a harmful allele exist in high frequencies? Wouldn't it decrease in frequency over time? It would, if not for the interaction of genotype and environment. Individuals with an Hb^S allele, it turns out, are resistant to malaria, a serious mosquito-borne disease which infects normal red blood cells with a tiny parasite that sickens or kills many millions of people every year. In an environment in which malaria is common, such as sub-Saharan Africa, individuals with one normal and one sickling allele have the advantage of resistance to malaria, yet do not suffer from sickle cell disease. Those with two normal alleles also do not have sickle cell disease, but they are more likely to be infected with malaria. Individuals with two Hb^S alleles resist malarial infection, but also have sickle cell disease. Thus, in a malarial environment, having one copy of each allele is the most advantageous genotype to have. Not only that, when a person with the $Hb^A Hb^S$, malarial-resistant genotype has children, 50% of them will inherit the Hb^S allele and thus be resistant to malaria, too. Only 25% of children born to parents that both have the $Hb^A Hb^S$ genotype will have sickle cell disease. It's a matter of odds—in an environment with constant exposure to malaria—a person is both more likely to survive to adulthood and have a greater number of children that survive if they have one copy of the sickling allele Hb^S, and so the Hb^S allele has increased in frequency since first appearing though mutation. In an environment without malaria, this allele provides no advantage, and extreme disadvantage if someone is unlucky enough to inherit two copies of this allele. It should be no surprise that the Hb^S allele is much rarer in non-malarial environments.

Some genotypes are deleterious (harmful) in any environment. It is estimated that most people have one or two rare alleles in their genome that would be lethal if two copies were inherited.[18] This is not usually a problem in humans, because these alleles are rare enough, and most populations have high enough levels of genetic variation that these alleles almost never end-up paired in an individual. Populations can have low amounts of genetic variation, however, if they are very small (such as endangered species) and/or have high amounts of inbreeding. When closely-related individuals have offspring, the chance for the offspring to inherit the same harmful allele from both the mother and the father is increased. This is an issue in animal breeding, such as in pedigreed dogs, which are often the result of extensive inbreeding, and in management of captive and zoo populations. Concern about genetic disease from shared, rare, negative alleles is one reason why the marriage of close relatives, such as first cousins, is taboo or illegal in many places. Historically and in some contemporary cultures, "consanguineous," or cousin marriage is more acceptable than it generally is in the United States today. The occasional such marriage is not a cause for genetic concern. In fact, there is also the possibility of inheriting two copies of a favorable allele. Extensive inbreeding over many generations, however, can have very negative consequences, as illustrated by the Habsburg royal dynasty, which inbred itself to extinction.[19]

Genetic disease in humans is generally not the result of inbreeding, except in isolated populations like the Old Order Amish.[20] Some human genetic diseases such as cystic fibrosis are caused by alleles that are relatively common in the general population. It is becoming more common for people to seek genetic testing before they have children, particularly if they are aware of genetic disease in their families, to determine if they might have a child with a genetic disease. While the technology does not currently exist to "fix" genetic disease alleles through genetic engineering, it is likely to be possible in the not-so-distant future. The ethics of engineering children for desirable traits (or the lack of deleterious ones) are controversial.

Cloning

While genetic variation between individuals is the norm, it is possible for individuals to have identical genomes. These individuals are called clones. Clones in science fiction are usually the same age, even if a clone was created using the DNA of an adult. Fictional clones are often evil by nature, and/or can access the thoughts or memories of their DNA donor. What is the nonfiction reality of cloning?

Clones of mammals are created by taking the DNA from an individual donor cell, inserting this DNA into a recipient egg cell from which the DNA has been removed, and then triggering an embryo to develop. The first successful clone using this method was a sheep named "Dolly," born in 1996.[21] Mammalian cloning currently has a low rate of success, though technology is improving.[22] The clones frequently fail to develop and those that survive to birth are often unhealthy. Despite these drawbacks, there are several purposes for which the cloning of animals is considered desirable. Cloning a particularly valuable livestock animal for breeding, copying a genetically-engineered animal for research, restoring an extinct species, and recreating a beloved pet are all objectives of various projects.

The ethics of cloning humans as reproductive clones, to create a child, or as therapeutic clones, to provide organs or tissues to the DNA donor are widely disputed, both in the United States and internationally.[23] Human clones already exist in the simplest sense, however, and have always existed. These clones are called "monozygotic," or identical, twins. Monozygotic twins can be very similar, but this is no surprise given that not only are they genetically nearly-identical (but not perfectly so, as mutations occur over the course of a lifetime),[24] they are almost always raised together and share their environment from conception through childhood. The more similar the genotypes and environments are, the more similar the phenotypes will be. If human reproductive cloning were to take place, the DNA donor's clone would be younger, as it would have to develop at a normal rate from an embryo, and it would share no memories, thoughts, or feelings with the donor. Claims of shared memories or telepathic abilities between twin siblings have never been scientifically validated, and there is no reason to believe clones would have these abilities either. The clone would be in effect a younger twin sibling for the donor, each of whom would have her/his own unique life experiences. In fact, for several reasons, human clones would be *more* different in phenotype than monozygotic twins. They would not share an environment either in the womb or while growing up, and because the donor DNA is injected into a donor egg cell, the clone will have developed in a different egg cell environment than the donor, including having different mitochondria (specialized part of a cell found outside the nucleus). This will likely result in very different epigenetic effects (development of new characteristics) in the clone than in the donor (see below).

While we may object to human reproductive cloning for other ethical reasons, we should not do so for fear that the DNA donor is somehow diminished by the presence of a clone, or that by creating clones, we are creating somehow less than fully-real people simply because they are not genetically unique. A clone would always be a fully autonomous, independent person. Genetic uniqueness is not the same thing as individuality and should never be considered as a necessity in order for a person to possess human rights.

Epigenetics

Genetically-identical individuals such as clones and monozygotic twins still have differences in their phenotypes. This is due in part to the phenomenon of "epigenetics." An epigenetic change is a heritable modification of the genome structure that is not a change in the DNA sequence itself.[25] Instead, chemical changes to the DNA molecule or the proteins around it lead to differences in the ways in which genes are expressed. An epigenetic modification to the DNA of a cell can be inherited by its daughter cells. These modifications can be involved in determining which genes the daughter cell will then express. Epigenetic modification may be a large part of what causes the daughter cell of a skin cell to function as a skin cell, and not a liver cell or muscle cell.[26] Epigenetic changes may also be inherited from one generation to the next through epigenetic modifications in the germ cells.

Epigenetic modifications producing changes to gene expression may result from environmental influences. Changes to gene expression in the brain can result from drug and alcohol abuse and may contribute to addiction and withdrawal symptoms.[27] Epigenetic modification can also occur as a result of diet,[28] such as during periods of famine, and may have serious health consequences. In a study of the Dutch famine of the winter of 1944–1945, poor nutrition in women who were pregnant resulted in long-term health effects for their children, including an increase in rates of coronary artery disease as adults.[29] There is some suggestion that there may be effects on the following generation, the children of the individuals who were in utero during the time of the famine, as well.[30] Epigenetic modification may also occur in response to stress or other experiences, modifying gene expression in the long-term with both psychological and physical effects.[31] In other words, our experiences have a profound impact in molding us, even at the molecular level.

Variation in epigenetic patterns has been well-documented in monozygotic (identical) twins,[32] and is potentially the cause of some different phenotypes between twins.[33] A clone will also have different epigenetic modifications to its genome structure than its DNA donor. A clear example of how this affects phenotype is in the cat clone "CC," born in 2001.[34] CC is a brown and white tabby, while her DNA donor is an orange, brown, and white calico. They have different color patterns because coat color is partially determined by events in development. The study of epigenetics is likely to have a major impact in the way geneticists view the relationship between genotype and phenotype.[35]

Gene-Environment Interactions

Now that we have discussed genetic variation, environmental variation, and epigenetics, let us conclude with examples of how these factors interact to produce the phenotype. Complex traits are often those of most interest to science and medicine. The underlying genetic influences on traits like obesity, autism, intelligence, athleticism, fertility, substance addiction, depression, and schizophrenia are eagerly sought, but these traits may not be highly heritable. Alcoholism, for example, has a heritability of about 50%. This means that genes (nature) and the environment (nurture) have been found to contribute equally to determine a person's tendency to develop alcoholism.[36] Some of these genes have been identified. In a study that identified an allele associated with higher rates of alcoholism, the gene in question is a receptor of an inhibitory molecule, GABA, in the nervous system.[37]

Obesity, type II diabetes, and related metabolic disorders are familiar examples of phenotypes that are influenced by the interaction of genes and the environment. Some individuals can easily maintain a healthy weight and metabolism, others struggle with diabetes and obesity, and still others have a healthy weight but have high levels of cholesterol in the blood. This is because these phenotypes result from complicated interactions that include genetic factors, nutrition, exercise, aging, and hormones. The recent obesity epidemic is due in part to shifts in the last century to an environment with greater availability (and often affordability) of fatty, sugary foods and in which exercise levels tend to be lower. This environment affects diet and exercise levels, but it also interacts differently with each person's unique genotype so that genes and the environment together play a role in creating the phenotype.[38]

While there are a few known cases of human obesity due to a mutation in a single gene,[39] these single-gene mutations account for the phenotypes of a negligible number of people with obesity. A large number of genes and regions of the genome have been associated with a risk of obesity, each having a small effect.[40] The effect of genotype on body mass index (BMI) has been estimated as being responsible for between 20% and 70% of variation in total body mass,[41] but much more research is needed to understand the effects of individual genotypes. Experiments in mice suggest that the effects of any specific gene depend not only on which alleles of that gene are present, but also the dietary environment, sex, and even which parent provided which allele.[42]

Individuals have no control over the genes that they inherit, but in the case of a phenotype like obesity, people can have some measure of control over their environments. Exercise may reduce the effects of an obesity-prone genotype.[43] Because nature and nurture interact in complex ways, the effect is not entirely predictable, though going for a walk instead of sitting on the couch, or choosing fruit over fast food for an afternoon snack, is likely to be beneficial to all genotypes. In the same way that a healthy diet and exercise can moderate "bad genes" with regard to obesity or heart disease, limiting alcohol consumption can be a personal choice to compensate for possessing alleles that are linked to higher rates of alcoholism and addiction.

DNA, Genes, and Alleles

a) An example DNA sequence. The letters each represent a nitrogenous base. Only one strand of the DNA double helix is shown.

A T C G G C A T C C T C T G G A T T A A A G C G T G A C T

b) The boxed letters represent a gene within the DNA sequence shown in (a). Genes are sections of DNA that code for protein or RNA molecules.

A T C G G C A T C C T C T G G A T T A A A G C G T G A C T

c. Two alleles of the same gene. Differences in a single base (in **bold italics**) are the simplest examples of alleles. In this case the upper DNA molecule has thymine (T) at the 10th position in the gene and the lower DNA molecule has cytosine (C). These two alleles might code for different proteins.

A T C G G C A T C C T C T G G A T *TA* A A G C G T G A C T

A T C G G C A T C C T C T G G A T *CA* A A G C G T G A C T

Figure 6.1.

CONCLUSION

Genes pass from one generation to the next, carrying instructions to each cell that describe how to produce the necessary molecules that carry out the complex business of creating and maintaining a living organism. Variation in DNA sequence between people is called "genetic variation," and it is this variation, along with variation in the environment, that results in the diversity of traits you see around you. Genotype and environment are closely entwined to produce the phenotype. Either nature (genes) or nurture (the environment) may be more important to determining a particular trait, but taken as a whole, it is the interaction between the two that makes us who we are. The relationship between nature and nurture is never simple, but always interesting.

NOTES

1. James D. Watson and Francis H. Crick, "Molecular Structure of Nucleic Acids; a Structure for Deoxyribose Nucleic Acid," *Nature* 171, no. 4356 (1953): 737–738.

2. Webb Miller, Daniela I. Drautz, Aakrosh Ratan et al., "Sequencing the Nuclear Genome of the Extinct Woolly Mammoth," *Nature* 456, no. 7220 (2008): 387–390; Evgeny I. Rogaev, Yuri K. Moliaka, Boris A. Malyarchuk et al., "Complete Mitochondrial Genome and Phylogeny of Pleistocene Mammoth *Mammuthus primigenius*," *PLoS Biology* 4, no. 3 (2006): e73, doi: 10.1371/journal.pbio.0040073.

3. International Human Genome Sequencing Consortium, "Finishing the Euchromatic Sequence of the Human Genome," *Nature* 431, no. 7011 (2004): 931–945.

4. S.M. Bakhtiar, A. Ali, S.M. Baig et al., "Identifying Human Disease Genes: Advances in Molecular Genetics and Computational Approaches," *Genetics and Molecular Research* 13, no. 3 (2014): 5073–5087.

5. Ernst Mayr, *The Growth of Biological Thought* (Cambridge: Harvard University Press, 1982), 720–722.

6. Robin D. Knight, Stephen J. Freeland, and Laura F. Landweber, "Rewiring the Keyboard: Evolvability of the Genetic Code," *Nature Reviews Genetics* 2, no. 1 (2001): 49–58.

7. Michael W. Nachman and Susan L. Crowell, "Estimate of the Mutation Rate per Nucleotide in Humans," *Genetics* 156, no. 1 (2000): 297–304; Yali Xue, Qiuju Wang, Quan Long et al., "Human Y Chromosome Base-Substitution Mutation Rate Measured by Direct Sequencing in a Deep-Rooting Pedigree," *Current Biology* 19, no. 17 (2009): 1453–1457; Michael Lynch, "Evolution of the Mutation Rate," *Trends in Genetics* 26, no. 8 (2010): 345–352.

8. Pascale Gerbault, Anke Liebert, Yuval Itan et al., "Evolution of Lactase Persistence: an Example of Human Niche Construction," *Philosophical Transactions of the Royal Society B: Biological Sciences* 366, no. 1566 (2011): 863–877; Sarah A. Tishkoff, Floyd A. Reed, Alessia Ranciaro et al., "Convergent Adaptation of Human Lactase Persistence in Africa and Europe," *Nature Genetics* 39, no. 1 (2007): 31–40.

9. Piri L. Welcsh and Mary-Claire King, "BRCA1 and BRCA2 and the Genetics of Breast and Ovarian Cancer," *Human Molecular Genetics* 10, no. 7 (2001): 705–713.

10. Laura Dean, *Blood Groups and Red Cell Antigens* , (Bethesda, MD: National Center for Biotechnology Information (US), 2005), http://www.ncbi.nlm.nih.gov/books/NBK2261/toc/.

11. Colin B. Begg, Robert W. Haile, Ake Borg et al., "Variation of Breast Cancer Risk among BRCA1/2 Carriers," *Journal of the American Medical Association* 299, no. 2 (2008): 194–201; Piri L. Welcsh and Mary-Claire King, "BRCA1 and BRCA2 and the Genetics of Breast and Ovarian Cancer," *Human Molecular Genetics* 10, no. 7 (2001): 705–713.

12. Douglas S. Falconer and Trudy F.C. MacKay, *Introduction to Quantitative Genetics* 4th ed., (Essex: Longman, 1996), 122–124.

13. International Human Genome Sequencing Consortium, "Finishing the Euchromatic Sequence of the Human Genome," *Nature* 431, no. 7011 (2004): 931–945.

14. Zahi Hawass, Yehia Z. Gad, Somaia Ismail et al., "Ancestry and Pathology in King Tutankhamun's Family," *Journal of the American Medical Association* 303, no. 7 (2010): 638–647.

15. Richard Bischof and Jon E. Swenson, "Linking Noninvasive Genetic Sampling and Traditional Monitoring to Aid Management of a Trans-Border Carnivore Population," *Ecological Applications* 22, no. 1 (2012): 361–373.

16. Andreas Keller, Angela Graefen, Markus Ballet al., "New Insights into the Tyrolean Iceman's Origin and Phenotype as Inferred by Whole-Genome Sequencing," *Nature Communications* 3 (2012): 698, doi: 10.1038/ncomms1701.

17. Paul S. Frenette and George F. Atweh, "Sickle Cell Disease: Old Discoveries, New Concepts, and Future Promise," *Journal of Clinical Investigation* 117, no. 4 (2007): 850–858; David C. Rees, Thomas N. Williams, and Mark T. Gladwin, "Sickle-Cell Disease," *Lancet* 376, no. 9757 (2010): 2018–31.

18. Alan H. Bittles and James V. Neel, "The Costs of Human Inbreeding and Their Implications for Variations at the DNA Level," *Nature Genetics* 8, no. 2 (1994): 117–121; Daniel L. Halligan and Peter D. Keightley, "How Many Lethal Alleles?" *Trends in Genetics* 19, no. 2 (2003): 57–59.

19. Gonzalo Alvarez, Francisco C. Ceballos, and Celsa Quinteiro, "The Role of Inbreeding in the Extinction of a European Royal Dynasty," *PLoS One* 4, no. 4 (2009): e5174, doi: 10.1371/journal.pone.0005174.

20. Kevin A. Strauss and Erik G. Puffenberger, "Genetics, Medicine, and the Plain People," *Annual Review of Genomics and Human Genetics* 10 (2009): 513–536.

21. I. Wilmut, A.E. Schnieke, J. McWhir et al., "Viable Offspring Derived from Fetal and Adult Mammalian Cells," *Nature* 385, no. 6619 (1997): 810–813.

22. Björn Oback, "Climbing Mount Efficiency—Small Steps, Not Giant Leaps towards Higher Cloning Success in Farm Animals," *Reproduction in Domestic Animals* 43, s2 (2008): 407–416; Nguyen Van Thuan, Satoshi Kishigami, and Teruhiko Wakayama, "How to Improve the Success Rate of Mouse Cloning Technology," *Journal of Reproduction and Development* 56, no. 1 (2010): 20–30; Sayaka Wakayama, Takashi Kohda, Haruko Obokata et al., "Successful Serial Recloning in the Mouse over Multiple Generations," *Cell Stem Cell* 12, no. 3 (2013): 293–297.

23. National Academy of Sciences (US), National Academy of Engineering (US), Institute of Medicine (US) and National Research Council (US) Committee on Science, Engineering, and Public Policy, *Scientific and Medical Aspects of Human Reproductive Cloning* (Washington DC: National Academies Press (US), 2002), http://www.ncbi.nlm.nih.gov/books/NBK223962/; United Nations General Assembly, Resolution 59/280, *United Nations Declaration on Human Cloning*, March 8 2005, http://www.un.org/en/ga/search/view_doc.asp?symbol=A/RES/59/280; Shaun D. Pattinson and Timothy Caulfield, "Variations and Voids: the Regulation of Human Cloning around the World," *BMC Medical Ethics* 5 (2004): 9, doi: 10.1186/1472-6939-5-9.

24. Carl E.G. Bruder, Arkadiusz Piotrowski, Antoinet A.C.J. Gijsbers et al., "Phenotypically Concordant and Discordant Monozygotic Twins Display Different DNA Copy-Number-Variation Profiles," *American Journal of Human Genetics* 82, no. 3 (2008): 763–771.

25. Andrew P. Feinburg, "Phenotypic Plasticity and the Epigenetics of Human Disease," *Nature* 447, no. 7143 (2007): 433–440.

26. Eva Jablonka and Gal Raz, "Transgenerational Epigenetic Inheritance: Prevalence, Mechanisms, and Implications for the Study of Heredity and Evolution," *Quarterly Review of Biology* 84, no. 2 (2009): 131–176.

27. David A. Nielsen, Amol Utrankar, Jennifer A. Reyes et al., "Epigenetics of Drug Abuse: Predisposition or Response," *Pharmacogenomics* 13, no. 10 (2012): 1149–60; Alfred J. Robison and Eric J. Nestler, "Transcriptional and Epigenetic Mechanisms of Addiction," *Nature Review Neuroscience* 12, no.11 (2011): 623–637.

28. Frank M. Ruemmele and Hélène Garnier-Lengliné, "Why Are Genetics Important for Nutrition? Lessons from Epigenetic Research," *Annals of Nutrition and Metabolism* 60, Suppl. 3 (2012): 38–43.

29. Rebecca C. Painter, Susanne R. de Rooij, Patrick M. Bossuyt et al., "Early Onset of Coronary Artery Disease after Prenatal Exposure to the Dutch Famine," *American Journal of Clinical Nutrition* 84, no. 2 (2006): 322–327.

30. Rebecca C. Painter, Clive Osmond, Peter Gluckman et al., "Transgenerational Effects of Prenatal Exposure to the Dutch Famine on Neonatal Adiposity and Health in Later Life," *BJOG: An International Journal of Obstetrics & Gynaecology* 115, no. 10 (2008): 1243–1249.

31. Divya Mehta, Torsten Klengel, Karen N. Conneely et al., "Childhood Maltreatment is Associated with Distinct Genomic and Epigenetic Profiles in Posttraumatic Stress Disorder," *Proceedings of the National Academy of Sciences of the United States of America* 110, no. 20 (2013): 8302–8307; Moshe Szyf, "The Early Life Social Environment and DNA Methylation:

DNA Methylation Mediating the Long-Term Impact of Social Environments Early in Life," *Epigenetics* 6, no. 8 (2011): 971–978.

32. Marcel W. Coolen, Aaron L. Statham, Wenjia Qu et al., "Impact of the Genome on the Epigenome is Manifested in DNA Methylation Patterns of Imprinted Regions in Monozygotic and Dizygotic Twins." *PLoS One* 6, no. 10 (2011): e25590, doi: 10.1371/journal.pone.0025590; Zachary A Kaminsky, Thomas Tang, Sun-Chong Wang et al., "DNA Methylation Profiles in Monozygotic and Dizygotic Twins," *Nature Genetics* 41, no. 2 (2009): 240–245.

33. Jordana T. Bell and Tim D. Spector, "A Twin Approach to Unraveling Epigenetics," *Trends in Genetics* 27, no. 3 (2011): 116–125; Emma L. Dempster, Ruth Pidsley, Leonard C. Schalkwyk et al., "Disease-Associated Epigenetic Changes in Monozygotic Twins Discordant for Schizophrenia and Bipolar Disorder," *Human Molecular Genetics* 20, no. 24 (2011): 4786–4796.

34. Taeyoung Shin, Duane Kraemer, Jane Pryor et al., "A Cat Cloned by Nuclear Transplantation," *Nature* 415, no. 6875 (2002): 859.

35. Eva Jablonka and Gal Raz, "Transgenerational Epigenetic Inheritance: Prevalence, Mechanisms, and Implications for the Study of Heredity and Evolution," *Quarterly Review of Biology* 84, no. 2 (2009): 131–176.

36. Mary-Anne Enoch, "The Influence of Gene-Environment Interactions on the Development of Alcoholism and Drug Dependence," *Current Psychiatry Reports* 14, no. 2 (2012): 150–158.

37. Danielle M. Dick, Howard J. Edenberg, Xiaoling Xuei et al., "Association of GABRG3 with Alcohol Dependence," *Alcoholism: Clinical and Experimental Research* 28, no. 1 (2004): 4–9.

38. K. Silventoinen, B. Rokholm, J. Kaprio et al., "The Genetic and Environmental Influences on Childhood Obesity: a Systematic Review of Twin and Adoption Studies," *International Journal of Obesity* 34, no. 1 (2010): 29–40.

39. Karine Clément, Christian Vaisse, Najiba Lahlou et al., "A Mutation in the Human Leptin Receptor Gene causes Obesity and Pituitary Dysfunction," *Nature* 392, no. 6674 (1998): 398–401; Carl T. Montague, I. Sadaf Farooqi, Jonathan P. Whitehead et al., "Congenital Leptin Deficiency is Associated with Severe Early-Onset Obesity in Humans," *Nature* 387, no. 6636 (1997): 903–908.

40. Felix R. Day and Ruth J. F. Loos, "Developments in Obesity Genetics in the Era of Genome-Wide Association Studies," *Journal of Nutrigenetics and Nutrigenomics* 4, no. 4 (2011): 222–238; Johannes Hebebrand, Anna-Lena Volckmar, Nadja Knoll et al., "Chipping Away the 'Missing Heritability': GIANT Steps Forward in the Molecular Elucidation of Obesity—but Still Lots to Go," *Obesity Facts* 3, no. 6 (2010): 294–303.

41. Hermine H. M. Maes, Michael C. Neale, and Lindon J. Eaves, "Genetic and Environmental Factors in Relative Body Weight and Human Adiposity," *Behavioral Genetics* 27, no. 4 (1997): 325–351.

42. Heather A. Lawson, Janet E. Cady, Charlyn Partridge et al., "Genetic Effects at Pleiotropic Loci are Context-Dependent with Consequences for the Maintenance of Genetic Variation in Populations," *PLoS Genetics* 7, no. 9 (2011): e1002256, doi: 10.1371/journal.pgen.1002256.

43. Shengxu Li, Jing Hua Zhao, Jian'an Luan et al., "Physical Activity Attenuates the Genetic Predisposition to Obesity in 20,000 Men and Women from EPIC-Norfolk Prospective Population Study," *PLoS Medicine* 7, no. 8 (2010): e1000332, doi: 10.1371/journal.pmed.1000332; Jeanne M. McCaffery, George D. Papandonatos, Dale S. Bond et al., "Gene X Environment Interaction of Vigorous Exercise and Body Mass Index among Male Vietnam-Era Twins," *American Journal of Clinical Nutrition* 89, no. 4 (2009): 1011–1018.

Chapter Seven

Genetic Determinism and Human Freedom

A Religious Response

Clifford Chalmers Cain

Genetics may be defined "as the biological science that deals with heredity: The nature and function of the biological material that transmits inherited characteristics."[1] "Genes tell cells how to behave, what proteins to make, and when to start and stop growing."[2]

Genetics indicates that behaviors—even perhaps religious beliefs (for example, the "God gene" MATb)—at the very least have genetic "tilts"[3] to them.[4] Some argue that genes "determine" behavior, even belief.[5]

Jane Kenney-Hunt's chapter points to the multitude of factors, based on "nature" and "nurture"—genetic endowment and environment—that enter into the behavioral and physical traits that actually result. *Genotype* (genetic endowment) influences *phenotype* (physical expression—traits or characteristics—of *genotype*). Her research and her presentation point to the utter complexity and deterring difficulty of predicting absolutely, guaranteeing unquestioningly, and riveting irrevocably, behavior or traits to their genetic components.

Hence, there is no "straight line from genes to behavior."[6] Genes play a crucial role, but a limited one, notes biologist Ruth Hubbard. That is, we are "bent" or "predisposed," but not determined, by our genetic endowment.[7]

Be that as it may, misunderstandings and false conclusions have arisen in the past decade about genetic power and control. Much earlier, B. F. Skinner[8] argued for genetic determinism, as currently does E. O. Wilson as revealed in his comment, "Our genes have us on a leash."[9] Dean Hamer adds, "We're a bunch of chemical reactions running around in a bag."[10] The suggestion is that our DNA looks "like a puppeteer pulling the strings that make us dance."[11] According to this understanding of humans (this "anthropology"), "the human being as a thinking, imagining, willing, and emotive subject relating to other human subjects, cultural life, and the global environment is ultimately reduced to what goes on in biochemical reactions at the molecular level."[12] Human freedom is therefore an "illusion."[13] As Francis Crick, in his book, *The Astonishing Hypothesis*, has stated:

> The Astonishing Hypothesis is that "you," your joys and your sorrows, your memories and your ambitions, your sense of personal identity and free will, are in fact no more than the behavior of a vast assembly of nerve cells and their associated molecules. As Lewis Carroll's Alice might have phrased it: "You're nothing but a pack of neurons."[14]

If this understanding is accurate, then "human action can therefore be [totally] explained and [fully] defined by the physical activity that takes place at the molecular level."[15]

Professor Kenney-Hunt's treatment of genes shows how and why this understanding is inaccurate. Genetic determinism is an exaggeration of the influence of genetic endowment, she argues. We humans are not entirely the "product of our genes," and socio-biology is overconfident and presumptuous in suggesting that we are.

If this were not the case, then behavior would be fully traceable to one's genetic make-up. If "genes made me do it," then a person's personal responsibility for his or her own actions is abrogated.

Free will is the basis of morals. If one is not free to choose, then one cannot be held accountable for her/his actions. In the early 20th century, and decades before contemporary genetic research, attorney Clarence Darrow (of 1925 Scopes Monkey Trial fame), argued in court that his two clients should not be convicted and punished for a confessed murder because they had no choice in the matter—they were driven to their deeds by environmental and genetic compulsion. Because they could not have chosen otherwise, they should not be found guilty.

The publication, *Attorney for the Damned: Clarence Darrow in the Courtroom*, revealed that Darrow's entire philosophy of criminal justice hinged on his notion that criminals had no free will: They couldn't choose to commit or refrain from crime, but were conditioned completely by their constitutions and environment."[16] In the case of murder mentioned above— the Nathan Leopold and Richard Loeb case (considered to be of the three most famous trials of the twentieth century)—two students at the University of Chicago decided on May 21, 1924, to kidnap a 14-year-old named Bobby Franks, to kill him by bludgeoning him with a chisel, and to drive to a lake in nearby Indiana and dump his body in a culvert.

Someone discovered the body, and, a few days later, a policeman found a pair of Leopold's glasses at the crime scene. Since the glasses had an unusual frame, and only three such pairs had been sold in Chicago, the glasses were traced to Leopold, who quickly cracked (as did Loeb), and both went to trial in August. Clarence Darrow was their attorney.

In the face of indisputable evidence, Darrow counseled his clients to plead guilty, hoping that this plea would save the two from the death penalty. In a remarkable 12-hour speech before the presiding judge, Darrow pleaded for their lives. He was successful, because the judge, who was weeping heavily at the end of Darrow's appeal, sentenced both killers to life in prison plus ninety-nine years.

In his closing argument, Darrow brought up his view that criminals have no choice about their actions. "The Leopold and Loeb case raised, in a well-publicized trial, Darrow's lifelong contention that psychological, physical, and environmental influences—not a conscious choice between right and wrong—control human behavior."[17] Here is what Darrow said on August 22nd, 1924, as part of his final words in behalf of his clients in *The State of Illinois v. Nathan Leopold and Richard Loeb* case:

> Why did they kill little Bobby Franks? Not for money, not for spite; not for hate. They killed him as they might kill a spider or a fly, for the experience. They killed him because they were made that way. Because somewhere in the infinite processes that go to the making up of the boy or the man something slipped, and those unfortunate lads sit here hated, despised, outcasts, with the community shouting for their blood.[18]

It was as if Darrow realized that science itself rules out any kind of free choice.

If genetic determinism is true, then the foundation of societies' criminal codes is obliterated. And religiously-speaking, if one has a genetic compulsion to, say, commit adultery, then how can the seventh commandment be binding on that person? How could it be, when he or she could not choose to obey it?

In the Christian tradition especially, the concept or doctrine of "sin" assumes that humans have freedom and therefore responsibility for their actions; "sainthood" assumes human freedom and character formation/development—persons elect to be righteous and strive for the highest spiritual plane; "sanctification" assumes human choice to do/be better, to move in the direction of "perfection."

Thus, free will is the underlying foundation, the cornerstone, of "sin," "sainthood," and "sanctification." The saints of the Church were persons who were distinctive by virtue of their virtue! Indeed, they chose to live lives of exemplary righteousness. How they decided amidst their freedom of choice options distinguished them and earned them the respect, and the "imitation-ability," of and for other Christians.

However, if their lives of "excessive moral achievement" were pro-grammed-in, rather than deliberately and freely cultivated, then they only became what they were "hard-wired" to be. By random good luck, or divine purposeful providence, or the fickle finger of fate, they were given in their very nature a spiritual advantage. They became what they were fated to be.

What reward should this merit?—certainly not adulation, certainly not distinction, certainly not adoration, certainly not sainthood. If the genetic determinists and the socio-biologists are right, then the category of "saint-hood" would need to be expunged—expurgated—from the historical and theological records and annals of the Church.

So, ethically, if we *are* our genes ("materialistic reductionism" or "reduc-tive materialism")—if "our genes hold us on a leash" (E. O. Wilson) or if "you're nothing but a pack of neurons" (Francis Crick)—then can unfaithful-ness be judged as bad, since adultery is in our genes?[19]

Can people be tried for crimes, if criminality is in our genes (my genes made me do it!)?

Should any college abandon its alcohol policy—"you may drink but not get drunk"—if alcoholism is in students' genes (I don't *choose* to drink to intoxication—I just can't keep it from happening!)?

Is a diet unethical, unfair and therefore inappropriate, not to mention doomed, if obesity is in my genes (I can't help it if I'm overweight!)?

Is disease in our genes (for example, the cystic fibrosis gene was discov-ered in 1989 by Francis Collins and a colleague)? If so, and therefore, should medical insurance be more costly for persons with penchants for disease as revealed in their "genetic print-out"? Further, could health insurance compa-nies refuse coverage for such persons in the first place?

Is spirituality in our genes? Geneticist Dean Hamer argues that faith is hardwired into our genetic make-up.[20] Some have it, some don't. So, is belief not a free choice, but a physical disposition?

As presented in Professor Kenney-Hunt's chapter, genetics research con-firms the precondition of human freedom that is essential for religion's stan-dards of morality. Genetics research shows that there *is* genetic influence, but *not* genetic determinism. Genes offer an outline, but not a blueprint; they provide a roadmap containing a number of possible paths, not a certain, direct, single route. "Genotype does not exhaustively determine pheno-type."[21] There is no straight line from genes to behavior, or genes to physical traits. One's genetic inheritance may be likened to a "weather report," for as geneticist R. David Cole cautions, "The genome predetermines all the poten-tial states of being and behavior, but it does not predetermine the person to any one particular state."[22] Theologian Ted Peters affirms this point toward the end of his book, *Playing God: Genetic Determinism and Human Freedom*, when he reveals:

> The task of this book has *not* been to rally the crowd one more time to give a cheer for freedom. Rather, we have tried to give answer to the modest question: Does the new knowledge deriving from the frontier of genetic research confront us with a genetic determinism that threatens our confidence in human freedom. We have seen that the answer has been no.[23]

Theological ethicist Paul Jersild adds, "It is not a matter of whether we are free in any absolute sense, but that we are sufficiently free to make moral responsibility a defining feature of what it means to be human."[24]

At the same time, scientific research raises questions that it cannot answer. "Limit questions," as physicist Ian Barbour calls them[25] are not within the purview of science to address. German Roman Catholic theologian Karl Rahner calls them "boundary questions,"[26] while Scottish theologian Thomas Torrance calls them "fundamental questions,"[27] while American Roman Catholic theologian David Tracy calls them "limit-situation questions."[28] These are questions that arise from the implications and complications of scientific research. Science, by its very method of observation, experimentation, and testing, is not equipped to address them. As Michael Crichton puts it in *Jurassic Park*, "What should I do with this power? . . . is the very question science says it cannot answer."[29]

In fact, these questions are often ethical: For example, is cloning good, or bad, or both? It can be good—beneficial—for example, when cloning bacteria is performed for the treatment of diabetes, Alzheimer's, and AIDS. However, cloning may be bad—not for the common good—for example, in the cloning of human beings. So, should we *do* it at all? If so, in what circumstances and for what reasons would it be justified? If not, in what circumstances and for what reasons should it be prohibited? What are the criteria that would warrant it or deny it?

It is clear that the scientific capability to manipulate genetic inheritance has proceeded at an alarming rate: Science is close to being able to replicate body parts, some say in a manner similar to the way that a tadpole or lizard or salamander can replace its tail when lost. This would certainly help soldiers who have lost limbs in Afghanistan and Iraq. But is this an entirely-good proposition?[30]

And speaking of the military, science is researching the ability to "produce" "super-soldiers" who can run faster, and longer, react faster and more accurately, are stronger, with a higher pain tolerance and threshold, who have sharpened senses to see, hear, and smell, who have the ability to carry-on with very little sleep, who have the ability/willingness to kill with little-to-no discretion, little-to-no remorse. Is this wholly-desirable?[31]

Beyond this, science is drawing closer to being able to "custom-make" children. Much in the way that the buyer can "assemble" the car he or she so desires—specially-ordered, custom-made—according to preferences and priorities, the prospective parents can specially-order, custom-make, their child(ren) by selecting (prenatally) traits such as gender, height, weight, attractiveness, intelligence, skill in athletics, musical ability, etc. In fact, Princeton molecular biology professor Lee Silver coined the term "reprogenetics" to refer to embryonic manipulation that is both therapeutic (ridding the fetus of predisposition toward specific diseases, for example) and enhancing (the list of traits specified above, for example):

> With reprogenetics, parents can gain complete control over their genetic destiny, with the ability to guide and enhance the characteristics of their children, and their children's children as well. [32]

Is such a notion of "designer genes" a good thing?

One blatant example of what can happen when ethical reflection and discourse are not in conversation with science is the eugenics movement of the late-nineteenth and early-twentieth century. "Eugenics" is a word which refers to the qualitative improvement of a species through genetic manipulation. Coined by English geneticist, Francis Galton, the word derives from the Greek for "well-born." [33] Of course, this kind of "selective breeding" to improve the quality of living things had long been performed in raising animals, such as cattle, and in growing crops, such as corn. Then this notion was applied to human beings. "Originally a socially progressive movement that embraced the ideals of a better society," [34] eugenics held the hope that "society could be engineered so that only the supposedly healthiest elements would reproduce" [35] and some subscribers believed that primarily feeble-minded persons (chiefly prisoners) should be sterilized so that their genetic inheritance would not be passed-on to future generations.

In this regard, when a case concerning a woman in Virginia who was classified as a member of "the . . . worthless class of antisocial whites" went to the United States Supreme Court, Chief Justice Oliver Wendell Holmes articulated the court's verdict in the spring of 1927: "It is better for all the world if . . . society can prevent those who are manifestly unfit from continuing their kind." [36]

This notion of building a better race—prevalent in North America and in England as well as some European countries as well—escalated in Nazi Germany to the goal of building a master race. Persons who were not Aryan—i.e., not tall, thin, athletic, blonde, blue-eyed, and "patriotic"—were seen as inferior. Jews, the physically-handicapped, Gypsies (Roma and Sinti), Communists, Jehovah's Witnesses, the mentally-handicapped and the mentally-ill, and children with birth defects and diseases, were especially targeted.

Ironically, it was the children who were targeted first in the T-4 "euthanasia" program beginning in 1939. It was believed that removing these "racially value-less children"[37] constituted both mercy toward them and an improvement for society. A year later, the program was expanded to adults, especially aimed at those with physical and mental defects (including alcoholism). At least eighty thousand handicapped adults were killed (while five thousand children had been euthanized or murdered).[38]

This "racial hygiene" (*Rassenhygiene*) was based on a "scientific" approach to "cleansing the racial stock of the country."[39] By weeding-out the inferior who continued to propagate and by weaning-off the parasites who drained society, the German race could be purified and German society benefitted. Thus, the elimination of such "lives unworthy of life" (*Lebensunwertes leben*) was deemed necessary, and in Germany the eugenics movement was wedded to antisemitism and the atrocities of the Final Solution.[40]

Although there were religious protests to this "genetic cleansing" (my phrase) from a few Protestants and substantially-more Roman Catholics (a number of whom were penalized with imprisonment at Dachau and other camps), the political situation was not amicable (to say the least!) to a conversation in the public forum between the application of scientific research and scientific capability, and ethical concerns and religious reservations.

But prior to its adoption by Nazi Socialism, eugenics research and its conclusions and proposals were not in intentional, public conversation with religion on the other side of the Atlantic as well. Indeed, when confronted with their actions at the Nuremburg War Trials, the accused Nazis pointed to the United States, England, and other European countries as having influenced their actions (as if that reference justified them). If it was okay there—with advocacy of sterilization and birth control to help undesirable personal traits wane in those locations—why was it not okay also in Germany, albeit in a more severe, thoroughgoing form?

Be that as it may, the implications and repercussions of scientific research must clearly be analyzed and responded to in light of the public good (morality) and reflection on the rightness and wrongness of actions (ethics).

Currently, scientific research in genetics has placed somatic cell genetic manipulation and germline cell genetic manipulation into the realm of possibility and probability and therefore, controversy. More moral scrutiny and ethical reflection are necessary. Somatic cell genetic manipulation refers to altering the genetic make-up of a given individual in such a way, and in the hope, of turning-on or turning-off a particular gene responsible (at least in part or in major part) for a specific positive or negative physical characteristic in that particular person alone. In a procedure called "gene transfer," "a gene is added to or replaces a gene in the tissue or an organ of an individual, and the effects of the transfer are limited to that individual."[41] On the other hand, germline cell genetic manipulation places alteration into the inheritance of future generations: Not a particular person alone is affected; rather, "the effects of the modification are transmitted to everyone in the generations that follow."[42]

A number of persons have little reservation about tinkering with the genetic material that could cause Alzheimer's, or Huntington's disease, or cystic fibrosis, or muscular dystrophy, or sickle-cell anemia, or any other of "the roughly twelve hundred disorders that geneticists associate with a single gene."[43] This tinkering, however, is not without risk. In some instances, such as cystic fibrosis, the technology has not been sufficient to be successful. In other instances, "inefficient transfer" has occurred. In other words, the modification must be successful, the reception of the modification must be positive, and then the altered or introduced gene must work when and where it is supposed-to. Consequently, there is a high-level of various risks inevitably involved.

Genetic enhancement—what some call, "inheritable genetic modifications"—is more problematic.[44] This meddling in genetic materials offers the "promise" (or at least the "hope") that widespread healing could occur in the face of disabling, deadly, even catastrophic diseases for future generations. In addition, it might mean that the human desire for stronger, healthier bodies, smarter minds, more attractive appearances, and longer lives might be fulfilled.[45]

At the same time, such enhancement could be used to "build" children the way we order cars—with all the desirable features, characteristics, and traits. Some find this unproblematic: "Why is it okay for people to choose the best house, the best schools, the best car, but not try to have the best baby possible?"[46] "If we could make our baby smarter, more attractive, a better athlete or musician, or keep him or her from being overweight, why wouldn't we?"[47]

On the other hand, some find this problematic: Would this denigrate a child into a commodity, and subject him or her to rejection because of undesirable traits? After all, we return merchandise that we have purchased, when the product doesn't meet expectations. Children cannot be sent-back to the manufacturer for correction, replacement, or our money back.

Because of this, some, such as theological ethicist Paul Jersild, advocate that genetic enhancements should be restricted to the healing of dire diseases.[48] Whether one would argue totally in-favor of germline genetic cell manipulation or be fully opposed—or take a position in the middle of the two extremes—it is hardly arguable that religion, morality, and ethics (plus our understanding of human nature—what does it mean to be human?) have a crucial and critical role to play in helping to guide our use of biotechnology.

Where are we going with biotechnology? Where is biotechnology taking us?[49]

NOTES

1. Paul Jersild, *The Nature of Our Humanity* (Minneapolis: Fortress Press, 2009), 55.
2. *Ibid.*, 58.
3. "Genetic tilts" is a phrase that I have found helpful in my conversations with my genetics colleague, Dr. Jane Kenney-Hunt. I find it more useful than "genetic inclinations" or "genetic predispositions" or "genetic predilections" because of its visual component of "leaning."
4. Andrew Newberg, Eugene D'Aquili, and Vicne Rause, *Why Won't God Go Away: Brain Science and the Biology of Belief* (New York: Ballantine Books, 2001).
5. Andrew Newberg; Dean H. Hamer, *The God Gene: How Faith Is Hardwired into Our Genes* (New York: Doubleday, 2004).
6. Paul Jersild, *op. cit.,* 61.
7. Ruth Hubbard and Elijah Wald, *Exploding the Gene Myth* (Boston: Beacon Press, 1999), 53–54).
8. B. F. Skinner, *Beyond Freedom and Dignity* (Indianapolis: Hackett Publishing Co., 2002 reprint; originally published 1971).
9. E. O. Wilson, *Consilience* (New York: Knopf Publishing, 1998), 127–128.
10. Dean H. Hamer, *op. cit.*; cf. *Time* (October 25, 2004), 65.
11. Ted Peters, *Playing God* (New York and London: Routledge, 1997), 177.
12. Jersild, *op. cit.,* 33.
13. Daniel Dennett, *Darwin's Dangerous Idea* (New York: Simon and Schuster, 1995), 81f; cf. E. O. Wilson, who says that "Our human freedom is only a self-delusion," in *On Human Freedom* (Cambridge, MA: Harvard University Press, 1978), 71.
14. Francis Crick, *The Astonishing Hypothesis* (New York: Scribner, 1994), 3; also, I am indebted to my Westminster College colleague, Professor of Psychology Ted Jaeger, for suggesting to me the current work of Michael S. Gazzaniga, who states that "free will is an illusion, but you're still responsible for your actions." Though he argues for brain-determined action, he contends that responsibility is learned at the social level. See Gazzaniga, *Who's in Charge?: Free Will and the Science of the Brain* (New York: HarperCollins, 2011) and "Free Will Is an Illusion, But You're Still Responsible for Your Actions" in *The Chronicle of Higher Education* (March 18, 2012).
15. Paul Jersild, *loc. cit.*
16. Douglas O. Linder, Law2.umkc.edu/faculty/projects/ft.
17. "Clarence Darrow, Criminality, and Free Will," Whyevolutionistrue.wordpress.com.
18. *Ibid.*
19. E. O. Wilson, *Sociobiology* (Cambridge, MA: Harvard University Press, 1976); cf. E. O. Wilson, *On Human Nature* (Cambridge, MA: Harvard University Press, 1978), 201, 176; Francis Crick, *loc.cit.*
20. Dean H. Hamer, *op. cit.*
21. Ted Peters, *op. cit.,* 51.
22. R. David Cole, "Genetic Predestination?," in *Dialog* (Vol. 33, No. 1, Winter, 1994), 20–21.
23. Ted Peters, *op. cit.,* 176.
24. Paul Jersild, *op. cit.,* 46.
25. Ian Barbour, *When Science Meets Religion* (New York: HarperCollins, 2000), 24.
26. Karl Rahner, *Foundations of Christian Faith* (New York: Seabury Press, 1978), 11f.
27. Thomas Torrance, *Fundamental Reality and Evangelical Theology* (Downer's Grove, IL: InterVarsity Press, 1982).

28. David Tracy, *Blessed Rage for Order*, (New York: Seabury Press, 1975), 98f; cf. T. Howland Sanks, S.J., "David Tracy's Theological Project ," *Theological Studies* (Vol. 54, 1993), 707; cf. Ian Barbour, *op. cit.,*24.

29. Michael Crichton, *Jurassic Park* (New York: Ballantine Books, 1990).

30. The "Regenesis" Program of DARPA—the Defense Advanced Research Projects Agency—is discussed in Paul Jersild, *op. cit.,* 95–96.

31. Jersild, *op. cit.*, 95.

32. Lee M. Silver, *Remaking Eden: Cloning and Beyond in a Brave New World* (New York: Avon Books, 1997), 8.

33. James R. Curry, *Children of God, Children of Earth* (Bloomington, IN: AuthorHouse, 2008), 150.

34. Ted Peters, *op. cit.,* 150.

35. Doris Bergen,*War and Genocide: A Concise History of the Holocaust*, second edition (Lanham, MD: Rowman and Littlefield, 2009), 12.

36. James R. Curry, *op. cit.,* 149.

37. Thomas Childers, *A History of Hitler's Empire*, second edition (Chantilly, VA: The Great Courses, 2001).

38. Doris Bergen, *op. cit.,* 128–133.

39. Thomas Childers, *op. cit.*

40. Richard Proctor, *Racial Hygiene: Medicine Under the Nazis* (Cambridge, MA: Harvard University Press, 1988).

41. Jersild, *op. cit.,* 108.

42. *Ibid.*

43. *Ibid.,* 109.

44. Audrey Chapman and Mark Frankel, eds., *Designing Our Descendants: The Promises and Perils of Genetic Modifications* (Baltimore: Johns Hopkins University Press, 2003), 4.

45. The President's Council on Bioethics, *Beyond Therapy: Biotechnology and the Pursuit of Happiness* (New York: HarperCollins, 2003), 21.

46. Lee M. Silver, *op. cit.,* 211.

47. Gregory Stock, *Redesigning Humans: Our Inevitable Genetic Future* (Boston: Houghton Mifflin, 2002), 188.

48. Jersild, *op. cit.,* 134.

49. Ted Peters, Paul Jersild, and Ronald Cole-Turner have written, in my opinion, the most accessible and most carefully-argued books on this topic of genetic manipulation or GE—Genetic Engineering—and are commended to the reader for further study: Ronald Cole-Turner, *New Genesis: Theology and the Genetic Revolution* (Louisville: Westminster/John Knox, 1993); Paul Jersild, *The Nature of Our Humanity*, (Minneapolis: Fortress Press, 2009); Ted Peters, *Playing God* , (New York: Routledge, 1997). I am deeply-indebted to them for their insights.

Chapter Eight

Intelligent Design

Rich Geenen

INTELLIGENT DESIGN — HISTORICAL CONTEXT

Prior to Charles Darwin's publication of the *Origin of the Species* in 1859, most Western thinkers, scientists included, were creationists who accepted the biblically-inspired worldview that the earth was created relatively recently (within a few thousand years) in pretty much its present form. Most people accepted that species were specially created by God as depicted in Genesis. Many were also swayed by theologian and pastor William Paley's design argument which suggested that given the similarities between a watch and a human eye, both must share an intelligent creator as a common cause.

Darwin's evolutionary theory rejected the need for such an intelligent creator. Instead, he suggested that unintelligent forces like natural selection could produce the order and apparent design we see in our biological world. As species reproduce, some natural variations in their offspring provide a benefit to some individuals over others depending on the environment in which they live. For example, relative to snowy environments, a hare which is white during snowy months has an advantage over one with brown coloration year round. These naturally selected individuals are more likely to live longer and reproduce, thus increasing the likelihood that their own genetic features will be passed along into the gene pool. Given long periods of time, Darwin argued, such changes can produce not only new traits in species, but also new species themselves. As he made clear in later works, even human beings, in his view, are the product of these natural evolutionary forces instead of being created directly by God's hand.

From its inception, Darwin's theory was controversial. Aside from scientific debates over the adequacy of the evidence for evolution and natural selection, some Darwinian critics assailed his theory on religious grounds.

Biblical literalists, for example, saw common descent of species (e.g. exist-ing species such as humans and apes sharing a common evolutionary ances-tor) as contrary to Genesis' depiction of God's creation of humans and other beings according to their "kinds." Other critics focused on alleged moral objections to Darwinian theory. If humans are nothing but "modified apes," then such a worldview, it was argued, threatens the moral status and impor-tance of human beings and undermines moral law.

Given this history and the rise of Christian fundamentalism in the United States in the early 20th century, it is not surprising, perhaps, that laws against teaching evolution existed in 20 states by the 1920's. The most famous trial involving such a law was the so-called Scopes Monkey Trial. In this trial, John Scopes, a high school science teacher, was accused of violating Tennes-see's Butler Act, which made it illegal to teach that humans had descended from lower species, a view thought to violate the Bible's teachings. Though Tennessee's Supreme Court upheld this law in Scope's trial, by the 1960's, only 3 states—Arkansas, Mississippi and Tennessee—retained so-called "monkey laws" which prohibited the teaching of evolution. Susanne Epper-son, a biology teacher in Arkansas, challenged her state's law in 1967. In 1968, the U.S. Supreme Court rejected the law in question, overturning the Arkansas Supreme Court on the grounds that anti-evolution laws were mere-ly an attempt to preserve literal, biblical creationism from a perceived con-flict with evolution.

After this defeat of anti-evolution legislation, biblical creationism gave way to so-called "creation-science" which attempted to defend God's crea-tion through scientific evidence rather than via mere appeals to the Bible. Young Earth Creationists, stemming in part from their literalist interpretation of biblical genealogies, believe that the earth is a mere several thousand years old. They have attempted to defend such claims by dismissing carbon dating and other geological scientific methods in favor of hypotheses for "catas-trophism"—the general view that massive geological catastrophes such as the Flood depicted in Genesis could explain biological and geological fea-tures of the world in a manner consistent with the earth's alleged young age. For example, some "creation-scientists" suggest that the more complex fos-sils we see in more recent rock layers of the earth in contrast to simpler organisms in older rock strata does not show that younger fossilized species evolved from older ones; instead, they suggest that they all lived at the same time and merely ended-up in different rock strata as a result of the Flood itself. Yet, despite creationists' attempts to redefine themselves in such ways, the creation-science movement, which sought equal time in the public school science classroom with evolutionary theory, was also eventually rejected by the courts by the late 1980's.

The modern intelligent design (ID) movement is a product of these histor-ical forces, and like its creationist predecessors, attempts to dismiss evolutionary theory in order to make room for scientific explanations more consistent with God and religion. Phillip Johnson, one of ID's founders and spokespersons, is a retired UC Berkeley law professor who insists that evolutionary theory is convincing to many, not because of the weight of the evidence for evolution, but instead, because of the naturalistic assumptions that scientists dogmatically make that help establish the arena in which competing biological explanations are considered. Johnson admits that if one *assumes* at the outset that neither God nor any other intelligent being can be considered as a scientific explanation, then evolution may well be the best scientific answer we can find. Yet Johnson insists that this naturalistic assumption used by many scientists today is dogmatic and unwarranted: Since it is an assumption that is not based upon evidence itself, it is really a mode of faith upon which current science rests. Further, it is a type of faith that unfairly biases science against religious views. Finally, since many people assume that science's answers are true or factual, in contrast to religion or philosophy which are understood as mere opinion or belief, science's unfair naturalistic assumptions about the world imply the fact that an active, theistic God does not exist.

Johnson's push is to make room for God as an explanation in science. To increase his chance of political success, Johnson attempts to unify theists of very different theological persuasions. Instead of focusing on the details of how and when God is supposed to have created the world (e.g. within the last few thousand years vs. billions of years ago), Johnson attempts to unite all theists together in opposition to evolutionary theory. Although many scientists insist that evolutionary theory is, in principle, consistent with religious views of creation (or at least those religious views which are not committed to specific unscientific claims such as a geologically young earth or the direct creation of all species in their present forms), Johnson himself insists that evolutionary theory is hostile to *all* theistic creation that moves beyond God as a simple first cause of the universe. This becomes clear in his broad description of creationism:

> All persons who affirm that 'God creates' are in an important sense creationists, even if they believe that the Genesis story is a myth and that God created gradually through evolution over billions of years. This follows from the fact that the theory of evolution in question is naturalistic evolution, meaning evolution that involves no intervention or guidance by a creator outside the world of nature. [1]

So, in Johnson's view, given that evolutionary theory makes no room for an active, theistic God intervening in the natural world (since such explanations are anathema to science's natural evolutionary picture), all theists who believe in such an active God should see evolutionary theory as a threat and should join ranks in the intelligent design movement which attempts to disprove crucial elements of evolutionary theory and the naturalism upon which, according to Johnson, it allegedly rests.

INTELLIGENT DESIGN: A PRIMER

Johnson invites theists to join him in supporting intelligent design in opposition to evolutionary theory. Yet this raises the obvious question, "What is intelligent design and what is the design inference upon which it is based?" Intelligent design is a broad movement which insists that certain natural phenomena such as cellular structures, DNA, the first human life, or even the *cosmos* itself, are better explained as the product of some intelligent design (e.g., an intelligent being such as God created this species, this eye, this universe and so on) rather than being caused by unintelligent forces such as those proposed by evolution (e.g., natural selection, genetic mutations, and so on).

To understand the intelligent design movement, it is helpful to draw from two philosophical predecessors, Aristotle and William Paley. Aristotle was not a design theorist; indeed, his god is not an active, creative god in the Judeo-Christian tradition. Even so, Aristotle's teleological worldview, that is, a worldview that appeals to nature's goals, functions and purposes, is helpful for understanding intelligent design.

Aristotle famously posited four causes or explanations (*aitia*) that must be addressed if we want a full understanding of natural phenomena—(a) the efficient cause—that which produces the effect; (b) the material cause—that from which a thing is made or composed; (c) the formal cause—the essential nature of the thing in question; and (d) the final cause (*telos*)—the purpose or goal of the entity in question or the mature state toward which a thing is naturally changing. For our purposes, we'll focus on two of these causes, the efficient cause and the final cause. The efficient cause is that which produces or initiates an effect such as a sculptor producing her statue. The final cause is the purpose for which the action is completed—for example, the sculptor may have been commissioned to produce the statue to commemorate a famous dignitary. It is important to note that in Aristotle's view, if we want full explanations of natural phenomena, we must not merely ask about what things are made from (the material cause) and what produces certain natural effects (the efficient cause), but we must also attempt to understand the natural goals or purposes of the phenomena in question. You get a more complete answer to the question about why the statue exists if you do not merely reply, "Because Smith created it," but instead continue the explanation by providing the goal or purpose for which it was made. Similarly, we get a more complete understanding of nature, in Aristotle's view, if we understand nature by virtue of its inherent purposes and goals. For example, to understand what a heart is, we must understand its teleological nature as the organ which pumps blood in the living organism—this purpose tells us what it means to be a heart.

Much of contemporary science has rejected Aristotelian teleology (that is, his attempt to understand nature in terms of its goals and purposes). Francis Bacon and other Enlightenment scientists opted for non-teleological explanations that have become the scientific norm. Indeed, evolutionary theory can be understood as a theory which attempts to explain *apparent* design found in nature as being the product of *unintelligent*, non-teleological forces instead. What appears to be the product of intelligent purposes, e.g., perhaps the human eye was created by God to allow humans to see, is instead postulated to be the product of unintelligent forces such as genetic variation and natural selection. Yet contemporary intelligent design proponents insist that intelligent agency, that is, creation of effects by intelligent beings in virtue of goals and purposes, is a perfectly legitimate form of scientific explanation. They seek to reestablish intelligent agency in science in order to allow God to be considered a scientific cause.

At this point, one might insist that introducing intelligent agency into science is problematic since it means appealing to some mysterious, occult mechanism that cannot be scientifically studied or tested. Not so, say ID proponents. We can and often do infer intelligent agency based upon our experience of intelligent beings and their effects.

Consider William Paley, an 18th century theologian and Christian apologist, and his famous rendition of the design argument. Paley argues as follows:

> In crossing a heath, suppose I pitched my foot against a *stone* and were asked how the stone came to be there, I might possibly answer that for anything I knew to the contrary it had lain there forever. . . . But suppose I had found a *watch* upon the ground, and it should be inquired how the watch happened to be in that place, I should hardly think of the answer which I had before given, that for anything I knew the watch might have always been there . . . [f]or this reason, and for no other, namely, that when we come to inspect the watch, we perceive—what we could not discover in the stone—that its several parts are framed and put together for a purpose. . . . This mechanism being observed . . . the inference we think is inevitable, that the watch must have had a maker— that there must have existed, at some time and at some place or other, an artificer or artificers who formed it for the purpose which we find it actually to answer, who comprehended its construction and designed its use. [2]

Paley insists that some natural phenomena such as the human eye can legitimately be inferred to be the product of intelligent agency given the similarity to human artifacts such as a watch. Contemporary ID proponents extend a similar line of reasoning. For example, Stephen Meyer compares a flower bed where the flowers are arranged to spell out a message with the "message" inherent in DNA:

> Since information requires an intelligent source, the flowers spelling "Welcome to Victoria" in the gardens of Victoria harbor, lead visitors to infer the activity of intelligent agents even if they did not see the flowers planted and arranged. Similarly, the specifically arranged nucleotide sequences, the encoded information, in DNA imply the past action of an intelligent mind, even if such mental agency cannot be directly observed.[3]

Using these and similar examples, intelligent design theorists insist that just as archaeologists can perform legitimate science when trying to distinguish intelligently-designed artifacts from natural, non-intelligent entities (e.g., stone tools from accidentally occurring stones shaped in similar ways), so too biologists and physicists should appeal to intelligent agency when this is the best explanation for the phenomena in question in their respective domains or when there is no known non-agent explanation available.

ID advocates are largely silent about who the designer is and how the designer creates, though it is clear from context that most ID advocates infer that the designer is God. As Paul Nelson states, "God is the principal cause invoked in non-evolutionary theories."[4] And, as leading ID advocate Michael Behe makes clear,

> Although there are, at least in theory, some exotic candidates for the role of designer that might be compatible with materialist philosophy (such as space aliens or time travelers), few people will be convinced by these and will conclude that the designer is beyond nature [i.e., supernatural].[5]

Yet many ID advocates are often less-willing to state this explicitly. Leading ID theorist William Dembski, for example, is often careful not to publicly equate the intelligent designer with God: "Notice that I never used the G-word in this whole talk," Robert Pennock quotes him as saying during a talk to science teachers.[6] So, the "official" ID position is that the intelligent designer needed to replace non-agent explanations in some areas of science is some intelligent being, but we know not whom or what.

In terms of what the intelligent designer is responsible for creating, we receive various disparate responses—anything from the origin of the universe, to the bacterial flagellum (a tail-like appendage on certain bacteria), to the human species, to the first living organisms and so on. The common themes here appear to be two sorts—(a) those traditional phenomena singled-out for importance by traditional Judeo-Christian religions (e.g., special creation of the human species); (b) natural phenomena of which current scientific research has less well-developed causal answers (e.g., micro-cellular entities such as the bacterium flagellum, the poster-child of ID theorist Michael Behe discussed below).

In terms of the unknown designer's mechanisms and methods of creating, we get no answers whatsoever, though given ID advocates' common belief that an all-powerful God is the true designer, perhaps they believe no mechanism is needed.

Since ID theorists propose so little information about the intelligent designer, the singular cause of their entire theory, and given that none of the designer's methods nor goals of creating are typically stated and supported, one might rightfully wonder whether a design inference under such ambiguous conditions could be made at all. Yet ID advocates typically insist that their lack of knowledge about who the designer is and how he/she/it creates is not problematic. This is so, William Dembski, an information theorist and leading ID proponent, assures us, because "intelligent design studies the *effects* of intelligent causes and not intelligent causes *per se*. Intelligent design does not try to get into the head of a designing intelligence; rather, it looks at what a designing intelligence does and draws inferences from there."[7] Just as we can infer that certain objects are artifacts without knowing their designers or their purposes (Stonehenge is an often cited example), so, too, we can know this of naturalistic objects such as the bacterial flagellum.

Yet to know that something is the product of intelligent design we must have some method of detecting intelligent design (also known as "agent causation"). Here, finally, is the area in which the intelligent design project has produced the most work (aside from mere criticisms of evolutionary theory which makes up a large part of ID literature). In the section below, we'll focus on micro-biologist, Michael Behe, and his "irreducible complexity" argument for intelligent design. In summary, Behe argues that because certain biological phenomena are so complex and need all of their parts in order to function, they could not have evolved at all. We'll also briefly examine William Dembski's explanatory filter which makes the related, but more general point, that if chance and necessity are ruled out as explanations for some phenomenon, then an intelligent being such as God is responsible instead.

DARWIN'S BLACK BOX—
BEHE AND IRREDUCIBLE COMPLEXITY

Darwin proposed that species evolve via slight modifications over long periods of time. Yet, if this is so, how might something as complicated as the human eye evolve? In order to address this challenge, Darwin did not trace the specific evolutionary pathways that led to the eye; instead, he cited various animals with eyes ranging from simple light-sensitive structures to the complex eye of vertebrates. Darwin's point was to suggest that very simple eyes or eye-like structures could serve as precursors—earlier building blocks, if you will—for those more complex structures such as human eyes which we see today. Given sufficient time (life has been evolving for billions of years according to evolutionists), natural selection can help to shape or fashion simpler eyes into something much more complex.

Though perhaps adequate for Darwin's time when molecular biology did not yet exist, Behe suggests that this tactic of alluding to possible precursors to a complex system without specifying the molecular causes that led to these changes, is no longer justified. Indeed, he suggests, that since evolutionists often are not able to answer all questions about molecular causes for complex biological phenomena, they are really just appealing to a mysterious "black box" when they claim that evolution can explain how eyes and other biological systems have evolved. Behe elaborates using vision as an example:

> Biochemists know what it means to "explain" vision. They know the level of explanation that biological science eventually must aim for. In order to say that some function is understood, *every relevant step* in the process must be elucidated. *The relevant* steps in the biological processes occur ultimately at the *molecular level*, so a satisfactory explanation of a biological phenomenon such as sight . . . must include a molecular explanation. [8]

Behe is suggesting a new sort of challenge for evolutionists, or at least a challenge at a new explanatory level. Darwin attempted to defend evolutionary theory by making a cumulative case appealing to evidences from a variety of areas. For example, he appealed to artificial selection—human breeding of plants and animals in order to produce certain favored traits—as an analogy for natural selection. He appealed to the fossil record of the time (much more sparse than the fossil record established today) as evidence that more recent fossilized species are more similar to current ones than those species which lived long ago. He appealed to similar bone structures in related species as evidence of their common descent. Behe, on the other hand, suggests that these and many other evolutionary evidences are irrelevant. According to Behe, evolution's true burden is to establish the molecular pathways responsible for the evolution of biological phenomena, since this is where the "relevant steps" of evolution occur.

> It is no longer sufficient, now that the black box of vision has been opened, for an "evolutionary explanation" of that power to invoke only the anatomical structures of whole eyes, as Darwin did in the 19th century and as most popularizes of evolution continue to do today. Anatomy is, quite simply *irrelevant*. So is the fossil record. It does not matter whether or not the fossil record is consistent with evolutionary theory, any more than it mattered in physics that Newton's theory was consistent with everyday experience. The fossil record *has nothing to tell us* about, say, whether or how the interactions of 11-cis-

retinal with rhodopsin, transducin, and phosphodiesterase [a molecular level interaction that allows for sight] could have developed, step by step. [9]

If Behe is right, then the majority of evolutionary evidences may be cast aside. Yet Behe insists that evolution is even worse off than this. Not only has he dismissed a vast array of evolutionary evidence as irrelevant, he also insists that there is a systematic roadblock that prevents evolution from producing certain biological systems altogether, namely, those which he calls "irreducibly complex" systems. It is to this argument that we now turn.

THE IRREDUCIBLE COMPLEXITY ARGUMENT

As discussed above, in Darwin's view, individual members of populations that are even slightly-more fit relative to their environment are more likely to survive and to pass down their genetic traits to their offspring. Such natural selection tends to promote small, gradual changes to populations over time which can build and develop into larger evolutionary changes, including the creation of new species. Darwin himself noted, however, that if there were some biological phenomena that came about in one grand step, then this would contradict evolutionary theory which, in Darwin's view, requires significant geological time through which natural selection can work. Small changes to a species accrue to larger changes over the long run. Given this Darwinian view of evolution, Behe suggests that if a complicated system were to come about, not through small successive alterations but through one grand step, then it could not be the product of evolution.

Behe's central argument is that he has discovered various biological phenomena that, indeed, could never come about except in one grand step, and hence that such phenomena are created by non-evolutionary forces, and more specifically, by an intelligent designer. The phenomena in question are complex systems whose parts are all required for the system to function, a feature Behe dubs "irreducible complexity" (IC). Behe elaborates: "By irreducible complexity, I mean a single system which is composed of several interacting parts that contribute to the basic function, and where the removal of any one of the parts causes the system to effectively cease functioning."[10] So, for example, if an arch is made out of stones and if each of these stones is required for the structure to function as an arch (e.g., if you remove one stone, the whole structure will fall), then this structure is irreducibly complex.

When speaking of IC biological systems, Behe argues as follows:

> An irreducibly complex system cannot be produced directly by slight, successive modification of a pre-cursor system, since any precursor to an irreducibly complex system is by definition non-functional. Since natural selection re-

quires a function to select, an irreducibly complex biological system . . . would
have to arise as an integrated unit for natural selection to have anything to act
on.[11]

In summary, Behe is telling us that an irreducibly complex system cannot
come about by gradual changes that have happened to an earlier precursor
(an earlier stage from which the later system developed). Behe's reason is
that the earlier precursor would have to be simpler in order to be a precursor,
but being simpler, it must lack at least one of the parts of the later system.
Yet by definition an IC system cannot function if it lacks any parts. In Behe's
view, this shows that IC systems could not have evolved since it is obvious
that natural selection cannot work for non-functioning entities. A non-functioning tail or eye simply could not evolve into anything else. Hence, evolution and natural selection cannot create irreducibly complex systems which
require all of their parts in order to function.

Behe further illustrates his point with the analogy of a traditional snap-
style mousetrap. Because the spring, base, hammer, etc., are necessary for the
mousetrap to function, evolution could not create a mousetrap (thinking, for
a moment, that the mousetrap is analogous to a living system) out of some
simpler precursor such as the base and the hammer without the spring. This
simpler system without the spring could not function as a mousetrap at all
since the mousetrap is irreducibly complex. Yet evolution cannot work on
non-functional systems—if they are non-functional, they cannot confer an
advantage that can be passed down to their offspring. Therefore, in Behe's
view, our mousetrap could not have evolved and neither can living biological
systems which are irreducibly complex.

At this point, Behe has set his own trap. Now all he needs to do is to
identify some irreducibly complex biological system and thereby evolutionary theory will fail, or at least, it will fail to provide an explanation for this
biological phenomenon.

Behe contends that irreducibly complex biological systems are found everywhere. Some of his examples include cilia (a hair-like structure found on
certain cells), the bacterial flagellum (a tail-like appendage that allows some
bacteria to swim), and aspects of blood clotting and photosynthesis. Indeed,
Behe claims, "Examples of irreducibly complexity can be found on virtually
every page of a biochemistry textbook."[12] If true, and if Behe's IC argument
is sound, then there are numerous biological systems that are the product of
some non-evolutionary cause.

At this stage, one might believe that the IC Argument, if successful,
would merely leave us in a state of uncertainty as to what caused these
alleged IC biological systems. Behe disagrees. To the contrary, he introduces
the notion of intelligent design as an alternative explanation. Such design
comes about when there is "purposeful arrangement of parts" by an intelli-

gent being.[13] For Behe, the move from the failure of Darwinian evolutionary theory to explain IC systems to intelligent design as the cause for such systems is immediate. For example, when discussing the cilium as irreducibly complex, Behe concludes: "We can go further and say that, *if* the cilium cannot be produced by natural selection, *then* the cilium was designed."[14] Why draw such a conclusion? Behe's implied reasoning seems to be the following: Darwinian evolution is the only reasonable non-design explanation for biological phenomena. Darwinian evolution fails *per* the IC Argument. The design hypothesis readily explains the biological phenomena in question, e.g., we know that intelligent agents produce complex machines, and IC systems such as the bacterial flagellum resemble such intelligently-designed products. Hence, where evolutionary theory falls short, intelligent design remains as the sole viable alternative and, in Behe's view, is evident to anyone who is not predisposed against such a reasonable inference. Behe himself concludes:

> There is an elephant in the roomful of scientists who are trying to explain the development of life. The elephant is labeled "intelligent design." To a person who does not feel obliged to restrict his search to unintelligent causes, the straightforward conclusion is that many biochemical systems were designed.[15]

DEBUNKING THE IRREDUCIBLE COMPLEXITY ARGUMENT

Behe's Irreducible Complexity Argument is deeply flawed in numerous ways: One major problem with his argument is that Behe is imprecise about what he means when he speaks of IC systems *functioning* and this imprecision undermines his argument. Recall Behe's definition of irreducible complexity and note the role that functionality plays: "By irreducible complexity, I mean a single system which is composed of several interacting parts that *contribute to the basic function*, and where the removal of any one of the parts causes the system to effectively *cease functioning*."[16] When Behe's argument is examined closely, one can quickly recognize that it employs two distinct senses of what it means to function, neither of which supports his argument. By functioning, Behe may mean one of two things—functioning in any way at all which I will call *functioning simpliciter*, or functioning in the manner characteristically associated with the system in question which I will call *characteristic functioning*. If something does not function in any way, then it has no function simpliciter—it is a functionless entity. Yet an entity could lose its characteristic function and still function in non-characteristic ways—e.g., a ballpoint pen which has lost its ink cartridge can no longer be used for its characteristic function of writing, but may be used for all sorts of other purposes such as a straw.

Which type of functionality, then, does Behe have in mind in his IC Argument? Behe's language often implies that he has only characteristic functioning in mind. For example, when speaking of a mousetrap as irreducibly complex, he notes only that all of the trap's parts are necessary for it "to trap a mouse."[17] Yet even if this were true (which many critics have challenged by showing how a mousetrap missing one or more parts could still function to trap a mouse), it would clearly not show that the mousetrap with the missing part could not function simpliciter (i.e., function in any way). There are many ways in which a mousetrap without a spring, for example, could function. One could use it as a doorstop, as a car ramp for a child's toys, as a shim for leveling a floor, and so on.

This point about the flexibility of functionality may seem obvious, yet it is crucial for assessing Behe's argument. If Behe merely wants to contend that there are biological systems whose parts are each necessary for them to function in their *characteristic* way, then Behe cannot validly infer that an IC biological system has no functional precursor; instead, he would only be entitled to conclude that a precursor to an IC biological system must not be able to function in the *same way* as the system into which it evolves. For example, if the tail of a bacterium is irreducibly complex, then a simpler precursor could not serve *as a tail*, but it could function for other purposes (indeed, parts of the bacterial flagellum are known to have a distinct prior function as a secretion system). But this claim, that the precursor to an IC biological system must have a distinct function from that system into which it evolves, does not pose a threat to evolutionary theory—in fact, evolutionary theory thrives upon the co-option of biological systems for new purposes. To use one of Stephen J. Gould's famous examples, the sesamoid bone in the panda's wrist was co-opted for a new function, namely, to help it to strip bamboo upon which it feeds, becoming a nominal sixth digit.[18] Similarly, biologist Kenneth Miller describes bones from the reptilian jaw that were gradually altered for a new purpose, to help transmit sound vibrations in the middle ear[19] (we'll return to the details of this example below). Hence, if Behe's IC Argument relies upon characteristic functioning, then it poses no threat to evolutionary theory.

Perhaps, then, Behe wished to contend that a biological system that is irreducibly complex could have *no function whatsoever* if any of its parts were missing. If this were true, it would indeed pose a challenge to evolutionary theory since evolution cannot work on completely non-functional systems (e.g., if something cannot function in any way it wouldn't even be alive and thus could not lead to evolutionary changes). However, Behe has never given any evidence to show that any biological system could have no functionality whatsoever if one of its parts was missing. Until and unless he is able to do so, he has provided no serious impediment to evolutionary theory.

Additionally, Behe's reasoning is flawed because it is based on an inaccurate view of evolution and natural selection. Recall Behe's reasoning that because an IC system needs all of its parts in order to function, therefore, any precursor would not be functional. This move is based on assumptions about evolution that are simply inaccurate. For example, to get to his conclusion, Behe is assuming that all evolutionary systems are produced by *addition* of parts. However, numerous critics have pointed out that this is not the case. A.G. Cairns-Smith and others use the example of the construction of stone arches to make the relevant point: In a completed stone arch, each stone is essential for the arch to continue to function as an arch—if you took out any one stone, the arch would collapse. Hence, the arch fits Behe's definition of an irreducibly complex system. Yet this does not mean that the arch could not have been produced by a series of gradual steps that parallel evolution as long as the building process involved the right supplemental framework. Indeed, this is precisely what builders do by using scaffolding as the arch is being produced in order to support the stone arch while under construction. When the builders are done, they remove the scaffolding and in this way an irreducibly complex system, the completed stone arch, is created by *subtracting* something from its "precursor," namely the scaffolding that is no longer needed. The very same logic can explain how evolutionary forces can produce an irreducibly complex system gradually over time by subtracting excess parts and leaving an irreducibly complex system analogous to the arch which now needs all of its parts in order to function.

Biologist Allen Orr provides another general explanation of how irreducibly complex biological systems could evolve without the hand of an intelligent designer:

> An irreducibly complex system can be built gradually by adding parts that, while initially advantageous, become—because of later changes—essential. The logic is very simple. Some part (A) initially does some job . . . Another part (B) later gets added because it helps A. This new part isn't essential, it merely improves things. But later on, A . . . may change in such a way that B now becomes indispensable. This process continues as further parts get folded into the system. And at the end of the day, many parts may all be required. [20]

Hence, Orr and others convincingly illustrate that Behe's argument is logically invalid. He has provided no critical argument showing evolutionary theory to be impeded in principle from creating IC systems.

So far, we have considered the logical underpinnings of Behe's argument and some of his critics' responses. Biologist Kenneth Miller responds to Behe's irreducible complexity argument by drawing from empirical data as well. Contrary to Behe, Miller believes the fossil record *is* relevant to understanding the process whereby evolution produces irreducibly complex systems. One specific example Miller uses pertains to the system of sound transmission in the middle ear of humans that includes three small bones, the *malleus*, *incus*, and *stapes*, responsible for transmitting sound vibrations. Such a system is irreducibly complex since hearing is not possible if any of the middle ear's parts are absent. Yet as Miller says, the fossil record itself demonstrates how this IC system evolved:

> During the evolution of mammals, over several million years, two of the bones that originally formed the rear portion of the reptilian lower jaw were gradually pushed backwards and reduced in size until they migrated into the middle ear, forming the bony connections that carry vibrations into the inner ears of present day mammals. This is an example of a system of perfectly formed interlocking components, specified by multiple genes, that gradually refashioned and adapted for another purpose altogether—something that evolution's critics claim to be impossible. Evidence of this sequence, which was worked out in detail by Arthur W. Compton of Harvard University, even includes a fossil species possessing a remarkable double articulation of the jaw joint—an adaptation that allowed the animal both to eat and hear during the transition, enabling natural selection to favor each of the intermediate stages.[21]

Here we have a case in which Behe's overreach becomes obvious. Even if the fossil record does not itself demonstrate genetic pathways and microbiological data, this doesn't indicate that the fossil record has no bearing on the manner in which IC systems have evolved. Miller cites the empirical evidence for the evolution of one such case. He further critiques Behe's argumentation explaining where Behe has gone wrong:

> Arriving at the irreducible complexity of the five-part auditory apparatus was easy for evolution because it doesn't work the way that its critics claim it must. To fashion the three-bone linkage that conducts sound from the eardrum, evolution didn't have to start with a non-working incomplete one-bone or two-bone middle ear. Instead, it started with a perfectly good working reptile-style ear, which had a single internal bone. Then it grabbed two other bones from a different organ, the jaw, and used them to expand and improve the apparatus.[22]

Miller concludes:

> Remember Behe's statement that "any precursor to an irreducibly complex system that is missing a part is by definition nonfunctional"? Well, there's just no other word for it—that statement is *wrong*. What evolution does is to add parts that expand, improve, and sometimes completely refashion living systems. Once the expansion and remodeling is complete, every part of the final working system may indeed be necessary, just as the *malleus*, *incus*, and *stapes* are. That interlocking necessity does not mean that the system could not have evolved from a simpler version—and in this case we know that is exactly what happened.[23]

In these ways, then, Behe's argument is unconvincing. The empirical case stands against him as shown by Miller and others, and Behe's own statement that the fossil record is irrelevant to the production of IC systems is belied by the evidence. Moreover, Behe's central argument is logically flawed as previously indicated. If Behe wants to claim that an IC system can have no precursor with the same characteristic function, then this doesn't threaten evolution that thrives off of co-opting precursors for new functions; but if Behe wants to claim that an IC system can have no precursor with any functionality whatsoever, then he has provided no evidence for such, and so his claims are unconvincing and unsupported. Given the obvious and central nature of these problems, it is, perhaps, surprising that Behe's arguments are the poster-child for the ID movement and receive as much attention and support as they tend to muster.

DISJUNCTIVE REASONING AND EXPLANATORY FILTERS

Aside from these critical objections to Behe's argument, there is a crucial final step that Behe and other design theorists make that is central to their argument and which must be examined. Recall that Behe moved from the allegation that evolution couldn't produce irreducibly complex systems such as cilia (hair-like structures on certain cells), to the conclusion that a designer must thereby be responsible for creating them. "We can go further and say that, *if* the cilium cannot be produced by natural selection, *then* the cilium was designed."[24] Such a move in logic is called a disjunctive syllogism: either P or Q; not P; therefore Q. This is a form of more general eliminative reasoning whereby all but one option is eliminated and that which remains is said to be the answer which is sought. This is also a very familiar strategy from the anti-evolution "creation-science" movement, for example, from their often-cited argument that because there are "gaps" in the fossil record, therefore God must have produced species rather than evolutionary forces. People like Philip Johnson still make this a cornerstone of their intelligent design argument. In fact, if you look at the collective works of intelligent design theorists, you will find that the bulk of information available fits into the "objections to evolution" category with comparatively little in the way of direct arguments for a designer him/her/itself.

Information theorist William Dembski defends this broader form of eliminative reasoning. He contends that there are three forms of explanation available for scientific phenomena—chance, necessity and intelligent agency. If we can rule-out chance and necessity with respect to the phenomenon in question, then we can justifiably infer that the phenomenon was the product of intelligent agency. Dembski himself appeals to Behe's bacterial flagellum (tail-like structure found on some bacteria) as one example of this argumentative strategy at work. Since we allegedly have no explanation of the flagellum via chance or necessity, it must be the product of intelligent design. Dembski and other ID proponents also frequently appeal to the SETI program—Search for Extra Terrestrial Intelligence—to help bolster their case. The basic argument offered is that if SETI scientists were to receive some extra-terrestrial signals that could not be explained as the product of chance or necessity, then they are justified in inferring that intelligent agency is the cause, e.g., perhaps the signal comes from some group of intelligent aliens. Moreover, though some celestial bodies such as pulsars (rapidly rotating neutron stars) emit radio waves and other electromagnetic energy in regular patterns, we would never expect them to emit highly complex mathematical signals. Thus, in *Contact*, Carl Sagan envisions extraterrestrials attempting to communicate by sending out a repeating transmission of the first few hundred prime numbers—a signal that indicates an intelligent source rather than mere chance or necessity. Using this as a model, ID proponents like Dembski suggest that information in biology can also be understood to indicate an intelligent designer when chance and necessity cannot explain the information's origin.

Despite the simplicity of Dembski's argumentative strategy, his eliminative reasoning in favor of an intelligent designer is unconvincing. First and foremost, it is simply not true that if all of our attempts at natural non-agent explanations have been ruled-out that there cannot be other non-agent explanations that exist that are more probable than God, aliens, or some other intelligent being. You simply cannot privilege intelligent agency in this way whereby agency or design is the default conclusion we should draw every time all of our available non-chance/non-necessity explanations come up short. This conclusion is obvious if we look back at the history of science and consider the numerous cases in which existing non-agent explanations were falsified without thereby showing that some unknown designer was thus the best explanation for the phenomenon in question. For example, prior to our understanding of epilepsy in terms of storms of electrical activity in the brain, we were not justified in concluding that because we had no explanations of seizures *per* chance or necessity, we should conclude that they were being caused by some unknown intelligent cause (God, demons, aliens, or the like). Often the most likely explanation is merely some non-agent explanation with which we are not yet familiar.

That we should be reluctant to appeal to agent causation in biology and physics is further supported by the poor historical showing of intelligent agency in these realms. Simply put, intelligent agency has had an abysmal track record with respect to the natural sciences. Natural phenomena such as earthquakes, lightning, fossils, and diseases were all at one time thought to be the product of agents such as the gods. Yet, over time, intelligent causation in the natural sciences has consistently been supplanted by non-ID naturalistic explanations that are now accepted as not mere theory, but as fact (e.g., germ theory of disease, theories of earthquakes and their relation to tectonic plates, etc.). Given the success of non-ID explanations in the natural sciences and the lack of success of ID explanations in these realms, one should reasonably infer that current gaps of scientific knowledge will indeed be filled-in via non-ID naturalistic explanations as well. Indeed, this is precisely the trend we see in the history of science with respect to past creationist challenges to evolution: For example, former "gaps" in the fossil record have been filled-in via more and more transitionary fossils rather than through the discovery of an intelligent designer and signs of his/her/its agency in the production of biological species.

Intelligent design theorists are correct to suggest that intelligent agency can be adduced with respect to certain natural phenomena—e.g., archeologists may insist that a stone object is a human-made tool or that a certain fire was the product of human causes. However, when we validly draw the inference that something is an intelligently-produced artifact, e.g., a Stone Age tool, we make this design inference on the basis of what we know about human beings and their marks of design. Even if we are unfamiliar with the specific architects of Stonehenge, for example, we *are* familiar with other human agents responsible for this sort of stone structure and we are familiar with their distinctive causal marks.

> Archeologists . . . routinely recognize as artifacts, objects that have no known purpose and whose functions we are unlikely ever to know. But in every instance we recognize them by the simple observation of marks: the pits, scratches, polish, grinding, burning, fracture, and so on that are the unambiguous indication of manufacturing.[25]

Further, if there were no marks to determine whether an entity were intelligently *versus* non-intelligently designed, then the design inference could only be made through tracing the causal history of that design. Niall Shanks makes this case forcefully when he imagines the possibility of a future biochemist who can create a functioning cell indistinguishable from one produced by the human body itself. Shanks contends:

> [W]hether a given cell under study was extracted from a human subject or intelligently designed in the laboratory to look just like it, is a matter that could be settled only through analysis of its causal history. This information will not be discernible simply by inspecting the cell itself. There is nothing analogous to the Breguet secret signatures[26] to be found there. The judgment would be in favor of human intelligent design, if the trail led back to the laboratory, to identifiable human designers with the biochemical and biological wherewithal to accomplish the feat. The judgment would favor intelligent human design precisely if the design questions could be appropriately answered and justified.

Then and only then, would we have a good account of the intelligent origins of the cell in question. [27]

Yet intelligent design theorists never offer any causal history whereby the alleged designer is supposed to have created some particular biological entity such as the bacterial flagellum. And, such an entity shows no "marks" of intelligent design on par with the marks left by our stone-age ancestors when creating stone tools and implements. As such, we are left with no rational argument to support the conclusion that such biological entities are the product of intelligent agency.

Finally, though the intelligent design movement tries to pass itself off as engaging in science, given that the designer itself is never specified, given that its means, mechanisms, motives and history are never stated, and given that the designer is allowed to be a supernatural being which can violate the very laws of nature upon which scientific testing rests, there is no way for intelligent design to be considered scientific. Rather, intelligent design is a specific philosophical theory with religious and philosophical origins which attempts to undermine scientific conclusions in order to make room for God's causal role in the physical and biological world.

CONCLUSION

Intelligent design offers itself as a competitor to evolutionary theory. If it wants to be taken seriously as such a competitor, it has a great deal of work to do. It doesn't win a victory over evolution by illustrating flaws in evolutionary theory any more than demonic possession would by showing that we have yet to fully understand some form of mental disease. If intelligent design wishes to make its case, it must move beyond eliminative reasoning that finds its roots in creation-science. It must also move beyond the basic arguments by analogy upon which it historically relies (Paley's comparison of a watch to the human eye, Meyer's comparison of DNA to words in a book, and so on). When there is only one type of cause for certain effects, arguments by analogy can be effective—e.g., if a house-fire shares a unique pattern of burn marks found solely in fires which are the product of arson, then one may reasonably infer that arson is the cause. Yet, often times, the world is more complex than this. Similar stomach pains can have diverse causes. As such, one cannot simply argue by analogy to say that because your stomach pains are similar to mine, e.g., in terms of intensity and duration, they must have a similar cause. Likewise, evolutionary theory illustrates that complex entities such as the human eye can, in principle, have causes beyond Paley's God or an unnamed intelligent designer. Yes, the eye is relevantly similar to a watch in terms of having parts that work toward a purpose, but to show that an intelligent being created the eye, in contrast to the eye's evolving via natural, non-intelligent forces, one must establish that the ID explanation is superior to the evolutionary explanation, a task that ID theorists have not successfully completed.

In order for one to prove that intelligent design is a better explanation than evolutionary theory for the human eye or the bacterial flagellum or other biological phenomena of this sort, intelligent design theory would have to make testable, falsifiable predictions. For example, if two coroners have different explanations for how a person died, one insisting on natural causes and another insisting on murder by a blunt instrument, then each would have to make testable predictions to help prove that his preferred explanation was superior. Intelligent design, simply put, fails to provide such testable predictions and in this way it fails to show that it is a better explanation than evolutionary theory. Evolutionary theory, on the other hand, makes ample testable predictions that are confirmed on a regular basis. The forces of evolutionary theory such as natural selection are regularly observed in the lab as illustrated by the growth of antibiotic resistance of some bacteria. Evolutionary theory predicts a certain order to the fossil record which is consistently confirmed by new fossil discoveries, and, indeed, which allows scientists to predict where further transitionary fossils can be discovered (the discovery of the transitionary species *Tiktaalik* is a famous case in point). Similarly, genetic information illustrates precisely the sorts of genetic similarities between different biological groups that are predicted by evolutionary theory. These and many other areas of scientific data are explained by evolutionary theory which helps to bolster its scientific credentials in contrast to intelligent design which, instead of generating genuine falsifiable predictions, falls back on assuming that when we don't know of a natural non-agent explanation, we can infer that some unknown designer was the cause.

Even so, some might still be persuaded by the "argument from fairness" with respect to giving intelligent design its due. In a Gallop poll taken in May of 2012, 78% of those Americans surveyed believe that God has some influence over the development of humans. Moreover, almost half, 46%, believe that humans were created by God in their present form in the last 10,000 years. [28] Why should their views and values be dismissed by scientists, and why should their views not be taught alongside evolution in the science classroom? Shouldn't all sides of this debate be taught? Isn't that being fair and balanced?

The quick answer to this question about whether intelligent design or creationism should be taught as science to our children in public schools is a resounding "no." Science is a field with a rigorous methodology. Scientific methodology has promoted copious discoveries about the natural world and how it works. Yet even though science's answers definitely conflict with many people's worldviews (e.g., science has proven without any doubt that the earth is billions of years old, contrary to what almost half of Americans currently believe), this doesn't give us a reason (or at least not a good reason) to refrain from teaching scientific truths as fact, nor a reason for teaching a non-scientific explanation like intelligent design as if it were something it is not—namely, science. To illustrate this latter point, consider how absurd it would be if our university medical schools had to teach all alternative forms of medicine practiced by different peoples of different cultures, religions, and beliefs. Demonic possession would be taught alongside scientific views on epilepsy, faith healing alongside surgical procedures, and herbal remedies alongside the administration of antibiotics. The stakes are simply too high for us to conflate scientific medicine with non-scientific beliefs in this way. Yet the stakes are also high when it comes to teaching our children. They deserve the best answers science can provide even if those answers challenge core religious beliefs of many people within our country.

Does that mean that children should not learn about intelligent design theory? Not at all. Aside from parental and religious instruction, even our public schools should provide an opportunity to engage in questions about intelligent design and broader questions about our world and our place in it. The design argument is one variety of philosophical argument about an intelligent being such as God being the cause of our origins. Such an argument should be able to be discussed and critically assessed if schools are able to provide such a philosophically-themed class (though obviously budget priorities do not always allow for such). Yet the intelligent design argument should never be passed off as science and should not take place independent of a renewed focus on scientific literacy, so that when students do make their own conclusions about the world and their origins, they can do so being properly informed.

NOTES

1. Phillip E. Johnson, "Evolution as Dogma: The Establishment of Naturalism." In *Intelligent Design Creationism and Its Critics: Philosophical, Theological and Scientific Perspectives*, ed. Robert T. Pennock (Cambridge, MA: MIT Press, 2001), 64.

2. William Paley, "The Argument from Design." In *Reason and Responsibility*, 10th ed., ed. Joel Feinberg and Russ Shafer-Landau (Belmont, CA: Wadsworth Publishing Company, 1999), 30.

3. Stephen Meyer, "The Origin of Life and the Death of Materialism." In *The Intercollegiate Review* 31, no. 2 (1996), 39–40.

4. Paul A. Nelson, "The Role of Theology in Current Evolutionary Reasoning." In *Intelligent Design Creationism and Its Critics: Philosophical, Theological and Scientific Perspectives*, ed. Robert T. Pennock (Cambridge, MA: MIT Press, 2001), 681.

5. Michael J. Behe, "Darwin's Breakdown: Irreducible Complexity and Design at the Foundation of Life." In *Signs of Intelligence: Understanding Intelligent Design*, ed. William A. Dembski and James M. Kushiner (Grand Rapids, MI: Brazos Press, 2001), 100–101.

6. William A. Dembski, quoted in Robert T. Pennock, "The Wizards of ID: Reply to Dembski." In *Intelligent Design Creationism and Its Critics: Philosophical, Theological and Scientific Perspectives*, ed. Robert T. Pennock (Cambridge, MA: MIT Press, 2001), 663.

7. William A. Dembski, "Introduction: What Intelligent Design is Not." In *Signs of Intelligence: Understanding Intelligent Design*, ed. William A. Dembski, and James M. Kushiner (Grand Rapids, MI: Brazos Press, 2001), 17.

8. Michael J. Behe, "Molecular Machines: Experimental Support for the Design Inference." In *Intelligent Design Creationism and Its Critics: Philosophical, Theological and Scientific Perspectives*, ed. Robert T. Pennock (Cambridge, MA: MIT Press, 2001), 246 (emphasis added).

9. *Ibid.* (emphasis added).

10. *Ibid.*, 247.

11. *Ibid.*

12. *Ibid.*, 252.

13. *Ibid.*, 254.

14. *Ibid.*, 251 (emphasis added).

15. *Ibid.*, 254.

16. *Ibid.*, 247 (emphasis added).

17. *Ibid.*, 248.

18. See Stephen J. Gould, *The Panda's Thumb: More Reflections in Natural History* (New York: W.W. Norton and Company, 1980).

19. Kenneth R. Miller, *Finding Darwin's God: A Scientist's Search for Common Ground Between God and Evolution* (New York: Harper Collins Publishing, 1999), 138–139.

20. Allen H. Orr, "Darwin vs. Intelligent Design (Again)." Quoted in Robert T. Pennock *Tower of Babel: The Evidence Against the New Creationism* (Cambridge, MA: MIT Press, 1999), 270.

21. Kenneth R. Miller, *Finding Darwin's God: A Scientist's Search for Common Ground Between God and Evolution* (New York: Harper Collins Publishing, 1999), 138–139.

22. *Ibid.*, 139.

23. *Ibid.*

24. Michael J. Behe, "Molecular Machines: Experimental Support for the Design Inference." In *Intelligent Design Creationism and Its Critics: Philosophical, Theological and Scientific Perspectives*, ed. Robert T. Pennock (Cambridge, MA: MIT Press, 2001), 251 (emphasis added).

25. Gary Hurd, "The Explanatory Filter, Archeology, Forensics." In *Why Intelligent Design Fails*. Ed. Matt Young and Taner Edis, (Piscataway, NJ: Rutgers University Press, 2006), 119.

26. A watchmaker's secret signature to ensure authenticity.

27. Niall Shanks, *God, the Devil, and Darwin: A Critique of Intelligent Design Theory* (New York: Oxford University Press, 2007), 169.

28. Frank Newport, "In U.S., 46% Hold Creationist View of Human Origins." *Gallup*, June 1, 2012, http://www.gallup.com/poll/155003/hold-creationist-view-human-origins.aspx.

Chapter Nine

Is the Intelligent Designer the Biblical, Traditional God?

A Religious Response

Clifford Chalmers Cain

As Dr. Geenen pointed out in the previous chapter, Intelligent Design—the idea that irreducible complexity provides incontrovertible evidence for a Designer—is the latest attempt to introduce "creation science" into public school curricula and require teaching it as legitimate science and as an alternative to evolutionary biology. Advocates believe that Intelligent Design fits the data more adequately than the alleged "blind chance" of natural selection and purposeless adaptation. Thus far, it has been unsuccessful chiefly because—when taken to court—the legal system at both the federal and state levels has rejected "creation science"/Intelligent Design as not truly being science and violating the First Amendment which is intended to preserve the separation of Church and state. [1]

Be that as it may, ID proponents continue to argue that it "explains" why things are as they are—and does so "better" than evolutionary science—through the action/intervention of a divine cause. As referenced in Chapter 8, biochemist Michael Behe of Lehigh University and a Fellow at Seattle's Discovery Institute (the premier ID organization in the United States) contends that ID is *better* science than evolutionary theory. [2] But most scientists believe that a divine cause—an Intelligent Designer—is unnecessary as an explanation and that science can account for what has come to be, by "natural" causes and not by a necessary appeal to "super-natural" ones.

The "good" thing about ID is that it allows "room" for a role for the Divine. What is, resulted from divine input, from the "design" provided and constructed by an intelligent Designer. But the "bad" thing is that it does so by enlisting and appealing to a transcendent, super-natural cause or primary causation. In this regard, Michael Behe argues that some aspects of life are characterized by "irreducible complexity." As an example, which Dr. Geenen mentions in the previous chapter, Behe examines the bacterial flagellum, a rotor-like device on the tail of a bacterium that provides propulsion. This motor is too complex to have come to be through incremental, chance development, he asserts, but must have been provided by a Designer. If any one part of the flagellum were missing, the motor would not work.

This was not due to indirect divine influence—one factor among perhaps many—but rather to direct divine input. The Designer imposed this onto/into the organism, and the "'coordinated functioning' of many parts that occurs in complex organisms is the result."[3]

Of course, most scientists[4] contend that natural causes and a lengthy period of time can account for the evolution of the bacterial flagellum. No super-natural agent—no cause coming from outside, whether an intelligent Designer or not—is necessary to account for this.

So, if/since theology and religion want to preserve a role for the divine in the world [this preservation is known as the Doctrine of Providence: The God who created (*creatio ex nihilo*) continues God's process of creation (*creatio continua*)], then the God who was at the beginning must also be active in the world since that time and in the present. God must be a "hands-on deity."[5] Thus, perhaps a better, more satisfactory "space" for divine causation would be as internal, secondary cause. What if God works from/on the inside—influencing/luring—rather than by imposing from the outside? What if God's activity is conceived as inside-out and not top-down? What if God's role is "evocation" rather than "control"?[6]

As indicated Chapter Five, process theology—a brand of theology emanating from North America—emphasizes God's activity as a divine influence alongside other influences. Here "God is not . . . a metaphysical *deus ex machina* called-in to shore up tottering metaphysical structures by supplying a desperately needed explanation. Rather, God is a factor in human experience and is found at work in the world."[7] God provides the best possibility for actualization that is available and relevant to the living creature at that moment in its history and development. " . . . God [is] deeply involved to persuade us to the good."[8]

However, God does not impose this possibility so that the creature must adopt it. The creature chooses what to adopt and how to be (become). So, God is a persuasive influence, not an irresistible dictator. God is not a deterministic deity, predestining all that occurs—how, when, and where—by God's omnipotent will.

There is real freedom, then. This does not compromise God's presence—immanence—in the world. God is pervasively and deeply present in all that is and is becoming. But God is not omnipotent. Instead, God is the source of potentiality and of novelty.[9]

In this theology, God affects the world, and God is affected by the world. Through God's primordial nature/dimension—the aspect of God that provides "initial aims" (the possibilities that influence the world)—God provides input to the world, and through God's consequent nature/dimension—the aspect of God that receives information from the world—God receives output from the world.[10] As a result, God and the world are interdependent.[11] God's primordial nature is an expression of God's creative love; and God's consequent nature is an expression of God's responsive love.[12] God as love includes both creative activity and empathic responsiveness.

Thus,

> It is as true to say that God is permanent and the World fluent, as that the World is permanent and God fluent. It is as true to say that God is one and the World many, as that the World is one and God many. It is as true to say that, in comparison with the World, God is actual eminently, as that, in comparison with God, the world is actual eminently. It is as true to say that the world is immanent in God, as that God is immanent in the world. It is as true to say that God transcends the World, as that the World transcends God. It is as true to say that God creates the World, as that the World creates God.[13]

God is, therefore, "the divine persuasion."[14] God contributes to the actuality of the world—in this sense, God's role may be that of helping the world in its becoming: God wants/intends certain things, but God does not guarantee—cannot guarantee—that those things will come to be. God influences, but God does not—cannot—determine.[15]

Process theology picks-up on both the God of the philosophers *and* the God of the Bible: As in how Greek philosophy colored Christian theology, God remains omnipresent and omnibenevolent, but God is not omnipotent. At the same time, as in the biblical texts, God is active in the world and in the lives of people, a *personal* deity.

By contrast, the Intelligent Designer is not the equivalent of the personal God of the Bible. The Intelligent Designer echoes Aristotle's impersonal Unmoved Mover or Aquinas's transcendent First Cause, rather than the God who hears the cries of the people and mixes it up with history and in nature to save them; who at the right time becomes incarnate in history in the first-century figure Jesus of Nazareth in order to liberate from sin; who is a jealous God who tolerates no idolatry; who is a God who loves, forgives, and punishes; who is a deity to whom humans may pray and expect both rapport and response; and who speaks through the prophets of old and changes his mind when the people repent. As German physicist Harald Fritzsch has affirmed, "[God] concerns Himself with the suffering and sorrows of the individual."[16]

Although there *have* been other movements from a "hands-on, anthropomorphic deity to a less-intrusive, more-abstract deity" in biblical history,[17] the Judeo-Christian tradition has consistently affirmed the notion of a God who is active in the world. Neither deistic nor pantheistic,[18] this doctrine of divine providence makes God a personally-related and presently-involved deity. ID invokes neither of these dimensions.[19]

ID believes that there is a necessary divide between theism and evolution, based on "naturalism." That is, the scientist begins with an assumption that there is no supernatural—no God—and this filter shapes what he or she finds and interprets. Therefore, the naturalistic scientist is the enemy of religious faith and theistic belief.

However, it is possible to distinguish between philosophical naturalism (ontological naturalism) and methodological naturalism. The former *is* what ID is concerned about—reality has no supernatural, no God; there is just the natural. But the latter is what *science* assumes as its necessary methodology in order to do what it does—observe the natural world, experiment, and test hypotheses by looking at/for naturalistic causes of naturalistic phenomena. Science brackets such supernatural considerations or beliefs and then examines "the natural" as if that were all that is. This has resulted in tremendous discoveries, breakthroughs, cures, and understandings of how nature—the natural—works.

But methodological or scientific naturalism does not *necessarily* mean philosophical or ontological naturalism.

The astronomer Arthur Eddington once told a parable that illustrates both the value and the limitation of the scientific method: Imagine a man using a fishing net with a three-inch mesh. He casts the net time-and-time-again into the sea and examines the results of his casting. Only items three inches and greater had caught in the net. Of course, the things that are thus fished are not unimportant. But should the man conclude that there were no fish smaller than three inches would not be accurate. His means of gathering information about life in the sea, his methodology using a specific net with particular features, was a reduction from other methods. One's fishing methodology determines what will be caught.

Thus it is with the scientific method—it is highly effective, but it is narrow, and intentionally reductionistic. Its reductionism is *methodological* reductionism. Science is not automatically and simultaneously *ontologically* reductionist. Since science is selective, it does not (cannot) claim that its picture of reality is complete.[20]

As a result, both science and religion are needed for a complete picture of reality. Both religion and science bring essential approaches and make necessary contributions to human understanding. As Einstein captured this insight, "Science without religion is lame; religion without science is blind."[21] And as Roman Catholic lay theologian Jack Haught comments,

We can affirm life and its complex designs on many levels without one level being opposed to the other. Physics, for example, can explain life's order and design quite adequately from a thermodynamic point-of-view without interfering with biological accounts. Chemistry, too, can explain life at its own level. And so can theology. Theology, as one level in a whole hierarchy of explanations, has a legitimate role to play in our accounting in depth for the fascinating design in life. *Problems arise only when experts on one level claim that theirs is the only and adequate explanation of life* [emphasis mine].[22]

Beyond this, the two disciplines can contribute to the improvement of the other: "Science can purify religion from error and superstition. Religion can purify science from idolatry and false absolutes. Each can draw the other into a wider world, a world in which both can flourish."[23]

As a result, ID is neither good science nor good theology. "Science" looks for naturalistic explanations for naturalistic events. "For science, nature must be treated as a 'closed system.'"[24] An appeal to a supra-naturalistic explanation is not within its frame of reference. Such an explanation is not testable nor verifiable through experimentation. Steven Goldman lists five criteria for a scientific hypothesis:

1. explanatory power
2. logical consistency
3. predictive power
4. facilitates a research program
5. testable/falsifiable[25]

A hypothesis must account for why something is as it is or happens as it happens. A hypothesis is logical and not contradictory to the data accumulated. A hypothesis effectively indicates or forecasts what will happen or recur in the future. A hypothesis gives rise to extensive research, which may (or may not) provide additional evidence for the validity of the hypothesis; indeed, it may show the invalidity of the hypothesis. Therefore, and lastly, a hypothesis asserts something that may be tested and may be demonstrated to be true (or false).

As a result, ID's appeal to such a transcendent cause—an Intelligent Designer—violates the very definition and methodology of "science." ID is not good science.

But also, it is not cogent, good theology. An Intelligent Designer is not a contemporary "twin" of the personal God whom faith affirms and worships. The latter is a divine Agent who mixes-it-up in the real world of personal lives and historical events and natural phenomena. (Of course, *how* this divine Agent does this is in need of a revisit and a revision. This has been attempted in the course of this book's conversation between science and religion and theological reflection on that conversation.) The personal God of the Abrahamic traditions may be beseeched, prayed-to, and thanked, and is believed to make some sort of palpable and faith-based difference in happenings—comings and goings—in the world.

The Cosmic First Cause of Aquinas or the Deistic God of the framers of the Declaration of Independence—though easier to reconcile with science[26] —is not consonant with the related, personal nature of the biblical God who in some version and in diverse ways is worshipped in churches, mosques, and synagogues.

NOTES

1. Ian Barbour, *When Science Meets Religion* (New York: HarperCollins, 2000), 96–97. Examples of the court cases are United States Supreme Court, *Epperson v. Arkansas*, 1968; *Edwards v. Aguillard*, 1987; *Kitzmiller v. Dover Area School District*, 2005. These court cases are mentioned and addressed in some detail in James R. Curry, *Children of God, Children of Earth* (Bloomington, IN: AuthorHouse, 2008), 163–185.

2. Michael Behe, *Darwin's Black Box* (New York: Free Press, 1996); he discusses "irreducible complexity" beginning on 39.

3. Ian Barbour, *op. cit.,* 97.

4. A leading example is Ken Miller, an evolutionary biologist (and devout Roman Catholic), who wrote the widely-used high school textbook in the video "Judgment Day" and at the center of the court case in Dover, Pennsylvania (see footnote above)—Kenneth R. Miller and Joseph Levine, *Biology* (Upper Saddle River, NJ: Prentice-Hall, 2007).

5. Robert Wright, *The Evolution of God* (New York: Little, Brown, and Co., 2009), 103.

6. Ian Barbour, *op. cit.,* 177.

7. Walter Stokes, "A Whiteheadian Reflection on God's Relation to the World," in Ewert H. Cousins, ed., *Process Theology: Basic Writings* (New York: Newman Press, 1971), 142.

8. David Tracy, *Blessed Rage for Order* (New York: Seabury Press, 1975), 180; cf. T. Howland Sanks, S.J., "David Tracy's Theological Project," *Theological Studies* (Vol. 54, 1993), 709.

9. John Cobb, *A Christian Natural Theology* (Philadelphia: Westminster Press, 1965), 152–153.

10. Alfred North Whitehead, *Religion in the Making* (New York: Macmillan Co., 1926), 152; cf. Cobb, *op. cit.,* 148.

11. Clifford Chalmers Cain, "God's Providence and Pastoral Care" (Vanderbilt University: Unpublished doctoral dissertation, 1981), 65.

12. John B. Cobb and David Ray Griffin, *Process Theology* (Philadelphia: Westminster Press, 1976), 43f.

13. Alfred North Whitehead, *Process and Reality* (New York: Macmillan Co., 1929), 528.

14. Alfred North Whitehead, *The Adventures of Ideas* (New York: Macmillan Co., 1933), 214.

15. Science here could, and would, ask for evidence: 'If God is a contributing cause, even without necessitating, then does this causation show up in scientific testing? And if not, then God's "contribution" itself is superfluous and should be excised from the equation.' While process theological categories such as "novelty" and "creativity" and "beauty" may not be fully satisfactory as an explanation or contention, the fact that the development of life on planet earth has very, very gradually moved toward greater consciousness and greater complexity and greater newness ("beauty") *may* allow room, but not proof, for God's involvement as the supplier of initial aims, that is, of creative impulses in causation.

16. Harald Fritzsch, *The Creation of Matter: The Universe from Beginning to End* (New York: Basic Books, Inc., 1984).

17. Robert Wright, *op. cit.,* 128.

18. Deism separates God from the world and God is therefore not involved in that world; God's transcendence is affirmed at the cost of God's immanence. Pantheism identifies God with the world, and therefore God is not greater than the world, but rather equal to it; God's immanence is affirmed at the cost of God's transcendence.

19. To be fair to ID—and this insight has been pointed-out to me by contributing author, Professor Rich Geenen—Michael Behe and William Dembski *do* believe that the Intelligent Designer is the Christian God, but refrain from making that connection and insist that the evidence only "proves" a Designer. Professor Geenen's perspective is that the reticence to "name" the God of the Abrahamic religions (i.e., an interactive deity) as this Designer is to make ID's conclusion/assertion "more judicially palatable" in a court of law.

20. Arthur Eddington, *The Nature of the Physical World* (Cambridge, England: Cambridge University Press, 1928), 16.

21. Albert Einstein, *Out of My Later Years* (The Estate of Albert Einstein, 1956).

22. John F. Haught, *Responses to 101 Questions on God and Evolution*, (New York: Paulist Press, 2001), 88. Dr. Haught's claim does not mean that no problems will arise among fields when each field refuses to claim that it is the *only* source of truth. On the contrary, there will be numerous times when the explanations given are incommensurate. However, his point is to encourage humility among all fields and to exorcise presumption and arrogance from any one of them: "Scientism" says that science is the only way to truth; "fideism" or "fundamentalism" makes the same claim for religion. *This*, then, leads to "problems" which "arise."

23. Pope John Paul II, "Message of His Holiness John Paul II," in *John Paul II on Science and Religion*, edited by Robert John Russell, William J. Stoeger, S.J., and George V. Coyne, S.J. (Vatican: Vatican Observatory, 1990), 13.

24. Steven Goldman, *Science Wars* (Chantilly, VA: The Teaching Company, 2006), 114.

25. *Ibid.*

26. Cf. Harald Fritzsch, a West German physicist at the University of Munich at the Max Planck Institute, who argues that religion can provide values and morals, but that the God of Christianity with "human features," concerned "with the suffering and sorrows of the individual" is problematic for reconciliation with science, and that the God of Spinoza and Einstein and Eastern religions "can be much more easily brought into harmony with the insights of modern science"—Harald Fritzsch, "Science and Religion Are Complementary," in *Science and Religion: Opposing Viewpoints* (San Diego: Greenhaven Press, 1988), 58.

Chapter Ten

Conclusions

Clifford Chalmers Cain

This study of the relationship between science and religion, and a conversation between the two fields, has resulted in several key insights and conclusions.

First, biblical literalism—fideism—is "out." This literalism not only creates (unnecessary) conflict with science, it also does not do justice to religion's scriptures themselves. Fideism, in shutting-off the mind in behalf of "blind faith," honors the power and authority of revelation but at the total rejection of reason. It takes one of the methodological criteria for religion—revelation—and eliminates the other three (reason, experience, and tradition).

Fideism's historical manifestation—Fundamentalism—was a reaction to developments in scriptural "criticism" (analytic comparison of texts in the context of their historical environment), "liberal" theology (theology in conversation with reason and with culture), and science (chiefly but not exclusively the theory of evolution). A series of pamphlets—entitled *The Fundamentals*—was published in 1910 and was intended to return the Bible to its unique authoritative status as the infallible, inerrant Word of God, to rein-in Christian theology to its traditional affirmations about the Virgin Birth of Jesus, the physical resurrection of Jesus, and a historical Second Coming, and to put science in its place (by asserting that all things that 'are' came into existence in a time period of six, 24-hour days—"like the Bible says").[1] Clearly, fideism and Fundamentalism are at odds with contemporary biblical studies and theology, and also with the carefully-articulated theories of science (a "theory" is not merely a hunch or a guess or pure speculation, but a meticulously-tested assertion about an aspect of the natural world).[2]

By dismissing reason in favor of "blind" revelation ("The Bible means precisely what it says and says exactly what it means," so there is no need for interpretation), and by casting aside Church tradition (literalism does *not* enjoy regularity and precedence in Christian history),[3] fideism and fundamentalism are not "reasonable."

Second, although science can help religion repent of fideism, religion can help science shun scientism. Scientism takes methodological reductionism and elevates it to the status of ontological reductionism. That is, its presupposition that for the purposes of its investigation it will remove from consideration any non-naturalistic cause for naturalistic phenomena under investigation (methodological reductionism), is then expanded to disallow entirely any other avenue to knowledge and truth. Therefore, religious statements, because they cannot be falsified or verified by empirical means, are categorically false and utterly devoid of meaning.

Third, it is critical that the concept of God be revised. Specifically, God's power must be re-conceived, for it is no longer tenable to assert a notion of God as a divine Regulator with infinite power and meticulous providence—everything that happens is, in fact, God's will and completely under God's direct, overwhelming control.

Instead, God's power must be reinterpreted in order to preserve the Doctrine of Providence (if Intelligent Designer and Deistic First Cause conceptions of God are to be avoided). The understanding of divine power must be based on persuasion, not coercion; on divine lure, not divine determinism; on God's enticement, not God's manipulation. Roman Catholic lay theologian, Jack Haught, captures the point in the following way: "A truly creative God is not coercive but persuasive. If God is creative love, the world will not be forced to fit into some preconceived plan. It will be gently lured toward such beauty [*read*: order, novelty, directionality] as we see in atoms, cells, brains, and societies."[4]

Fourth, "process theology" provides an appropriate and helpful model for this reconsideration, this re-visioning. For, as we have seen, process theology describes a God who passionately influences the world but does not omnipotently determine outcomes in it. God affects the world in this way, and God is affected by the world. That is, in every situation, in every "moment of concrescence," God is providing an impetus toward what is good and best for the "actual occasion" (living thing) in that moment. However, the actual occasion does not *have* to choose that influence, for the living thing has free will. But if the actual occasion elects not to make incarnate that particular lure, God does not "give up" on the situation. God returns in the next "moment" with an evocation that is now appropriate for that subsequent situation.

Though God is unfailingly present, and God is utterly benevolent, God is not irresistibly all-powerful. God *does* have power, but just as a reservoir only has so much water, or a runner only has so much speed, so God only has so much power. Thus, God is intimately and extensively involved with life in the world, but God is not an autocrat who rules with ruthless, dictatorial power. God is a persuader, not an intruder: God provides guidance from within rather than intrusion from without, "gently informing the *cosmos*" rather than serving as a "dramatic interruption."[5]

Fifth, this whole "process" has as a corollary benefit the suggestion of some entrances into the quagmire of theodicy—the Problem of Evil: How can widespread suffering and intense pain *and* an "omni-God" (a deity who is omniscient, omnibenevolent, omnipresent, and omnipotent) simultaneously exist? Or, as physicist and theologian John Polkinghorne has put it, "How can a world of cancer and concentration camps be the creation of a God at once all-powerful and all-good?"[6]

Theodicy was Darwin's greatest dilemma *scientifically* (the "red in tooth and claw" dimension of nature),[7] *culturally* (the brutal carnage of the tribe in Tierra del Fuego that he observed while on his five-year voyage on *The Beagle*), *personally* (the tragic death of his daughter, Annie, which thoroughly devastated him and from which he never fully recovered), and *theologically* (reared on William Paley's "theology of design," he "gave up on the idea of divine design in evolution because of the clumsy, wasteful, blundering, and cruel works of nature.")[8]

In Darwin's own words,

> There seems to me too much misery in the world. I cannot persuade myself that a beneficent and omnipotent God would have designedly created the *Ichneumonidae* with the express intention of their feeding within the living bodies of caterpillars, or that cats should play with mice. Not believing this, I see no necessity that [for example] the eye [or anything else] was expressly designed.[9]

Among other things,[10] theodicy is also one of the greatest challenges that religion (especially the Western religions, Judaism, Christianity, and Islam) faces in the current century.

A God with limited power—not limited by any external thing, not self-limited, but with the power to persuade but not to coerce—means that God is not the source or cause of pain and suffering (not as punishment for sin nor as a trial that can test faith), but instead works in history and nature for human good and the world's good through the power of influence. The abuse of human freedom, for example, is responsible for much of the evil that causes suffering and pain in the world.[11]

In *Night*, Holocaust survivor Elie Wiesel's famous book about his concentration camp experience, he relates the story of a young boy who is hanged for some infraction of the rules or at the whim of a Nazi guard. Because he is young and not very heavy, his neck is not immediately broken when the trapdoor beneath him gives way, so he twitches in a grim and ghastly way at the end of the rope, his body contorting and jerking for what must have seemed an eternity.[12]

In the midst of that trauma—both the boy's and the onlookers'—the question flares up from the crowd, "Where is God? Where is God now?" And someone from among the spectators shouts, "There God is! God is hanging there on the gallows!"[13]

The most common interpretation of this proclamation is that it announces the death of God: Faith in God has been sacrificed in the misfortune and misery of countless events like the Holocaust. God has died on the gallows of Auschwitz and elsewhere in innumerable situations where people have experienced apparently meaningless pain and suffering and in some instances where that pain and suffering were the result of a calculated, evil plan of extermination. "How can there be belief in God after Auschwitz?" was the profound, perplexing question that arose following the Holocaust.[14]

However, there might be another interpretation: To suggest that God is on the gallows might not symbolically mean that faith in God has died, murdered like the young boy by the maliciousness of evil in the world. Rather, it might mean that God is literally with the victim, sharing his suffering and taking that painful human experience into God's experience. God identifies with the suffering in the world; God does not cause that suffering.

This means that God is with humans in their suffering as a source of empathy, love, and support. God did not cause their pain and suffering; God did not even allow it to occur. Rather, it happened despite God's preference for the contrary. God is an influence in the world, but God does not control what happens in the world in response. Sometimes God's will (God's preference) is chosen and honored, sometimes not. When it is, God's will is done on earth; when it is not, God's will is not.

This understanding of a God who acts through influence—whose power is encouraging or enticing rather than coercive or manipulative—is a concept of God that could resonate today with science, with theodicy, and with environmental challenges.

Regarding the last of these—the various dimensions of the ecological crisis—the model of a caring, serving, luring, working-with (rather than lording-it-over) God would or could encourage *Homo sapiens sapiens*—made in the divine image—to clearly and faithfully reflect God by using *their* power to nurture, care for, and serve ("encourage") nature/creation rather than to dominate, subjugate, conquer, and coerce it. Given the enormity, complexity, and urgency of environmental problems, this "imitation of God" in whose image humans were created could go a long way toward healing, rather than continuing to damage, the creation which God, like a divine Gardener, has cultivated, fertilized with "initial aims" (urges toward actualization), and attempted to guide as a persistent influence in the process of change and growth.

NOTES

1. *The Fundamentals*, ed. by A.C. Dixon and Reuben A. Torrey (Los Angeles: The Bible Institute, 1910–1915), contained 90 essays in 12 volumes written by 64 authors to preserve conservative, orthodox doctrines and beliefs. This publication was the brainchild of brothers Lyman and Milton Stewart. As a result, the earth is therefore considered to be but 6,000 years old (the seven-day creation having begun on Sunday, October 23, 4004 B.C., according to seventeenth-century British theologian, Bishop James Ussher), and human beings were believed to be created as a special act of God 'back then' in the same form as they are today.

2. Kenneth R. Miller, *Only a Theory: Evolution and the Battle for America's Soul* (New York: Penguin Group, 2008).

3. For example, the early Church Father and first systematic theologian of the Church, Origen, and later the primary theologian of the early Middle Ages, Augustine, advocated a metaphorical *hermeneutic* (principle of biblical interpretation) in understanding the meaning of biblical texts.

4. John F. Haught, *Science and Religion* (New York: Paulist Press, 1995), 180.

5. *Ibid.*, 94.

6. John Polkinghorne, *The Faith of a Physicist* (Princeton: Princeton University Press, 1994), 82.

7. Predator/prey relationships like the fox eating the rabbit and the wasp laying eggs in the caterpillar, the dog-eat-dog survival mentality, and evolutionary dead-ends and blind alleys; 99% of all the species which have lived on earth are now extinct—James R. Curry, *Children of God, Children of Earth* (Bloomington, IN: AuthorHouse, 2008), 177.

8. Ted Peters, *Playing God?* (New York and London: Routledge, 1997), 58.

9. Charles Darwin, quoted in John C. Greene, *Darwin and the Modern World* (New York: Mentor Books, 1963), 44.

10. Along with the contentious relationship between science and religion; religious pluralism—diverse truth claims among world religions and within specific religions; and the ecological challenges that beset planet earth—and the need for spiritual values and religious resources to motivate and help the healing of the environmental crisis in the name of both sustainability and God.

11. Human freedom, and its abuse, might account for a lot, but not all, of the evil and suffering in the world: Natural evil—suffering resulting from disease, earthquakes, tornadoes, etc.—is not explained by moral evil (the abuse of human freedom). But, in this instance as well, God does not control nature, only influences it.

12. Elie Wiesel, *Night* (New York: Hill and Wang, 2006), 64.

13. *Ibid.*

14. Richard L. Rubenstein, *After Auschwitz* (Indianapolis: Bobbs-Merrill, 1966), 70f.

Contributors

Clifford Chalmers Cain is Harrod-C.S. Lewis Professor of Religious Studies at Westminster College of Missouri. He is interested in contemporary religious thought, the interface between science and religion, and the contributions of world religions to ecology. His recent trilogy in environmental theology—*An Ecological Theology, Down to Earth*, and *Many Heavens, One Earth*—is now joined by this seventh book, *Re-vision*.

Gabe McNett is Associate Professor of Biology at Westminster College of Missouri. His research has involved the evolution of ecological and behavioral differences in birds and insects. In particular, he has studied animal communication in the form of feather coloration and color vision in birds, and the use of micro-scale vibrations in insects. More broadly, his emphasis has been on field-based studies of how the local environment affects communication behavior and efficiency, and ultimately how ecological differences affect the evolutionary process.

Jane Kenney-Hunt is Assistant Professor of Biology at Westminster College of Missouri and has authored over 20 peer-reviewed publications. Her research and writing are primarily in the field of evolutionary and quantitative genetics, with a focus on complex traits and gene-by-environment interactions.

Laura Stumpe is Assistant Professor and Director of the Physics Program at Westminster College of Missouri and has taught Physics and Astronomy at the college level for eight years. She has done experimental and theoretical research studying the magnetism in superconductors, colossal magnetoresistive materials, and semiconducting superlattices.

Rich Geenen is Professor of Philosophy at Westminster College of Missouri and worked under distinguished Professor Christopher Shields, now at Oxford University. He wrote his doctoral dissertation on the metaphysics of Plato's theory of forms and enjoys teaching courses across the philosophical spectrum, ranging from philosophy of religion to ancient philosophy to applied ethics. Recently, he has become interested in the philosophical and religious assertions of Intelligent Design and their criticisms.

Index